Global and Insurgent Legalities

A series edited by Eve Darian-Smith and Jonathan Goldberg-Hiller

BRENNA BHANDAR

Colonial Lives of Property

Law, Land, and Racial Regimes of Ownership

DUKE UNIVERSITY PRESS

DURHAM AND LONDON   2018

Library of Congress Cataloging-in-Publication Data
Names: Bhandar, Brenna, [date] author.
Title: Colonial lives of property : law, land, and racial regimes of ownership / Brenna
    Bhandar.
Description: Durham : Duke University Press, 2018. | Series: Global and insurgent
    legalities | Includes bibliographical references and index.
Identifiers: LCCN 2017049756 (print)
LCCN 2018000886 (ebook)
ISBN 9780822371571 (ebook)
ISBN 9780822371397 (hardcover : alk. paper)
ISBN 9780822371465 (pbk. : alk. paper)
Subjects: LCSH: Colonization. | Right of property. | Land tenure—Law
and legislation. | Indigenous peoples—Legal status, laws, etc. | Race
discrimination—Law and legislation.
Classification: LCC JV305 (ebook) | LCC JV305 .B43 2018 (print) |
DDC 333.309171/9—dc23
LC record available at https://lccn.loc.gov/2017049756

Cover art: *Latitude: 31°21′7″N / Longitude: 34°46′27″E*. Preparations for planting
the Jewish National Fund (JNF) Ambassador Forest at the site of the former
homes of the Abu Jāber, Abu Mdīghem, and Abu Freiḥ families, of the al-Tūri
tribe, al-ʻAraqîb, October 9, 2011. © Fazal Sheikh, from *Desert Bloom*, the second
volume in *The Erasure Trilogy*, Steidl Publishers, 2015.

FOR my mother Hargian and
my late father Ragbier

Contents

Acknowledgments

CONVERSATIONS WITH FRIENDS AND COLLEAGUES ABOUT THE IDEAS explored in these pages and encouragement to pursue them have been invaluable. Sincere thanks to Nasser Abourahme, Jose Bellido, John Borrows, Emilio Dabed, Janelle Dwyer, Denise Ferreira da Silva, Peter Fitzpatrick, Roderick Ferguson, Zeina Ghandour, Alexandre (Sandy) Kedar, Robert Knox, Peter Lagerquist, Robert Nichols, Kris Peterson, Alain Pottage, Kaushik Sunder Rajan, Jordy Rosenberg, Leticia Sabsay, Susan Schuppli, Nimer Sultany, Eyal Weizman, and Oren Yiftachel. Hoda Rouhana, Reem Botmeh, Nidal Rafa, and Linda Tabar were immensely generous with their time, knowledge, and hospitality on an initial trip to Palestine in 2010, and their introduction to the legal and political absurdities of the occupation made a deep and lasting impression on me.

Suhad Bishara and Hassan Jabareen were immeasurably helpful in guiding my research in the Naqab. The insights offered by researchers, lawyers, and journalists at Adalah, who kindly hosted me as a visitor in spring 2014, were inspiring and instructive. Thabet Abu Ras and Khalil Al-Amour generously gave their time and thoughtful advice in helping to arrange interviews undertaken in the Naqab, and patiently acted as translators on several occasions. I am deeply indebted to the activists, lawyers, and advocates who gave their time and offered their insights during interviews held in Haifa, Bir Al

Sabe / Be'er Sheva, Jerusalem, Ramallah, and Vancouver. I am indebted to Elian Weizman and Ofer Neiman for their excellent and timely translations of several Israeli High Court judgments that were essential for the research.

I want to give special thanks to friends and family who read earlier drafts of the manuscript, offered incisive thoughts, and have encouraged me to think more deeply about things: Donatella Alessandrini, Davina Bhandar, Avery Gordon, Adam Hanieh, David Lloyd, Elena Loizidou, Hyo Yoon Kang, Michael Ma, John Milloy, Haneen Naamnih, and Rafeef Ziadah. While I doubt that I have been able to incorporate all their insights and answer all their queries, their views have undoubtedly enriched the book and my experience of writing it.

In the final stretch of completion, Paula Ascorra Costa and Ricardo Espinoza Lolas graciously gave us a safe place to stay while the tectonic plates off the coast of Valparaiso released massive and troubling amounts of energy. Thank you!

I was very fortunate to have the opportunity to present different parts of the book as works in progress at various institutions, and thank the organizers for inviting me and attendees for their thoughtful questions and comments: Al-Quds Bard College of Arts and Science, hosted by Emilio Dabed and Nicola Perugini; the Knowledge/Value Workshop at UC Davis, organized by Kaushik Sunder Rajan and Mario Baggioli; Botanical Conflicts Conference at Goldsmiths organized by Shela Sheikh; the Rethinking Property Workshop at Humboldt University, Berlin, organized by Robert Nichols; the World Picture Conference, Cambridge, UK, organized by J. D. Rhodes; the Victoria Colloquium on Political, Social and Legal Theory at the University of Victoria, organized by Rebecca Johnson; and Aeyal Gross, who generously hosted an informal seminar (accompanied by a terrific supper) at his home in Tel Aviv.

The SOAS School of Law generously funded a research trip to the archives at the University of British Columbia, and another to Palestine/Israel.

Earlier versions of some of the material in chapters 2 and 4 were published as articles: "Title by Registration: Instituting Modern Property Law and Creating Racial Value in the Settler Colony," *Journal of Law and Society* 42, no. 2 (June 2015): 253–82; "Possession, Occupation, Registration: Recombinant Ownership in the Settler Colony," *Settler Colonial Studies* 6, no. 2 (2016): 119–32; and "Status as Property: Identity, Land and the Dispossession of First Nations Women in Canada," *Darkmatter* (2016).

Courtney Berger has been very supportive of this project from the first time we spoke about it, and I cannot thank her enough for her openness, encouragement, and advice. Eve Darian-Smith and Jonathan Goldberg-Hiller, the series editors, embraced this project with editorial verve. Two anonymous reviewers offered excellent suggestions on how to improve the draft manuscript and provided thoughtful, productive criticisms.

I feel particularly indebted to Jonathan Goldberg-Hiller, who has offered extensive comments and suggestions on this book in various incarnations and, moreover, has thought through its content with me and dispelled many doubts along the way.

Finally, the book would not have materialized without the boundless care and support of Alberto Toscano. His consistent enthusiasm for this project, infinite curiosity about the world, and expansive intellectual generosity have been a crucial and joyful source of sustenance.

Introduction

Property, Law, and Race in the Colony

To think about distant places, to colonize them, to populate or
depopulate them: all of this occurs on, about, or because of land.
The actual geographical possession of land is what empire in the
final analysis is all about. At the moment when a coincidence occurs
between real control and power, the idea of what a given place was
(could be, might become), and an actual place—at that moment the
struggle for empire is launched. This coincidence is the logic both
for Westerners taking possession of land and, during decolonisation,
for resisting natives reclaiming it.
—Edward Said, *Culture and Imperialism*

In *Culture and Imperialism*, Said reversed the tide against a literary criticism that had long approached European literature as having nothing to do
with empire and imperialism. As he noted, "[t]o read Austen without also
reading Fanon and Cabral—and so on and so on—is to disaffiliate modern culture from its engagements and attachments."[1] As Said excavated in
unsparing detail, the English novel (in particular) as a "cultural artefact of
bourgeois society" fortified the "structures of attitude and reference" that
were of central import to imperial (and colonial) endeavors. The novel, as a
cultural form, contributed to the sedimentation of narratives and language
as the means through which land, territories, and entire geographical regions were rendered as colonial possessions.

The novel became a powerful means of both expressing and consolidating a European, colonial vision of the world, while often, as Said explored, disavowing the very existence of a colonial relation. Alongside other cultural and political forms, it served to identify the true subjects of history, and thus it is no mystery as to why property ownership and propriety form such a colossal backdrop or, in some cases, explicit focus of so many key works of nineteenth-century English literature. Property law was a crucial mechanism for the colonial accumulation of capital, and by the late nineteenth century, had unfolded in conjunction with racial schemas that steadfastly held colonized subjects within their grip. Property laws and racial subjectivity developed in relation to one another, an articulation I capture with the concept of racial regimes of ownership. As a juridical formation, racial regimes of ownership have retained their disciplinary power in organizing territory and producing racial subjects through a hierarchy of value constituted across the domains of culture, science, economy, and philosophy.

In Walter Scott's *Waverley*, the historical fictionalization of the dramatic events of the 1745 Jacobite rebellion, to take one example, a multitude of different forms of land tenure covering the Scottish highlands, lowlands, English rural estates, and lavish homes in the city are thoroughly entwined with the character, habits, cultural practices, and kinship of owners, landlords, tenants, and laborers alike. Waverley initially confronts the brutish character of the Scottish highlanders—and their primitive, quasi-feudal system of landholding—before developing a benevolent respect for their ways; however, this does not ultimately change the narrative thrust that sees the onward march of progress (dramatized in the resounding defeat of the rebellion) as one defined by the development of an English agrarian capitalism.

In Maria Edgeworth's *Castle Rackrent*, published prior to Scott's *Waverley* and widely regarded as the first historical novel, the cultural, economic, and affective dimensions of the relations between the Anglo-Irish colonial rentier class and the Irish underclass charged with the upkeep of the estates is rendered in glaring terms. The power that generations of one family of owners wield, in spite of desperately negligent management practices, over the lives of those in their service is brought into stark relief with the story of the landlord family's eventual decline. The novel is written in the shadow of the Act of Union, and the crisis in property ownership occasioned by it.

Edgeworth addresses the dispossession of the Irish Catholic bourgeoisie and the possession of their lands by the Irish-Anglo class by treating the estate "as a microcosm of the nation itself."[2] As with so many genre-defining novels of the nineteenth century, relations of ownership provide the lens through which economy, cultural practices, state governance, military exploits, kinship, and relations of intimacy—nineteenth-century social formations—are revealed, explored, and, in Edgeworth's case, parodied to some extent.

Property constitutes a central part of the narrative foundation in a way that is so ubiquitous, it is akin to the furniture in the drawing room of a manor house, shoring up and naturalizing possession and occupation. If the possession of land was (and remains) the ultimate objective of colonial power, then property law is the primary means of realizing this desire. (Colonial endeavors that were focused on the exploitation of capital markets often relied on property laws in a more expansive sense for their realization and operation.)[3] Further, as we will see throughout the exploration undertaken in this book, laws of property also reflect and consolidate language, ways of seeing, and modes of subjectivity that render indigenous and colonized populations as outside history, lacking the requisite cultural practices, habits of thought, and economic organization to be considered as sovereign, rational economic subjects, much like Scott's highlanders.

To study modern laws of private property ownership without accounting for the significance of the colonial scene to their development is to disaffiliate the development of modern law from its deep engagements with colonial sites in ways that parallel the literary disavowals of colonialism diagnosed by Said. There cannot be a history of private property law, as the subject of legal studies and political theory in early modern England that is not at the same time a history of land appropriation in Ireland, the Caribbean, North America, and beyond. A central argument developed throughout this book is that modern property laws emerged along with and through colonial modes of appropriation. For instance, as explored in chapter 2, the system of formal ownership prevalent in many (if not most) common-law jurisdictions, which requires the registration of land title in a state-regulated system, was implemented first in the colony of South Australia, and then British Columbia, decades prior to being implemented on a national scale in the United Kingdom. In South Australia, the sovereignty of indigenous nations was vitiated by a colonial vision of that space as lacking in civilized inhabitants, and therefore empty and ripe for appropriation. As Nasser Hussain so cogently argued, colonial spaces were ones in which questions of law shaped the practice of colonial rule; and the development of legal doctrines in the colony "in turn, affected the development of Western legality."[4]

Property law holds a unique and distinctive place in Enlightenment thought and ensuing discourses of modernity. It operates as a set of both techniques and mechanisms encapsulated in legislation, legal judgments, and myriad everyday practices of ownership that have structured colonial capitalist modes of accumulation.[5] It is also a central fixture in philosophical and political narratives of a developmental, teleological vision of modernization that has set the standard for what can be considered civilized. The nearly uniform justification for casting indigenous populations as premodern was found in the absence of private property laws and particular forms of cultivation. As Peter Fitzpatrick has argued, law—and property law specifically—became "integrally associated with the mythic settling of the world—with its adequate occupation and its bestowal on rightful holders, the Occidental possessors and owners."[6] The English common law of property became the sine qua non of civilized life and society, an axiom sharpened at the expense of indigenous peoples throughout the colonial world. As explored in each chapter, the evolution of modern property laws and justifications for private property ownership were articulated through the attribution of value to the lives of those defined as having the capacity, will, and technology to appropriate, which in turn was contingent on prevailing concepts of race and racial difference. The colonial encounter produced a racial regime of ownership that persists into the present, creating a conceptual apparatus in which justifications for private property ownership remain bound to a concept of the human that is thoroughly racial in its makeup.

Thus not only was property law the primary means of appropriating land and resources, but property ownership was central to the formation of the proper legal subject in the political sphere.[7] Analyzing the techniques of ownership that remain a primary mode of dispossession in settler colonies cuts across the economic, cultural, political, and psychic spheres of colonial and postcolonial life. Modernity ushered in a relationship between ownership and subjectivity, wherein the latter was defined through and on the basis of one's capacity to appropriate. While the relationship between property ownership, propriety, and the proper subject of law has been excavated by other scholars, this book departs from the existing literature in the field by focusing on the centrality of race to the formation of modern legal subjectivity.[8] Drawing on the work of Stuart Hall, Cheryl Harris, Cedric J. Robinson, and others, I develop the argument throughout the book (and in further detail below) that legal forms of property ownership and the modern racial subject are articulated and realized in conjunction with one other.

RACIAL REGIMES OF OWNERSHIP

Being an owner and having the capacity to appropriate have long been considered prerequisites for attaining the status of the proper subject of modern law, a fully individuated citizen-subject. In the colonies specifically, one had to be in possession of certain properties or traits, determined by racial identity and gender, to own property. In this way, property ownership can also be understood as complicit in fabricating racial difference and gender identities. Fanon wrote incisively of how the ontology of settler and native was produced through a system of property: "The settler and the native are old acquaintances. In fact, the settler is right when he speaks of knowing 'them' well. For it is the settler who has brought the native into existence and who perpetuates his existence. The settler owes the fact of his very existence, that is to say his property, to the colonial system."[9] Here, Fanon pointedly reveals the centrality of property ownership to the life and existence of the settler, and in *Black Skin, White Masks* renders bare the core racial dimension of colonization. As Fanon's first published work, *Black Skin, White Masks* presented an excoriating critique of the psychoaffective and phenomenological dimensions of life for the colonized in Martinique and upon his arrival in France. Thinking through his concept of "epidermalization" (whereby the racial schema of colonization is grafted onto the figure of *le nègre* and resides parasitically on black skin), alongside the critique of colonial and anticolonial bourgeois nationalism in the later *Wretched of the Earth*, one gleans how relations of ownership, propriety, and racial subjectivity can be better grasped through a more expansive understanding of property law as a form of colonial domination.

The relationship between a racial concept of the human and property relations has long been the subject of critical histories of the transatlantic slave trade.[10] The brutal rendering of black lives as objects of economic commerce produced a racial regime of ownership whose legacies remain very much alive in the economic, social, and legal value accorded white lives over black lives (along with the racial and gendered legacies of contractual forms of domination present in the history of indentured labor, particularly with Chinese and Indian workers in the Americas).[11] However, while it may be intuitive to locate the origins of a racialized system of ownership in the transatlantic slave trade, Cedric J. Robinson has argued otherwise. "Simply put, the Atlantic slave trade was not the first slave system, nor the first slave system engaged in by Europeans, nor the first slave system of Europeans or their ancestors, and not the only slave system to produce a racialist culture."[12] Relatedly, Cornel West has also argued that racism predates capitalism, finding its roots "in the early encounter between civilizations in Europe, Africa and Asia, encounters which occurred long before the rise of modern capitalism."[13]

What distinguishes the emergence of a modern racial regime of ownership in settler colonies, and indeed those places where slavery was a core part of economic development, is the articulation of a commodity form of real property in conjunction with a globalized "economy of difference."[14] The racialism that had thoroughly infused social relations in feudal Europe was globalized with the advent of modern colonialism.[15] The transatlantic slave trade, and the appropriation of indigenous lands that characterized the emergence of colonial capitalism on a worldwide scale, produced and relied upon economic and juridical forms for which property law and a racial concept of the human were central tenets. Scientific techniques of measurement and quantification, economic visions of land and life rooted in logics of abstraction, culturally inscribed notions of white European superiority, and philosophical concepts of the proper person who possessed the capacity to appropriate (both on the level of interiority and in the external world) worked in conjunction to produce laws of property and racial subjects.

This book excavates the juridical formation constituted by modern property law and the racial subject, by examining the development of the specific legal form of private property relations in the settler colonial sites of Canada, Australia, and Israel/Palestine. In thinking through the relationship between modern forms of property and race, it becomes clear that this juridical formation has played a central role in the historical development of racial capitalism. The multitude of rationales for the colonial appropriation of indigenous lands (upon which slavery in the Americas was contingent), and the concomitant development of liberal democracy in the settler colony required legal and political narratives that equated English common-law concepts of property with civilized life, and were coupled with a belief in the inherent superiority of people whose cultural and economic practices bore resemblance to a burgeoning agrarian capitalism in England. Colonialism took root on the grounds of this juridical formation, twinning the production of racial subjects with an economy of private property ownership that continues to prevail over indigenous and alternate modalities of relating to and using land and its resources.

In many ways, Cheryl Harris's article "Whiteness as Property" remains unsurpassed in the novelty of the theoretical framework she developed for understanding how whiteness has come to have value as a property in itself, a value encoded in property law and social relations. Harris analyzes how the system of chattel slavery was premised upon the appropriation of indigenous lands, pointing to the deployment of different racial logics in the treatment of black slaves as objects of property and indigenous nations as lacking the cultural practices of white Europeans that defined them as inferior, and consequently as non-owners of their land. She critically interrogates the way in which the concept of race interacted with conceptions of property, to "establish and maintain racial and economic subordination."[16]

More specifically, Harris argues that the propertizing of human life—the lives of black slaves—forms the historical basis for the merger of white identity with property. Slavery created a form of property that would eventually become contingent on race; by the latter half of the seventeenth century in the United States, "only Blacks were subjugated as slaves and treated as property."[17] Writing incisively about the legacy of race-based chattel slavery, she maps the transition from whiteness as status property to whiteness as an entitlement to social goods that persists as the unspoken backdrop to contemporary litigation over affirmative action policies. Whiteness, argues Harris, shares the critical characteristics of property. The right to use and enjoyment, the reputational value, the power to exclude, are all characteristics of whiteness shared by various forms of property. Whiteness is, on Harris's analysis, an analogue of property.

While the arguments pursued in this book are in debt to and inspired by Harris's work, the analysis offered here also parts company in some significant ways. I develop the idea that modern concepts of race and modern laws of property share conceptual logics and are articulated in conjunction with one another. For instance, as I argue in chapter 2, the violence of abstraction that transformed land more fully into a commodity over the course of a long transition (from feudal land relations to forms of ownership that facilitated agrarian capitalism and market capitalism) has a counterpart in racial thinking that figured entire populations in a hierarchy of value with whiteness at its apex. As Ruth Wilson Gilmore has written, "racism is a practice of abstraction, a death-dealing displacement of difference into hierarchies that organise relations within and between the planet's sovereign political territories."[18] This is certainly not to suggest that all logics of abstraction are the same, but I argue that the commodity logic of abstraction that underlies modern forms of private property shares conceptual similarities with the taxonomization and deracination of human life based on racial categorizations, the early traces of which are evident in the work of natural historians such as Linnaeus.

It is, then, more than an interaction between race and property that I excavate in this work; my argument is that racial subjects and modern property laws are produced through one another in the colonial context. In relation to the appropriation of indigenous lands, Harris argues that "only particular forms of possession—those that were characteristic of white settlement—would be recognised and legitimated."[19] This is certainly true; however, in my view it was not solely whiteness or the cultural practices of whites that determined the kinds of use that would give rise to the right to own land. I argue in chapters 1 and 3 that the types of use and possession of land that justified ownership were determined by an ideology of improvement. Those communities who lived as rational, productive economic actors, evidenced by particular forms of cultivation, were deemed to be proper subjects of law and history; those who did not were deemed to be in need of improvement as much as their waste lands were. Prevailing ideas about racial superiority were forged through nascent capitalist ideologies that rendered race contingent on specific forms of labor and property relations. Property ownership was not just contingent on race and notions of white supremacy; race too, in the settler colonial context, was and remains subtended by property logics that cast certain groups of people, ways of living, producing, and relating to land as having value worthy of legal protection and force.

To understand the relationship between the production of racial subjects and property law, how it functions in colonial contexts at different historical moments, and how it continues into the present, it is necessary to grapple with a formation whose genesis cannot be reduced to any one singular system or structure. As pointed out by scholars theorizing the relationship between race and class, neither phenomenon is reducible to the other; political ideologies, economic rationalities, and cultural and juridical practices operate in conjunction to produce structures of domination that work through and continually reproduce relations of class, racial difference, gender, and sexuality. The production of racial subjectivity and the constitution of private property relations are articulated conjointly, in ways that are neither inevitable nor transhistorical. Rather, the juridical formation that I refer to as the racial regime of ownership requires continual renewal and reinstantiation to prevail over other ways of being and living. I draw on Stuart Hall's theorization of articulation, and Cedric Robinson's conceptualization of racial regimes in order to emphasize three different aspects of the constitutive relationship between modern property laws and the racial subject: the noninevitable yet nonarbitrary nature of this juridical formation; the (consequential) necessity for this formation to be continually renewed in the colonial drive to appropriate indigenous land; and the recombinant nature of the constituent parts of the racial regime of ownership.[20]

Race, for instance, as a concept is a variable amalgam of social, cultural, and biological markers and, practically speaking, amasses in its arsenal a range of different traits including "colour, physiognomy, culture, and gene pools" in order to differentiate.[21] While very broad shifts in dominant conceptions of race can be traced, it is also true that modern concepts of race draw on this wide range of factors for their rationalization. Biological and cultural explanations for racial difference are not mutually exclusive. Avery Gordon observes that the biological justification for racial inferiority "was a relative newcomer" in the nineteenth century. And while the "authority of Western science as the unquestioned standard of Western civilized knowledge" certainly set scientific racism apart from earlier forms, she argues that both "prescientific Western theorizing" that attributed racial difference to divine will, and biologically based racism posited the notion that "the inferior could be redeemed either by religious conversion or . . . by assimilation to the conquering tribe, empire or group."[22] Racial regimes of ownership make use of the plasticity inherent in both of its constitutive dimensions—race and property—and deploy rationalizations for the way these phenomena are articulated in conjunction with one another in a recombinant manner, using both scientific and prescientific modes of thought as a matter of brutalizing convenience.

As discussed above, Cheryl Harris has described race as an analogue of property in the sense that it shares many of its critical characteristics. The presumption that race is natural, much like private property ownership, is one that many scholars of critical race theory and scholars of property continue to spend time and effort undoing. The need to denaturalize race and property ownership, to reveal the techniques of their fabrication, and the historical sediment that haunts contemporary structures of racial oppression and appropriation are testament to their continual reiteration and reinvention. As such, the different manifestations of the racial regime of ownership explored in this book do not fall neatly into a chronology. The very nature of the appropriation of indigenous lands justified by the tripartite reliance on possession, use, and the abstract proof of ownership in the form of registered title exemplifies the fractured and disjointed nature of temporality in the colonial context. For instance, as we will see in the case of the Bedouin, explored in chapter 3, the Israeli state has relied on the absence of registered title along with an ideology of improvement that privileges European forms of cultivation as proof of ownership, along with continual attempts to physically remove Bedouin who are in occupation of their own land.

In thinking about racial subjectivity and modern property laws as articulations that are realized in conjunction with one another, Stuart Hall's theorization of the relationship between race and class is indispensable. Drawing on methods developed by Marx, Gramsci, and Althusser, Hall elaborated a theory of how race and economic structures are practically and conceptually connected to one another, and how this relationship produces specific forms of racism at different historical junctures. He rejected the economic reductivism of orthodox approaches to Marxist theory (which reduce the causes of race and racism to economic determinants or to the functional demands of social domination) and instead grasped the complex relationship between race and class through examining how they are articulated together as historically specific social forms of identity and domination. While class as a concept is not strictly analogous to property, it is a relation determined by, among other things, one's position as a producer in a hierarchy of ownership, alienation, and exchange and, further, intersects with race, gender, and sexuality in how it is lived. In this way, class is rendered as a core part of social formations very much in the way that property ownership operates as a legal, social, political, and economic relation in contemporary social formations, and we could say more specifically, juridical formations. Hall's analytical trajectory is thus particularly relevant for this study, which seeks to trace how modern legal forms of property ownership emerge in colonial capitalist contexts, articulated with and through modern concepts of race and racial difference that appear as specific juridical formations.

Drawing on the work of Gramsci, Hall writes that the concept of the social formation enables an understanding of how economic, political, and ideological relations constitute complexly structured societies, "where the different levels of articulation do not by any means simply correspond [to] or 'mirror' one another" but produce uneven, nonlinear, and sometimes contradictory effects. "Racism and racist practices," writes Hall, "frequently occur in some but not all sectors of the social formation; their impact is penetrative but uneven."[23] We will examine the relevance of Hall's observation below, where I draw out some examples of the uneven and sometimes contradictory ways in which juridical formations of race and property law appear in different settler colonial contexts.

While Hall stresses the contingency present in the development of social formations, he also (drawing on Althusser) defines the social formation as a "structure in dominance," in order to emphasize its determinate and systemic qualities.[24] The concept of the social formation is taken by Hall as an analytic to theorize a relationship between race and class, to open up the question of value to factors normally excised from Marxist understandings of the general operation of the law of value, such as the cultural and racialized nature of labor practices.[25] The more general point is that both social and juridical formations take shape within particular economic systems, in relation to both specific cultural norms and practices and different regimes of race, gender, and sexuality.

In his 1985 essay on Althusser, Hall identified articulation as a new concept, one that facilitates analysis of how political and economic and, I would add, juridical practices are "condensed" into forms of domination over particular social groups and classes.[26] The concept of articulation opens an avenue for understanding how different practices operate as a series of interconnected but differentiated processes. Here, we can draw an analogy with the limits of considering property as having distinct economic and juridical forms that are separate from the social, historical, and political milieu in which they exist; a conceptual error, ironically perhaps, committed by both Marxists and legal positivists. Paul Hirst pointed to the fallacious tendencies among some Marxist legal theorists (namely, Evgeny Pashukanis and Karl Renner) to reduce conceptions of legal subjectivity and juridical forms of property to their existence as mere expressions of economic exchange. While the very problem of what capital is cannot be separated from the modes of its legal organization, legal forms are not solely determined by economic processes of production or exchange. Juridical forms of property, in all their complexity and plasticity, have been central to multiple modes of capital accumulation (and dispossession), as Balibar has noted. To that end, I want to emphasize that juridical forms of property reflect much more than the life of property as a commodity form of exchange.[27] Indeed, even within Marxist discourse, the term "juridical form" denotes not formal structures but a variety of "political, juristic, philosophical theories, religious views" and "the reflexes of all these actual struggles in the brains of the participants" in the making of political struggles, in the making of history.[28] My use of the term "juridical" denotes the fabrication of legal techniques that define legality and illegality, produce legal subjects, operate as a form of governance, and in all of these guises functions as a form of disciplinary power.

The concept of articulation as conceived of by Hall expresses the noninevitable—yet nonarbitrary—nature of social formations; here I consider it in terms of the means by which racial regimes of ownership must be continually sustained and renewed by specific social, economic, and juridical practices:

> By the term "articulation" I mean a connection or link that is not necessarily given in all cases, as a law or fact of life, but which requires particular conditions of existence to appear at all, which has to be positively sustained by specific processes, which is not eternal but has constantly to

be renewed, which can under some circumstances disappear or be overthrown, leading to the dissolving of old linkages and the forging of new connections—rearticulations. It is also important that an articulation between different practices does not mean that they become identical or that the one is dissolved into the other. Each retains its distinct determinations and conditions of existence.[29]

Hall's conceptualization of articulation presents a means of understanding how the relationship between race and class cannot be cast as inevitably taking any particular form; there is no "necessary correspondence between one level of social formation and another" that is determined primarily by an economic base. There is also, however, no necessary noncorrespondence between different levels of a social formation, contra post-Marxist claims for total contingency. There are, rather, as Hall puts it, "no guarantees" that a given class or social group will respond to economic relations in a particular way, or that the "ideology of a class" necessarily corresponds with the position they hold within economic relations of capitalist production. In part, this is because class conflicts are not "wholly ascribable within 'social relations of production.'"[30] Race and racism, gender, and sexuality shape the nature and form that class relations take and, significantly, how they are experienced.

Analogously, there are no guarantees that a given articulation of race and property ownership will appear in the same configuration across time or jurisdictions.[31] In part this is because of the sheer heterogeneity contained within articulations of race and property ownership, occasioned by the resistance, refusal, negotiation, or recognition and acceptance of colonial relations of ownership by First Nations and other racialized subjects in settler colonial contexts. As we will consider in the conclusion, the continual renewal of racial regimes of ownership is not an inevitability, as political imaginaries that exceed the confines of this juridical formation demonstrate. The more immediate focus here, however, is on the specific processes of colonial land appropriation and the historical emergence and contemporary dominance of markets in land-as-commodity that work to articulate a racial concept of the human in conjunction with modern laws of property. This conjuncture is continually renewed through the persistent but differentiated reiteration of a racial concept of humanity defined in relation to logics of abstraction, ideologies of improvement, and an identity-property nexus encapsulated in legal status.

The task that Hall set for himself was to think about how race and class are theoretically connected to one another. The conclusion he reaches, that there is no necessary correspondence, but also no necessary noncorrespondence, between different levels of any given social formation (between, for instance, race, class, and gender) opens up space for considering how social relations do not inevitably adhere across time and space to a particular form. The noninevitability and contingent, yet nonarbitrary character of the articulation of race and class, for Hall, reveals the potential for political transformation and rupture. This emphasis on the possibilities of transformation is shared by Cedric Robinson, whose concept of the racial regime incorporates a recognition of how radical traditions of resistance exist in relation to the production of race and racism. Despite the many significant differences between the work of Hall and Robinson, not least their remarkably divergent relationships to Marxist traditions of thought, there is a contact point in their explorations of the potentiality for political transformation and change that exist in the structures, systems and relations of domination.

Cedric J. Robinson argues that racial regimes are "unstable truth systems."[32] Writing against the tendency of American race studies to obscure the chaos and contingency that characterize historical research, he critiques the inevitable "unitarianism where all the relations of power collaborate in and cohabit a particular discursive or disciplinary regime." Robinson seeks to open a space for thinking the "coincidences of different relations of power" that might collide, interfere with, or even "generate resistance."[33] Simply exposing how race is a fabrication, and how raced subjects are invented, is not a sufficient means for explaining racism and racial difference. Rather, one must be attuned to the contingencies, "the intentional and unintended," the fractured and fragmented means by which relations of power and cultural forms coalesce in racial regimes.[34]

In *Forgeries of Memory and Meaning*, Cedric J. Robinson examines early American cinema and the burgeoning American film industry at the turn of the twentieth century as a site where a new racial regime, one that persists in our present moment, came to dominate representations of race and racial difference. To quote from Robinson: "Moving pictures appear at that juncture when a new racial regime was being stitched together from remnants of its predecessors and new cloth accommodating the disposal of immigrants, colonial subjects, and insurgencies among the native poor. With the first attempts at composing a national identity in disarray, a new whiteness became the basis for the reintegration of American society."[35] Robinson analyzes how a racial regime is produced at a historical moment of uncertainty and flux, and appears in the emergence of a new technology that builds upon the racial representations of preexisting cultural forms (the world exhibition, for instance) and capitalist infrastructure and investment in new media.

Robinson criticizes both Marxist and Foucauldian approaches to the study of race and racism. Whereas Marxist accounts of race reduce its production down to an originary point—the commodification of African bodies during the slave trade—Foucauldian approaches elide the complex, contradictory, and contingent nature of how race comes to operate as a form of domination. "It is as if," writes Robinson, "systems of power never encounter the stranger, or that strangers can be seamlessly abducted into a system of oppression." These readings of race leave no space for understanding how racial regimes, described by Robinson as "makeshift patchworks masquerading as memory and the immutable . . . possess history."[36] These histories of how race is produced, when examined carefully, throw up moments of resistance and rupture that are also part of the constitution of racial regimes. In obscuring this complexity, resistance remains nothing more than a "fugitive consideration," a description replete with double meanings given the fugitive was an exemplary figure of resistance and rebellion against the established order during the era of slavery and has been reprised recently in works of critical theory that seek to analyze and revivify traditions of radical thought and praxis.

The forgetting of these histories of resistance not only attests to the kind of willful blindness engendered by racist ideologies but warps our understanding of how racism maintains its lethal grip over political, cultural, and social spheres. This is not a simple dialectic of opposing forces, of racist representations of people of color on the one hand, and resistance to it on the other; nor is it simply a matter of relations of power that capture us within their web in some a priori fashion, even though that is also true sometimes.

There is a dialectic at play in Robinson's analysis of racial regimes, but one that is sufficiently plastic to permit the possibility of unforeseeable rupture and change; where negation (racist representations of black life, for instance) and the negation of negation (antiracist resistance) are mired in other dynamics, such as deterioration and neglect. He describes, for instance, the decline of late nineteenth- and early twentieth-century antiracist imagery in black film, even while these instances of antiracist resistance were part of what a white supremacist vision, typified by films such as *Birth of a Nation*, were responding to and attempting to suppress. Robinson identifies contradictions and complex historical processes by reading across archives, with an interpretive gaze defined by the view that individuals and collectives have never been wholly determined by dominant racial paradigms. His method requires us to think race as produced by regimes of disciplinary power and capitalist modes of production and accumulation that are, in turn, composed of individual acts and collective agency, rebellion and rupture, across domains of science, economy, philosophy, and culture.

Robinson examines, for instance, how the emergence of the moving motion picture coincided with Jim Crow, a system of legalized segregation that was a central pillar in the South's strategy of economic development.[37] Robinson argues that the Jim Crow era was marked by a coalescence of infrastructure development (railroads) built with unfree (predominantly black) convict labor and capital investment (by railroad corporations and their complements) in the sponsorship of world fairs and exhibitions, sites where the new racial regime was on display and, after such events as the 1893 Chicago world's fair, transposed into an array of racist films.[38] This mapping illuminates the interconnectivity of a legal system that provided the scaffolding for new forms of racial capitalism in the era of Reconstruction, the use of exhibitions and fairs to fetishize and commoditize the cultural production of racist caricatures, and how the emergent motion picture industry became the eventual landing place for the newly consolidated figure of the Negro.

Whereas race is, as Robinson notes, mercurial and mutable, racism based on the idea of white supremacy is the constant and persistent factor characterizing the modern racial regime.[39] In this book, I take Robinson's theorization of racial regimes into the domain of property. Whereas ownership is mutable and mercurial, despite several hundred years of its naturalization as a concept by political philosophers, capitalist entrepreneurs, and jurisprudents (men who often occupied all three roles at once), private property persists as a political and legal form that characterizes and defines the modern era in many ways. The analogy between race and property is productive insofar as we regard both forms as historically contingent rather than natural; and as being produced by and through complex interrelations between capital, science, and culture.

Following Robinson, it becomes clear that the means by which racial regimes of ownership take shape require us to consider how it is not always the case that an ideology of white supremacy determines a particular economic or legal form in a straightforward or easily discernible causal sense; indeed, as discussed in chapter 1 in relation to the actions of colonial surveyor Joseph Trutch, a racial discourse of white supremacy coalesces with individual greed and the desire for personal advancement in decisions taken with respect to the surveying of indigenous lands in British Columbia and the redrawing of reserve boundaries. In this instance, racialized relations of power allow his greed and ambition to flourish. Conversely, nationalist discourses of racial and ethnic supremacy in settler colonial contexts are not always realized, in the first instance at least, through commodity forms of property. As explored in chapter 3, the ethnonational imperatives of the Israeli settler state have, until very recently, prevented a rational market in private land ownership from emerging. Racial regimes of ownership develop in uneven and sometimes contradictory ways; in the settler colony, state authorities and capitalist classes have utilized different juridical forms of property to secure, in most instances, "actual geographical possession" and, significantly, economic control over land.

PROPERTY

Property is notoriously difficult to define, particularly when we account for some of the more conceptually innovative scholarship in the field of intellectual property. In relation to real property, or land to be more specific, the literature on theories of property is truly vast. My aim here is not to provide (yet another) overview or discussion of the field of property theory but rather to identify the approach to property taken in this study. To begin with, I can be explicit about types of property that are not addressed in this book. I do not discuss, for instance, communal forms of property. While

I critique the manner in which courts have defined aboriginal title, I do not engage with indigenous concepts of ownership and relationships to land. There are examples of course, of alternate ways of holding property, as recent scholarship on the commons attests to. However, the racial regimes of ownership that I trace in this book persist as hegemonic juridical formations in liberal democratic settler states and beyond. The key political and philosophical question that I address by way of conclusion is how to resist contemporary forms of dispossession without replicating logics of appropriation and possessiveness that rely upon racial regimes for their sustenance.

While I do not focus on state property, in the colonial context, there is an intimate bond between state property and private property ownership, the latter often materializing only on the basis of sovereign colonial claims to underlying or radical title to territory. There is an undeniable relationship between the sovereign assertion of control over territory and the mechanisms through which the state organizes individual property ownership, which is primary to the overall apparatus of governance that characterizes the colony. The concept of possession in one register is taken as analogy in another, the rhetorical force of mastery deployed across a multitude of incongruent fields of ownership. As Ranajit Guha, in his classic study *A Rule of Property for Bengal*, observed, the English did "often speak of the Company's territories as an 'estate.' . . . England was thus required to assume the responsibilities of an improving landlord in Bengal."[40]

This book examines private property relations and their articulation with concepts of race through an examination of their historical trajectories in several different colonial sites, primarily South Australia, British Columbia, and the Naqab, the southern desert region of Israel/Palestine. I also draw on the work of scholars exploring property relations in other colonial sites, including colonial Bengal, Hawai'i, and other regions of Australia. (As I discuss below, the development of racial regimes of ownership cannot be neatly partitioned between settler colonial and colonial contexts.) I do not attempt to provide, nor do I draw on a singular, overarching theory of property or model of ownership. Rather, I trace the legal and philosophical justifications for appropriation and private ownership as they appear at distinct historical conjunctures of colonial settlement. The approach taken here can thus be contrasted with major works of property theory, which tend to examine the important role of property law in society, competition between individual interests and government regulation, the historical development of prevailing forms of ownership, property's relationship to social and cultural norms, and the role that property relations play in the distribution of social goods.[41]

Many of the key works of contemporary property theory of the last decades have charted a progressive path for considering the power of property law in maintaining economic inequality and, relatedly, in both producing and relying upon particular cultural and social norms. Joseph W. Singer, for instance, problematizes the dominance of the "ownership model" in prevailing understandings of property law, revealing how the latter is in reality troubled by restrictions and regulations on the (perceived) absolute right of an owner to do whatsoever she pleases with her property.[42] Property law is, rather, relational in the sense that it involves competing interests between people in relation to control over and the use of space and resources such as land.[43] Nicholas Blomley has revisited his earlier work on the contested nature of the boundary between public and private property, which he explores through interviews with private renters and owners on the perception of private and public property in light of their encroachment onto public boulevards through gardening and planting flowers. Blomley demonstrates that relationality is indeed a complex phenomenon, one that challenges the notion that property is constituted through a conceptual and spatial fixity, and that understanding relationality requires grounded research into the everyday property practices of particular communities.[44] The boundary in this particular instance demonstrates that ownership (whether it is ostensibly private or public) can be a space of overlapping interests and negotiation.

The ownership model is often contrasted with another idea of property, derived from the work of Hohfeld in particular, which is property ownership as a bundle of rights that can be rearranged and redistributed depending on the social and political norms that legislators aim to promote through the state regulation of property.[45] Laura Underkuffler emphasizes that the degree to which each of these rights is protected varies; the "stringency" with which each of these rights in the bundle, such as the right to use, possess, exclude, devise, alienate, etc., can be understood as existing in a hierarchy whereby some rights (such as the right to exclude) are more powerful than others.[46] The bundle of rights theory of ownership is often upheld as an alternative to the ownership model, which is premised on the idea that the owner has, or ought to have, an absolute degree of control over the object of ownership. This alternative model is often proposed without fully considering, in my view, the dramatic if not revolutionary changes in political economy that are the precondition for a substantive rebundling of property rights in a capitalist system of private ownership.

However, as property theorists have emphasized, this is a matter not only of economy but of the social and political imaginaries that subtend and structure contemporary property laws. Singer takes great care to emphasize the particular set of images that dominate American consciousness when it comes to "imagining the meaning of property," namely, the idea that ownership translates into an absolute right to do what one desires with the object of ownership, and near-total control over the object of ownership.[47] Given the importance of the social imaginary to the forms that ownership takes, he argues that "disputes over property use can be solved only by reference to human values, to a normative framework that helps us choose between freedom and security."[48] But what if the very concept of freedom to use property as a social good or resource in the American political and legal landscape is itself thoroughly tainted by a racial regime of ownership that was forged through slavery and the colonization of indigenous lands? This is the question posed by Saidiya Hartman, who, in the wake of W. E. B. Du Bois, points out that freedom for the previously enslaved meant entering new forms of debt bondage and exploitative labor relations. The freedom to contract (of the self-owning subject), a corollary of the freedoms associated with those of the owner of property, meant and still means, for vast numbers of people, the freedom to alienate one's labor in a highly stratified, racialized, and gendered labor market. In arguing for a balance between the owner's freedom to use his property and another's security from the harm that may be caused by the exercise of that right, a question arises about the very nature and concept of freedom that is being deployed here.

We could also ask whether the prevailing and persistent idea that ownership means absolute control over a thing has somehow shed its history as a primary technique of subjugation over the bodies of black people that facilitated massive amounts of capital accumulation by white plantation owners during the birth of the United States as a nation. How does this particular idea of ownership as absolute control appear in social relations structured by race and gender? (Cheryl Harris, as discussed above, offers an answer in her theorization of whiteness as property.) Furthermore, what happens if we consider the dominant field of perception that continually posits black bodies as a threat to the security of others? Is it possible that freedom to use property, to alienate it, and to freely enter contractual relations, and the other side of that coin, security from harm, are both still enmeshed in the racial and colonial legacies of property law formation in settler colonies, such as the United States? My intention here is not to pose these questions to Singer's text, because the parameters of his careful and detailed problematization of dominant conceptions of ownership are clearly set out, but rather to indicate the shift in orientation that my investigation reflects.

A sizeable body of sociolegal and critical legal scholarship on aboriginal rights has undertaken the task of deconstructing the Eurocentrism and cultural bias of settler courts and the contours of legal recognition. This literature has challenged the way in which aboriginal rights to land and resources have been defined according to English common-law ideals of cultivation, abstract representations of land in the form of registered title, and so on. While many of these scholars readily assume that the basis of the importation of common-law concepts of property into the content of aboriginal title is Eurocentric if not racist, this literature provides little if any theorization of how racial subjects are produced by these modes of legal recognition, and does not consider the constitutive relationship between property law and racial subjectivity.[49] It is as if acknowledging the fact that the history of land law in the settler colony had a racialist or racist dimension is sufficient for understanding how property law operates as a form of colonial domination. The omission of race and racial subjectivity as concepts worthy of serious theoretical reflection bears some resemblance to the acceptance of capitalism as the inevitable political landscape in which forms of legal mis- or nonrecognition could be ameliorated (an assumption forcefully challenged by Glen Coulthard's *Red Skin, White Masks: Rejecting the Colonial Politics of Recognition*). I seek to examine the shared logics of racial subjectivity and private property ownership that have been central to the development of racial capitalism.

Accordingly, this book is in dialogue with the research trajectories set by legal scholars dealing squarely with histories of racial oppression and private law domains such as property or contract, and scholars engaging with global histories of racial subjectivity and capitalism than with legal literature on aboriginal rights jurisprudence.[50] Most recently, Patrick Wolfe, in *Traces of History: Elementary Structures of Race*, argued that race is the idiom and modality through which colonization takes place on a global scale. Wolfe employed the idea of regimes of race to express the comprehensiveness that a "given regime of race coordinates and mobilises," and along with racial doctrine, "economic, political, moral, mythic, legal, institutional, sexual and aesthetic" dimensions constitute the regimes of race that operate as "instrument[s] of overlordship."[51] Race, for Wolfe, is a contested set of practices, a never-ending project through which labor and land appropriation throughout the colonial world is structured and rationalized.

The focus of this book is on the political ideologies, economic rationales, and colonial imaginaries that gave life to juridical forms of property and a concept of human subjectivity that are embedded in a racial order. This work can thus be distinguished from property theory emanating from the legal field in that my primary concern is not with assessing the relative merits and justness, emanating from concerns for legal and political equality, of contemporary property relations generally, and particularly in relation to First Nations. I turn to the more general question of property law and political transformation only in the conclusion. A work of property theory that engages very directly with the question of how property law can or ought to be reconfigured in specific political contexts, including the transformation of the racial regime of apartheid in South Africa, is André van der Walt's *Property in the Margins*. I discuss van der Walt's scholarly and political intervention in depth in the conclusion. Writing in the aftermath of the transition from apartheid to a liberal democratic constitutional order, to which the reform of property law was pivotal, van der Walt seeks to examine what justice demands of property law: "[C]ertain justice-driven qualifications of and amendments to the property regime are so fundamental that they cannot be accommodated within or explained in terms of the current doctrine—they require a rethink of the system, a reconsideration of the language, the concepts, the rhetoric and the logic in terms of which we explain and justify choices for or against individual security and systemic stability in the property regime."[52] Van der Walt explicitly distinguishes his work from the body of property theory that examines the limits of property within the presumed stability of political, economic, and social structures.[53] By way of conclusion, I discuss van der Walt's argument that in order for genuine political transformation to occur, the perspectives and political imaginaries of those without property, those in the margins, must replace the lexicon of rights embedded at the core of much property doctrine.

COLONIAL MODERNITIES AND SETTLER COLONIALISM

As noted above, articulations of race and property law do not emerge in a consistent, linear, or even fashion. The temporalities of colonialism, as with modernity itself, are multiple and uneven. Contrary to the colonial (and imperialist) narrative that modernity unfolds in a linear, developmental fashion, with the non-European world placed either at some earlier stage of development or outside history altogether (as with Hegel's infamous description of Africa in *The Philosophy of History*), there is no "homogenous 'law of development'" that can determine and define what constitutes improvement or indeed progress.[54] Postcolonial critiques of modernity, as David Lloyd observes, "supplement the recognition of the internal contradictions of modernization with the apprehension of other forms of unevenness, forms of unevenness that call into question the historicist narrative that understands modernity as the progress from the backward to the advanced, from the pre-modern to the modern."[55] As noted above, property law plays a significant role in the colonialist narrative of modern progress. The imposition of modern laws of private property are cast in developmental terms, shifting from early modern justifications for ownership based in possession and use to more abstract forms of ownership embodied in systems of title by registration. However, as we see in the settler colonial context, rationales for property ownership do not adhere to this developmental narrative. In this way, examining property laws in settler colonial contexts, and specifically rationales for ownership (including forms of ownership recognized in aboriginal title doctrine) presents an exemplary instance of how fractured and multiple the temporalities that characterize modern colonialism are.

Settler colonialism, as a structure, a continually unfolding process (a much-quoted observation of Patrick Wolfe), requires flexibility in the legal devices and rationales it utilizes to maintain state control—and possession— of indigenous lands. This is quite evident in the Palestinian context, where the perceived demographic threat of the Palestinian population leads the Israeli state to truly rely on a combination of older and newer rationales for appropriation and ownership, coupled with a range of other legal orders including military, land use planning, and criminal laws. These recombinant forms of appropriation and ownership, and the racial logics articulated through them, produce uneven landscapes and scenes of dispossession. In this way, this book is not a comparative analysis of different jurisdictions, but an exploration of how property, and its legal form, emerges in conjunction with modern concepts of race at different moments and in different settler colonies.

While the book focuses on settler colonialism, the economic, political, and social conjunctures that produce juridical formations of modern property law and race cannot be confined to the settler colonial context. One could certainly examine colonial and postcolonial contexts and find such articulations. However, the similarities in the development and contemporary expression of the relationship between modern property laws and race in settler colonies point to specificities and commonalities that are significant when considering how demands for justice and movements for decolonization confront the racial regimes of ownership that have so fundamentally shaped the nature of dispossession of indigenous and racialized migrant populations, the latter of which Jodi Byrd has termed "arrivants."

The place of law and the specifically juridical forms that colonial governance assumes in the settler colony inform a wide and rich terrain of literature on various aspects of settler colonialism. The nature of the political and legal recognition, misrecognition, and nonrecognition of First Nations in North America, for instance, has been addressed through analyses of the structures of indigenous self-governance, membership, and citizenship; land appropriation and status; and sovereignty and its ontologies of racialization and possession.[56] Land, territory, and the forms of life attached to, or embedded within them are a permanent site of contestation and struggle between settler state authorities and First Nations. Audra Simpson and Glen Coulthard, among others, have deftly explored the complex, and sometimes contradictory, political forms of refusal and rejection of the colonial politics of recognition that characterize many First Nations' resistance to colonial settlement. While this book does not address itself explicitly to the discourse of recognition or the problem of sovereignty, in my view, property ownership and appropriation are quite central to the form that the legal recognition of indigenous rights has taken in common-law jurisdictions such as Canada and Australia. As I have argued previously, property ownership and a dynamic of appropriation are both primary to a Hegelian dialectics of recognition, evident in juridical forms of recognition and nonrecognition.[57]

The continual struggle for ownership and control over indigenous land distinguishes settler colonialism from the postcolony. This is not to say that the legacies of territorial reorganization and the partitioning of land during colonial rule do not continue to plague postcolonial nation-states, creating sometimes lethal conflicts over land and resources; however, in the settler colony the colonial animus is driven by the need to control the land base for the continued growth of settler economies and for the security of settler populations.[58] Land, which is "necessary for life" as Wolfe puts it, thus becomes a site of contestation for nothing less than life itself.[59] As I demonstrate throughout this book, property law has proved itself to be one of the most significant orders, an amalgam of legal techniques, through which colonial appropriation of land and the fashioning of colonial subjectivities take place and are secured. Jodi Byrd articulates the "aggregation" of the global nature of forms of settler colonization and their deployment of racialization and property: "[r]acialisation and colonization should thus be understood as concomitant global systems that secure white dominance through time, property, and notions of self."[60]

The focus on land and property relations in this study intervenes against a theoretical tendency, a mode of thought, identified by Jodi Byrd, through which the conflation of racialization and colonization works to erase the central function played by territoriality in colonization and contemporary modes of dispossession. She asks, "what happens to indigenous peoples and the stakes of sovereignty, land, and decolonisation when conquest is reframed through the global historicities of race?"[61] Byrd deftly reveals how indigeneity comes to function, across a broad spectrum of continental philosophy and critical theory, as a "transit," in the sense that a wide range of historical experiences of exclusion and racism, in the multicultural liberal settler society, may acknowledge (and indeed, as Byrd points out, lament) the originary violence of colonial settlement only to move beyond it, as if it could be surpassed. Although indigenous dispossession is a constitutive part of the ground upon which other forms of racial subjugation take place in the settler colony, indigeneity becomes a space that is traversed, and often rendered as an artifact of the past. Examining how race and racialization are articulated through legal forms of property rooted in a spectrum of early modern and late modern rationalities shows how there is not a temporality of transit at work in the concept of the racial regime of ownership developed here, but rather the constant presence of territoriality, land, and possession.

The temporalities of property law's iterations and operations in the settler colony can be grasped by observing the difference between the myth of modernity instantiated in the wide-scale imposition of the English common law of property as the means through which the undeveloped would enter the pale of civilized life, and the actual use and manipulation of a wide range of rationales for the assertion of both colonial sovereignty and individual private ownership (which are of course dependent upon one another to a great extent) that do not adhere to a linear, teleological development of property law. The chasm between the myth of developmental progress and the often contradictory deployment of early and late modern rationales for ownership reflects the rather fragmented character of the temporalities of modernity itself. The chapters in this book thus do not adhere to a chronology, but attempt to trace three different economic, political-philosophical, and cultural rationales for specific legal modalities of ownership that appear at particular historical junctures in settler colonies: the ideology of use that casts both land and its native inhabitants as in need of improvement, the logics of abstraction that underlie increasingly commodified visions of land and human life from the seventeenth century onward, and the use of the juridical concept of status to bind together identity and property relations.

The inclusion of Israel/Palestine in this study presents an exemplary instance of the temporally fragmented and nonlinear nature of the racial regimes of ownership that typify the settler colony. There is a common tendency among some scholars of Israel/Palestine to assert that Israel is the last settler colony, engaging in practices of colonial settlement that were accomplished in North America and Australia in the nineteenth century. These assertions imply that colonization was accomplished in these older settler colonies and that somehow their past is Palestine's present.[62] Contrary to this view, I seek to emphasize that the juridical techniques of appropriation and dispossession utilized across the settler colonial sites that I examine continue to inform the ongoing processes of settlement and displacement in Canada, Australia, and elsewhere.

At the same time, it is undeniable that, as David Lloyd and Patrick Wolfe have written, "the twenty-first century context in which Israel is seeking to complete the seizure of what remains of Mandate Palestine differs crucially from the nineteenth-century context in which settlers in Australia and North America completed their seizure of the Native estate."[63] I don't entirely agree that the settler states of Australia and North America have "completed" their seizure of indigenous lands, in the sense that First Nations continue to mount effective forms of resistance against this long history of appropriation, and because these settler states are imposing new means of appropriating and reappropriating indigenous lands that are consistent with the organization of contemporary land markets.[64]

Notwithstanding this point, Lloyd and Wolfe present one of the most persuasive and insightful theorizations of how Israel's contemporary modes of settlement exist in relation to ongoing modes of appropriation and dispossession in other settler colonies. They argue that settler colonialism "is not some transitional phase that gives way to—even provides a laboratory for—the emergent global order." Rather, it is "foundational to that order."[65] New modes of accumulation, the "second enclosure" heralded by the ongoing privatization of public goods, which are aptly described by Lloyd and Wolfe as "public patrimonies of the modern liberal state that emerged from an earlier moment of enclosure and dispossession," are positioned in a relation of continuity with the very neoliberal settlement practices of Israel through the common objective of managing surplus populations.[66]

Lloyd and Wolfe argue that in both older settler colonies and Israel/Palestine, the native population has invariably occupied the place of a surplus population, necessitating the creation of a wide range of "techniques of elimination." The logic of elimination is as much figural as it is literal, and is as present in attempts to assimilate indigenous populations into nationalist iconography and multicultural narratives as it is evident in the techniques of spatial confinement. The massive differences between the nineteenth century, the era dominated by the growth of industrial capitalism, and contemporary modes of neoliberal capitalism require close attention to the ways in which modes of appropriation, rationales for ownership, and the legal form(s) of property have adapted themselves to the imperatives of colonial domination.

CHAPTER OVERVIEW

In chapter 1, I examine the enfolding of the valuation of land and the attribution of lesser value to the lives of indigenous populations in a racial regime of ownership based on an ideology of improvement. I analyze the policies of preemption and homesteading as the primary legal devices used to appropriate indigenous land in British Columbia. I also look at the actions and attitudes of colonial administrators, in particular Joseph Trutch, whose land surveys created the conditions for appropriation to take place on a greater scale than prior to his interventions. The ideology of improvement that informed the legal policies and colonial attitudes toward First Nations and their land finds one of its historical antecedents in Ireland. I trace the history of the articulation of racial inferiority with particular forms of land use through the work of William Petty and examine the manner in which he justified the fusing together of the value of Irish land with the value of Irish people. The technologies of measurement utilized to survey the land and its productivity are examined alongside Petty's view of the Irish peasantry as racially inferior and brutish. By way of conclusion, I analyze the Supreme Court of Canada judgment *Tsilhqot'in v. British Columbia* [2014] 2 S.C.R. 257, where the court expands the concept of aboriginal title to include indigenous conceptions of land use and ownership. I argue that while the court's modification of the doctrine of aboriginal title is legally and politically significant, it remains tethered to a racial, anthropological schema in its conceptualization of the claimants' mode of land use and ownership as seminomadic.

In chapter 2, I explore the commodity logic of abstraction that finds expression in a system of landholding that is premised on the erasure of prior interests in land. The system of title by registration that was implemented in the colony of South Australia in 1858, some seventy years prior to being fully implemented on a national level in the United Kingdom, reflects the commodity vision of land that British land reformers carried with them to the colony. In fact, the use of a system of individual fee simple titles, captured in a state-run registry, was a key means of diminishing indigenous systems of land tenure that did not conform to an economic and legal system based on an ideology of the possessive individual. Further, I argue in chapter 2 that the abstract logic of the commodity form found its counterpart in another form of abstraction, related to the racial classification of human life. The burgeoning pseudoscience of racial classification incorporated abstraction as a mode of ostensibly scientific thought, underpinning methods of measurement and the evaluation of human value based in anatomy and biology.

The racial regime of ownership consolidated at this historical conjuncture, in the mid-nineteenth century, certainly reflects a transition to a more abstract basis for ownership that is, in the settler colony, rendered possible by the racial taxonomization of human life that placed aboriginal people low on the scale of civilization. However, as I have argued above, the articulation of property law and race in racial regimes of ownership does not adhere to a linear, developmental temporality. By examining the contemporary status of title held by Palestinians in East Jerusalem, it becomes clear that possession, a much older rationale for ownership diminished by a logic of registration, retains its force as the primary colonial animus in Israeli attempts to displace Palestinians from the city of Jerusalem.

Chapter 3 follows the ideology of improvement to Palestine. I examine how Zionist settlers in the late nineteenth and early twentieth centuries viewed existing modes of cultivation in Palestine, and the notion that Palestinian modes of land use reflected an inferior intellectual capacity and less developed culture. Land that required improvement was a consequence of its stewardship being in the hands of people who themselves required improvement. I argue in chapter 3 that the establishment of agricultural settlements during this early period of settlement in Palestine provided a basis for the

Zionist narrative of a successful return to the land; a negation of exile that was realized through working the land. Cultivation was the means through which Zionist political claims could be realized territorially. Further, I examine how cultivation retains its force primarily as an ideological phenomenon rather than a reflection of actual economic and social realities, playing a significant role in land claims by Bedouin communities, for whom specific forms of cultivation remain a key legal threshold for proving historical occupancy and ownership of their lands.

Chapter 4 departs from the rationales analyzed in chapters 1 through 3, to focus on a racial regime of ownership characterized by what I refer to as the identity-property nexus. In chapter 4, through a largely historical analysis of Canadian Indian Act legislation, I examine how the colonial determination of the legal status of First Nations men and women, through the juridical category of the Indian, bound together legal identity and access to land. The concept of status articulates a nexus, a juridical knot, between identity and relations of ownership. I argue that this modern legal concept of status is in part the inheritance of modern property law as figured through the self-possessive individual. As such, I excavate the racial and gendered ontology of the self-possessive subject, as the ideal status against which the juridical category of the Indian was legislatively defined.

Avtar Brah makes a crucial intervention in conceptualizations of race by arguing that race represents gendered phenomena. Race is articulated with "socio-economic, cultural and political relations of gender, class and other markers of 'difference' and differentiation."[67] Race is thus articulated with gender, sexuality, class, and other modalities of difference in racial regimes of power, a fact explored and excavated by numerous feminist traditions of thought.[68] As I explore specifically in chapter 4, the nexus of identity-property relations that is captured by the use of legal status to dispossess First Nations women in Canada of their land and communities provides a stark instance of how a racial ontology of the human that informs the proper subject of ownership is thoroughly gendered. Relatedly, colonial representations of indigenous land as feminized, available for appropriation, or as waste land in need of being rendered fertile through cultivation, inform the discussion in chapter 1. While the primary focus in the book is on race and its articulation with private property relations, I have attempted to address the way in which gender is articulated within racial regimes of ownership by devoting a specific chapter to the topic.

The formations that I analyze appear across jurisdictions and at different moments of time. The voracious nature of capitalist forms of property does not adhere to a linear or teleological model of development. Expressed with and through ethnoracial nationalisms in the settler colony, the objectives of possessing and exploiting indigenous lands require a panoply of property logics that at times, as discussed above, can retard or hamper the development of rational markets in land. Possession, no longer the strongest basis of a property claim in many common-law jurisdictions, remains quite central to property relations in the settler colony. In Palestine, asserting colonial control over land and public space requires the displacement and dispossession of Palestinians, even in the face of formalized and well-documented ownership. In other words, even where indigenous ownership conforms to European standards of proof, the imperative to legally possess and displace indigenous populations from their land overwhelms more contemporary rationales for ownership. In Canada, attempts by the federal government to settle land claims through the conversion of lands held under aboriginal title to fee simple is perhaps another means of ultimately gaining possession of indigenous lands—bringing it within the mainstream market in land renders it in a form capable of being bought up by nonindigenous proprietors, unlike lands held under aboriginal title.

This book cannot do justice to the violence of dispossession of First Nations in Canada and Australia, and Palestinians living in exile, or in the West Bank, Gaza, or Israel. The effects of dispossession and displacement on indigenous people have not been captured in this analysis of the legal techniques and political-economic formations utilized by settler colonial authorities to continue their occupations. Similarly, I do not in this book discuss modes of resistance to colonization. To be very clear, this should not lead the reader to infer that in my view, settler colonial projects have been successful in their genocidal ambitions. This book is about a juridical formation that emerges with the advent of modern property laws and modern conceptualizations of race. The striking similarities in the articulations of modern property law and racial logics across the settler colonial jurisdictions examined in this book, despite the differences between these sites, reveal how the repertoire of legal techniques used to appropriate land and the philosophical rationales underlying them are not, necessarily, infinite in number. This book is an attempt to better understand what I refer to as racial regimes of ownership in the hope that they can be dismantled.

Contemporary struggles over property in urban areas often revolve around the concept of use. If people can use empty residential buildings for shelter, particularly when there are severe housing shortages in many major cities, shouldn't their interests in property prevail over that of a genuinely absentee owner?[1] The Plataforma de Afectados por la Hipoteca (PAH), to take one salient example, base their struggle for social housing on the idea that the social uses of property (residential housing stock in particular) should have greater weight in defining property interests than property's function as an instrument of financial investment and expropriation. In the face of a massive number of foreclosures and evictions in Spain in the aftermath of the 2008 financial crisis, PAH has sought to reinvigorate the provisions in the Spanish Constitution that explicitly protect the right to housing, and to challenge the primacy of the ideology of ownership itself.[2]

The relationship between the uses of property and property ownership has a complex history, which persists into the present. The question of whether the use of a thing gives rise (or ought to give rise) to an ownership interest has long been a matter of great contestation and revolves around the social, political, and economic value attributed to the particular form of use at issue. For instance, the Franciscans famously distinguished their use of property for the fulfillment of the necessities of life from the actual ownership of that same property in view of their order's prohibition on accumulation.[3] The question of whether Franciscan monks ought to be allowed to use property without being ensnared within legal relations of ownership or, indeed, whether their use de facto constituted an ownership interest was continuously posed by powerful clergymen and the pope during the thirteenth and fourteenth centuries.[4] Ultimately, while the Franciscans' use of property was juridically defined as being above and beyond the legal domain, Thomas Frank argues that the undertaking to live in poverty was understood as reaping a spiritual dividend. There was a "high degree of exchangeability between material goods and spiritual performances," with the Franciscans' use of property dependent on the license freely given to them by the legal owners, the Roman Catholic Church.[5]

The separation of interests between those who use property or benefit from its use and those who are the legal owners also lies at the basis of the modern law of trusts. The modern trust is a legal device that has evolved over time in order to split beneficial (or equitable) ownership from legal title to property, which has its origins in the Roman law concept of "the use." Translated into the Norman idiom of the medieval period, the *cestui que use* denoted one who was the beneficiary of property legally held by another.[6] With the modern trust, the use of property for the good of beneficiaries covers a very wide spectrum indeed, encompassing both charities on one end and private trusts used to accumulate vast amounts of wealth, while often avoiding various liabilities, on the other.[7] Precisely because of the contested nature of use and its relationship to legal ownership—the question of how property can and ought to be used, by whom and for whose benefit—this conjuncture remains a potentially fruitful arena for reshaping prevailing property norms.

Despite the flexible and variable nature of the relationship between use and ownership, the physical occupation and use of land as a basis for ownership has been defined quite narrowly by an ideology of improvement in settler colonial contexts. Despite the widespread adoption in Canada, many states in the United States, and Australia, among other places, of a system of title by registration in the late nineteenth and early twentieth centuries (explored in chapter 2), the concept of use retains its place at the heart of indigenous struggles for land. The social use of property (i.e., use that is not solely defined by economic productivity and profit), and the use of property to meet the basic necessities of life, such as shelter, form a part of contemporary struggles to redefine relations of ownership in urban spaces.[8] However, it is clear that historically speaking, in common-law jurisdictions, use that would justify an ownership right was defined by cultivation, and cultivation was understood within the relatively narrow parameters of English agrarian capitalism. In settler colonies, early modern property logics that posit cultivation as the basis of an ownership right shape the criteria for establishing indigenous rights to land, which, in the context of a land market where contemporary ownership is governed by a system of registration, produce anachronistic legal tests and legal subjectivities in the domain of aboriginal title.

It is instructive, in considering how use remains a central characteristic of aboriginal title in the Canadian context, as elsewhere, to consider the ideology of improvement that came to shape property law from the seventeenth century. The logics of quantification and measurement that subtend the ideology of improvement required new mechanisms for creating and attributing value to people and the land to which they were connected. We see in the work of early political economists such as William Petty the formulation of a scientific approach to the measurement of the value of land and people. The convergence of medical scientific understandings of the human body, and anatomy specifically, with a method of evaluation based on mathematics produced new forms of valuing land, produce, and people, and in turn justified new and emergent forms of colonial governance.

The imperative to quantify and measure value created an ideological juggernaut that defined people and land as unproductive in relation to agricultural production and deemed them to be waste and in need of improvement.[9] The creation of an epistemological framework where people came to be valued as economic units set the ground for a fusing together of ownership and subjectivity in a way that had devastating consequences for entire populations who did not cultivate their lands for the purposes of commercial trade and marketized exchange. These populations were by definition uncivilized and could be disposed of, cast out of the borders of political citizenship. The brutal displacement and dispossession of thousands of Irish that preceded the displacement of First Nations from their lands, based on the political arithmetic of Petty and those influenced by his work, such as John Locke and Adam Smith, is testament to the violence engendered by methods of measurement and quantification, and conceptualizations of value defined primarily by economic productivity.

In this chapter, I argue that in the settler colony, use remains at the core of prevailing definitions of aboriginal title. Governed by an ideology of improvement, the manner in which First Nations have historically used their land and whether it conforms to an idea of cultivation and settlement that emerged during the transition to agrarian capitalism in England has formed a primary criterion in adjudicating aboriginal title claims in the Canadian context, and as we will explore in chapter 3, in the Israeli/Palestinian context as well. Indigenous ways of using and owning land that don't conform to this ideal of settlement have been relegated to a prehistory of modern law.[10] This ideology of improvement is one that binds together land and its populations; land that was not cultivated for the purposes of contributing to a burgeoning agrarian capitalist economy by industrious laborers was, from the early seventeenth century onward, deemed to be waste.[11] Whereas wasteland was free for appropriation, those who maintained subsistence modes of cultivation, for instance, were cast as in need of improvement through assimilation into a civilized (read English) population and ways of living. In this chapter, the racial regime of ownership that articulates both land and its people as in need of improvement reappears across many colonial jurisdictions at different historical junctures, each with their own specificities.

In seventeenth-century colonial Ireland, the value of land and populations was assessed on the basis of their productivity, the former measured according to agricultural output and the latter by their capacity to cultivate. In Petty's writings we see the beginnings of what could be termed an early labor theory of value, rendering the value of both land and human life as equivalences based on the cultivation of land. The subsequent evaluation of both uncultivated land and the people associated with subsistence modes of life as waste is distinct, however, from the concept of a surplus population, as elaborated by Marx. The colonial compulsion to improve the native was not conditioned by the need to create a reserve army of labor. Rather, what is evident is a desire to expel or criminalize populations who are not settled on the land and who do not engage in marketized forms of cultivation. The lack of fixity or the nomadic character of populations has long been a basis for their criminalization and expulsion from the body politic. Foucault points to the first economic analyses of delinquency in eighteenth-century France, which identified the vagabond as a criminal element in society who deserved to be stripped of civil status: "[E]ntry into the world of vagabondage is the main thing to be punished; entry into the world of delinquency is the fact of travelling around, of not being settled on an estate, of not being defined by a job. Crime begins when one has no civil status, that is to say geographical location within a definite community, when one is 'disreputable (sans aveu).'"[12] The eighteenth century witnesses both the criminalization of groups of people not tethered or fixed geographically to regular work, as well as the rise in statistical forms of knowledge aimed at the governance of these (and other) populations. While Foucault does not address the colonial context, the criminalization of mobile groups of people found its legal expression, in the colonial context as elsewhere, in the crime of trespass. First Nations who, prior to the arrival of settlers, engaged in mobile and seasonal forms of cultivation and labor were rendered as inherently inferior, demonstrably lacking the norms of propriety required for full civil status. The Irish were viewed, from the beginnings of colonial settlement in the seventeenth century, as somewhat less than human on account of the lack of permanence that characterized the dwellings of laborers. In the nineteenth century, the racial difference of First Nations, based on the nature of their land use, is cast by the surveyor Trutch in British Columbia in civilizational terms; and finally in the twenty-first century, race appears primarily as a discourse of cultural difference in the case of the Tsilhqot'in land claims. The figure of the seminomad, recuperated and rehabilitated in recent indigenous rights litigation, bears the mark of this globalized history of exclusion.

This chapter proceeds in three parts. In the first part, I trace the history of the ideology of improvement through the work of William Petty. While Baconian influences on his thought are undoubtedly relevant, I focus here on the way in which Petty conceives of wealth and value in the *Political Anatomy* and *Political Arithmetick*. The fusing together of the value of land with the value of people emerges in the context of colonial Ireland, where early attempts to measure land with the use of a cadastral survey coincided with the desire to measure the value of the population on the basis of their consumption and productive labor. In the work of Locke and Blackstone, the attributions of savagery and underdevelopment to populations not engaged in waged labor or capitalist agrarian production as set forth by Petty are historicized and spatialized. The Indians of North America, lacking the laws of private property, inhabit a premodern space, a time and place before the advent of civilization.

In the second part of the chapter, I examine colonial settlement in British Columbia, and the widespread use of preemption and homesteading as the primary legislative devices used to settle unceded aboriginal lands. An examination of the attitudes and actions of colonial administrators, notably Joseph Trutch, reveal how First Nations' land was surveyed and remapped in the service of consolidating colonial sovereign control over it. We glean insight into how both the land and First Nations were viewed by colonists such as Trutch, who was motivated as much by individual greed for personal profit as grand civilizational and imperial objectives. Possession and the acquisition of aboriginal land, the necessary precondition for the development of agriculture, industry, and the accumulation of wealth by individuals as well as the colonial states they represented, shaped land law in colonial British Columbia, as elsewhere. What is of interest here is the major role that the ideology of improvement played in this process, and the way in which it enfolded the valuation of land and indigenous populations into one juridical formation, governing colonial spaces through a racial regime of ownership predicated on cultivation and racial hierarchies determined by this form of land use.

By way of conclusion, I examine the aboriginal title case of *Tsilhqot'in v. British Columbia* (2014). I analyze key judgments of the Supreme Court of Canada relating to section 35 jurisprudence on aboriginal title, and consider the Supreme Court's redefinition of the concept of aboriginal title to include the practices, forms of land use, and worldview of seminomadic peoples. In augmenting the concept of aboriginal title in this way, I argue that the Supreme Court has taken a significant step forward in taking into account aboriginal perspectives within the parameters of a colonial legal paradigm and yet remains tethered to an anthropological schema that can only recognize indigenous difference in terms of the language of nomadism. This theme is then explored in relation to the dispossession of the Bedouin in southern Israel in chapter 3.

The concept of improvement as the defining criterion for establishing a legitimate right to property finds its clearest expression in the work of

Locke. However, the fusing together of the value of land and people, and the conceptualization of value according to specific ideas of improvement, emerges in the work of William Petty, whose *Political Anatomy of Ireland* and *Political Arithmetick* forged a new way of conceiving of and valuing wealth (and, significantly for my purposes, its constituent components including land and populations) in the space of the colony of Ireland. As I argue below, the ideology of improvement came to be governed by a logic of calculation and measurement. The approach taken by Petty reflects the influence of Baconian natural history on his thought; emerging ideas about taxonomy and classification, the use of mathematics to compile statistical knowledge of the human body and populations, coalesce with the desire to increase individual and national wealth. What emerges, as we see below, are new ways of quantifying both land and people, binding the value of one to the other. One of the first devices of measurement utilized to change the fabric of Irish society and economy was the land survey.

THE POLITICAL ANATOMY OF COLONIZATION

Labour is the Father and active principle of Wealth, as Lands are the Mother.
—William Petty, *Economic Writings*

William Petty was an inventor, an entrepreneur, a physician, and a progenitor of modern political economy. It was his appointment as physician-general to the army in Ireland, and to General Ireton, the commander in chief in 1651 that first took him to Ireland.[13] This appointment marks the beginning of a long period of time in which Petty would have a profound influence on the appropriation of Irish lands and the displacement and dispossession of countless communities. The use of the survey as a technology for quantifying the value of land was refined by Petty in the Irish context, and deployed in many different colonial contexts thereafter.

By the mid-seventeenth century, Ireland lay, in the eyes of the English colonial power, a conquered and defeated territory. What remained as a prime concern to the English, however, was how to render the Irish into a complete state of submission; as conflict raged between Protestants and Catholics all over the European continent, there was fear of ongoing conflict with the Irish. The mass displacement and transportation of the Irish to England was viewed as a potential solution to war, but one that carried its own risks: " 'The unsettling of a nation,' they [the colonial council] pointed out, 'is an easy work; the settling is not,' and the transplantation could have but one result—the permanent mutual alienation of the English and the Irish, and the division of the latter between a large discontented garrison beyond the Shannon and scattered bands of pillaging Tories on this side of the river."[14]

By 1687 Petty would have devised a plan that involved forcibly transporting up to a million Irish from their native lands. His plan was based not solely on the fear of religious foment, however, but on a calculation. The value of the Irish was quantified according to their potential labor value, a calculation based on the idea that mathematical rules could provide a neutral, objective means of producing knowledge, useful for creating and measuring wealth.[15] Viewing the Irish population as an amalgam of economic units was bound to his valuation of the land, which began with the Civil Survey.

Petty's partitioning and parcellization of Ireland began when he was appointed in 1654 to undertake a survey. The urgent need to survey and value the land was driven by the debt owed by the British Crown to the army, and the "private adventurers" who had defeated the Irish in the war of 1648. Approximately one-eighth of all of Ireland was set aside to pay those who had privately invested in the bloody suppression of the Irish in exchange for land. In order to pay the arrears in property, there was a need to survey, map, and value all of the appropriated land. Petty proposed a survey of Ireland, to be followed by a mapping exercise. This initial survey then was quite unrelated to the mapping exercise; Fitzmaurice notes that it was called a "Civil Survey" as it involved the making of lists of descriptions of existing estates and territory, their acreage and value. Fitzmaurice notes that "the Civil Survey was simply a specification of lands, recorded in lists, with brief descriptive notes as to acreage and value, and partook of the character of what in modern days is called a valuation list or register. There were no maps attached to it, and the scheme of the general map, though present to the minds of the authors of the 'Grosse Survey,' had hitherto never been effectually carried out, though commenced here and there."[16]

Petty was at the forefront of the Downs Survey, commenced in 1655, which was a large-scale mapping exercise based on a cadastral survey of the land. As Linebaugh and Rediker have noted, "the Downs Survey facilitated a massive land transfer to private adventurers, soldiers, who were part of an 'immigrant landlord class.'"[17] Like other colonial surveyors of subsequent generations such as Joseph Trutch, Petty used his position as surveyor to amass a personal fortune. By 1688, he had been granted 160,000 acres in the county of Kerry.[18] He exploited Irish forests in the three baronies he had gained possession of, Iveragh, Glanaroughty, and Dunkerron, in order to make a quick profit.[19] While the ironworks he started were not as successful financially as he had initially hoped, they still yielded a profit for the enterprising colonist.[20]

In addition to appropriating Irish lands as payment to the English adventurers, Petty's assiduousness in pursuing the general survey of Ireland was a part of his larger objective of devising a means of calculating national wealth. A key component in assessing national wealth, in Petty's view, meant accounting for rent. Rent from lands formed a major plank in his method of calculation of national wealth, because it was a source of revenue through taxation, and because it reflected the size and productivity of the population.[21] As noted above, the size of the population was also a determining factor in the capacity of a nation to generate wealth. Poverty, as defined by Petty, was "fewness of people."[22]

The excision of "a sixth part of the rent of the whole, which is about the proportion, that the Adventurers and Souldiers [sic] in Ireland retribute to the King as Quit Rents" was in Petty's view the most secure way of generating the "publick charge."[23] Petty's ruminations on the most expedient form of tax collection involve a discussion of taxation on agricultural yield and, relatedly, the differential profits generated by a farmer as opposed to a landowner who rents his land to a tenant farmer. Who bears a greater taxation burden, the landowner who expends nothing on labor and yields no profit from the agricultural production of his tenant, but who collects a rent from a tenant, or the landowner-farmer who "with his own hands plants a certain scope of Land" with crops?[24] In this context we see one aspect of what is a major contribution to political economy, an early labor theory of value. What allows Petty to assess and evaluate these differences is not the price paid for agricultural yield or rent in gold or silver coins, but the "two natural Denominations ... Land and Labour."[25] Land and labor ought to be the measures for the value of rent, and for the price of land itself. "[T]hat is, we ought to say, a Ship or garment is worth such a measure of Land, with such another measure of Labour; forasmuch as both Ships and Garments were the creatures of Lands and mens [sic] Labours thereupon: This being true, we should be glad to fine out a natural Par between Land and Labour, so as we might express the value by either of them alone as well or better than by both, and reduce one into the other as easily and certainly as we reduce pence into pounds."[26]

Land and the labor of men ought to be conceptual equivalents; they are inextricably bound to one another. The improvement of one requires the improvement of the other. If men are not industrious and productive workers of the land, the land will be, like them, worth less, perhaps even worthless. Petty writes with unconcealed contempt of the "poor" Irish who farm and labor in sufficient quantities for subsistence but seemingly aspire to nothing more than that. Describing their existence as nothing short of brutish, Petty writes that the "Bulk of the Irish . . . are wretched Cabin-mens, slavishly bred."[27] The "nasty Cabbins . . . by reason of the Soot and Smoaks . . . and the Narrowness and Nastiness of the Place . . . cannot be kept Clean nor Safe from Beasts and Vermin, nor from Damps and Musty Stenches." They lived in a backward condition that required improvement if Ireland were ever to develop its natural fitness for trade.[28]

Land and the men who labored upon it were inextricably bound to one another in Petty's new method of valuation of wealth. The measures of wealth were land and people, and both were reduced to economic units. Another example of how land and the lives of men were reduced to economic equivalents of each other can be seen in Petty's method of valuing the fee simple title to a piece of land. He relates the value of land and the value of people through time, measured by the life span of men as workers. He takes three generations of men—grandfather, father, and son—and reasons that the land value is equal to the number of years its owners will be able to use and improve it (based on an estimation of the number of years that all three generations who are in a continual line of descent will coexist as producers). Here is where the rudimentary statistical information garnered in the Bills of Mortality generates the beginnings of data collection for the purposes of political economy and population control.[29]

In *The Political Anatomy of Ireland* the treatment of men, women, and children (or families) as economic units is honed to a crude science. Having accounted for the number of people based on religious belief, the number of families, and the relative wealth of families based on the type of dwelling (and the number of chimneys of each dwelling), Petty values the population according to their labor and the cost of reproducing the lives of laborers. In the *Verbum Sapienti*, the second chapter, titled "The Value of the People," reads like a slightly delirious set of calculations. Estimating the value of people's productive output, the cost of their labor, and the value of stock ("wealth") of the nation, Petty concludes that "6 Millions of People [are] worth 417 millions of pounds Sterling" and that accordingly, each one of them is worth "69¹ [pounds]."[30] This leads him to make concrete suggestions about how the cost of reproducing labor could be reduced (by, for instance, limiting the number and duration of meals laboring men normally consume) in order to increase wealth. The ideology of improvement tied the industriousness of individuals and national interests together, reflected in the metaphor of the beehive inscribed in Petty's coat of arms.[31]

This reductively economistic view of human life that was directly related to the value of land was at the same time racial and gendered in its conceptualization. Although Petty did not seem to attribute Irish laziness to the state of their bodily constitution, he did see Irish and English difference as somehow inherently biological.[32] His solution for quelling Irish rebellion involved the intermarriage of English women and Irish men, and Irish women to English men, who would raise their children to be English speaking, and the "whole Oeconomy [*sic*] of the Family" would be English.[33] The deficiencies of the Irish could be ameliorated by mixing their blood with that of the English. This appears as a precursor to the full-blown blood quantum racism in Australia in the nineteenth century, where the prevailing policy for several decades was to assimilate aboriginal communities starting with mixed-race children, who were perceived as closer to being white on account of their parentage. Petty's suggestion of mixing Irish and English blood through reproduction, in order to produce a more industrious and disciplined population, is akin to the method an agricultural scientist might utilize in the interbreeding of plant species to improve yield.

Intermarriage with the English was just one means of improving the Irish. In the report issued in 1676 from the Council of Trade in Ireland to the lord lieutenant and council, authored by Petty, he renders a list of "considerations relating to the Improvement of Ireland." These recommendations include the improvement of household dwellings, the planting of gardens (as stipulated by the Statute for Hemp and Flax), and the protection of "industriousness," among other things. Generally, Petty proposed that economic growth in Ireland depended on the settling and anglicizing of the Irish population.[34]

While modern biological racism had yet to emerge, conceptions of racial difference and, crucially, European superiority were conditioned at this time by the concept of land use described above. While Petty saw the Irish as capable of improvement, Jews were cast outside this paradigm altogether on account, at least in part, of their tenuous relationship to the land. In his *Treatise of Taxes*, he distinguishes Jews not only on the basis of communal and religious difference, but on the basis of their chosen livelihoods, which in his view rendered them justifiably liable to higher taxes in well-populated countries: "As for Jews, they may well bear somewhat extraordinary, because they seldom eat and drink with Christians, hold it no disparagement to live frugally, and even sordidly among themselves, by which way alone they become able to under-sell any other Traders, to elude the Excize, which bears but according to mean expenses; as also other Duties, by dealing so much in Bills of Exchange, Jewels, and Money, and by practising of several frauds with more impunity then others; for by their being at home every where, and yet no where they become responsible almost for nothing."[35]

The anti-Semitic trope of the wandering Jew that was all too familiar by the seventeenth and eighteenth centuries colors Petty's assessment of Jews in Europe. Avoiding tax by not participating in the general economy, with no attachment to the land, Jews were cast outside the bounds of legibility within the primary economy of landowners and laborers. Much like the Jewish characters in paradigmatic eighteenth-century novels such as *Waverley* and *Ivanhoe* by Sir Walter Scott, the figure of the Jew is rendered, in ways reminiscent of Foucault's vagabond, as one who deserves to be stripped of civil status and political rights due to an apparent lack of geographical fixity. It is also this form of anti-Semitism that arguably informs the Zionist emphasis on laboring on the land as key to the redemption of the Jewish people in Palestine, explored in chapter 3.

Petty's political arithmetic was influenced by the revolution in scientific method heralded by Francis Bacon's *Novum Organum*. As is widely recognized, Petty (along with many other of his contemporaries) was inspired by Bacon's intellectual agenda, which emphasized the importance of an empirical method and the centrality of experimentation to the study of natural history.[36] Bacon lamented the sedimentation of ideas whose presuppositions were merely taken for granted on the basis of their age, and the repetition of syllogisms based on abstract logic rather than observation and induction.[37] Bacon set out to devise a scientific method that would "equip the human understanding to set out on the ocean"; presumably Bacon meant the ocean of knowledge, but recognizing the influence of his method on colonial explorers and collectors of exotic specimens of plants and animals would foreshadow a much more literal application of his method throughout the colonial world.[38]

The influence of Baconian empiricism on Petty's work can be seen in the construction of mathematical data based on a keen observation of the Irish peasantry. The approach taken in the *Political Anatomy of Ireland* reflects his training as a physician; he observes the land and its inhabitants, collects whatever data were available about the people as a population, gives a diagnosis of the factors preventing improvement in Ireland, and gives a prescription for amelioration. In conceiving of the anatomy of the Irish economy, Petty's work focuses on the constituent parts of this body politic and also considers it as a whole. Individual habits of consumption, hours of labor and rest, and ways of living are analyzed in conjunction with economic categories and political interests. The peculiar mixture of mathematical accounting and scientific method that reduced human life to economic units was, in part, what marked the ingenuity of Petty's method.

The economic context in which Petty was writing was one to which the colonies had become quite central. Colonial trade in the seventeenth century not only was understood to increase consumption and the presence of consumer goods for an increasingly affluent class, but became a central pillar in Petty's calculations of English national wealth.[39] This was not, however, only a matter of inclusion in emergent methods of calculation; both the voyages of discovery and colonial spaces were central figures in both the scientific and economic imaginaries of the sixteenth and seventeenth centuries. Bacon was of the view that voyages of discovery had generated new insight into natural history, and that it was thus imperative for scientists to embrace a new method of analysis adequate to these new worlds. As noted by R. Hooykaas, Bacon believed that "surely it would be disgraceful if, while the regions of the material globe—that is, of the earth, of the sea, and of the stars—have been in our time laid widely open and revealed, the intellectual globe should remain shut up within the narrow limits of old discoveries."[40]

The growing importance of trade and commerce to political economists' theories of how to produce national wealth was an important dimension of the ideology of improvement. Paul Slack notes that increasing affluence in English society in the 1700s led writers to link "material satisfactions . . . to developing notions of linear improvement, advancement, or betterment in human affairs."[41] Those who adopted Baconian scientific methods in their approach to political and economic affairs, such as Petty, connected scientific advancement to material improvement. Improvement, whether it related to agricultural husbandry or increased commerce and trade, took on the cast of a linear, civilizational advancement. By the time Adam Smith penned *The Wealth of Nations*, civilization was not only linked to particular ways of holding and using land but was an explicit reflection of the existence of commercial trade.

As I've explored above, both race and the space of the colony figure quite centrally in Petty's emergent political economy. The ideology of improvement is grafted onto emerging ideas of racial difference, providing both the rationale for the perceived inability of particular populations to enter the pale of industrious, civilized life and the justification for the appropriation of their lands. Prior to the emergence of modern scientific racism in the nineteenth century, the use of classification as the primary means of ordering plant, animal, and human forms of life became the means of differentiating among different races. For instance, as Siep Stuurman has argued in relation to the racial thinking of François Bernier, a seventeenth-century doctor and career traveler, race was primarily conceived at this time on the basis of physical differences in skin color, facial features, and hair.[42] In Stuurman's analysis of Bernier's essay, "The Division of the Earth According to the Different Types of Races of Men Who Inhabit It," originally published in 1684, Bernier's classification of humankind into four or five "Species or Races" anticipates eighteenth-century racial anthropology. However, Bernier also locates the racial difference of Africans, who constitute a separate race, in the "blood or semen" of their bodies. Although these bodily fluids are the "same colour" as those of other species of human, herein lies the cause of their physical differences.[43]

These beginnings of racial classification and taxonomy reflect the fact that the predominant way of seeing human life within emergent political economies of land, labor, and commerce was inextricably tied up with colonial spaces. As I have argued above, a concept of value emerged that linked the improvement of land through particular kinds of use (cultivation for commercial purposes) to the improvement of populations who were not capitalist tenant farmers or engaged in waged labor within emerging capitalist agrarian markets. Further, in relation to both the Irish context of the seventeenth century and the settlement of British Columbia in the nineteenth century, those who were not productive and industrious cultivators of land (or landowners, or engaged in commercial ventures of some kind) were deemed to be lacking in the qualities befitting the civilized.

In many critical engagements with the significant role of the law of property in colonial settlement, the work of John Locke is given primary attention. As the political philosopher, legislator, entrepreneur, and colonial administrator who established land policy in the colony of Virginia, this is unsurprising. However, in focusing on Locke's rationales for the accumulation of private property and the contours of the proper subject of ownership without examining the work of Petty, it is difficult to fully appreciate how effectively Locke naturalized the rationales for colonial land appropriation found in Petty's work. Petty's political arithmetic is striking for the rather explicit and unabashed reduction of human life (and people's relations to land and labor) to economic criteria. Moreover, while one can measure and quantify the value of land based on economistic criteria, one cannot measure blood as a means of quantifying some illusory concept of race. Emergent concepts of race and racial inferiority were smuggled into new forms of value, constructed, ostensibly, on logics of measurement and quantification. This becomes much more explicit in the nineteenth century with the emergence of racial science, explored in chapter 2.

HISTORICIZING THE EQUATION:
PRIVATE PROPERTY = CIVILIZATION

Before turning to aboriginal rights jurisprudence in the Canadian context, a brief excursion into the work of Locke, whose notion of wasteland would come to legally justify the dispossession of indigenous peoples throughout North America and beyond, is necessary. It is the writings of Locke and subsequently Blackstone that provide the legal architecture for dispossession based on the concept of use elucidated above. In other words, it is in the work of Locke and Blackstone that we see the ideology of improvement achieve its full expression in the laws of property. Like Petty, Locke was influenced by the scientific method of Bacon, immersed as he was in devising new means of improving productivity and wealth (both individual and national).[44] But I want to suggest here that the abstract, economistic logic of Petty appears naturalized and historicized in the work of Locke, who more explicitly articulates modern property logics through racial difference.

Locke, whose theory of ownership and consciousness makes a longer appearance in chapter 4, is well known for the moral and legal justification he devises for private property ownership. In his attempt to secularize the divine foundations of property law, he asserts that when man mixes his labor with the earth, this gives rise to a right in that land that he has improved.[45] While God gave to mankind the world in common, the capacity and ability of man to create and produce his world according to a rational order meant that his industry would justify the private appropriation of land.

Industry and improvement were defined solely in terms of the use of land for agricultural purposes. The value of uncultivated land is so little, writes Locke, that "Land that is left wholly to Nature, that hath no improvement of Pasturage, Tillage, or Planting, is called, as indeed it is, wast [sic]; and we shall find the benefit of it amount to little more than nothing."[46] However, while in Petty we see the economic imperatives that ground the ideology of improvement, in Locke and Blackstone, improvement as a legal concept, one that is constitutive of the racial regimes of ownership emerging in North America, is cast almost entirely in civilizational terms.

Locke queries whether the "thousand acres . . . [of] wild woods and uncultivated waste of America left to Nature, without any improvement, tillage or husbandry . . . will yield the needy and wretched inhabitants as many conveniences of life as ten acres of equally fertile land doe in Devonshire where they are well cultivated."[47] Indeed, the appropriation and cultivation of land was integral to the progression from a state of nature to a civilized state of being. Owning land in common, without individual private ownership, reflected a "state of primeval simplicity."[48] Furthermore, the earth was given by God to industrious and rational men: men who "subdue the earth" and "improve it for the benefit of life."[49] Industrious men who cultivated God's earth existed in contradistinction to those who roamed the earth freely and did not enclose the land. In order for the fruits of the earth (or the earth itself) to really improve one's life, it was requisite to own that thing exclusively: "The fruit, or venison, which nourishes the wild Indian, who knows no inclosure [sic], and is still a tenant in common, must be his, and so his, i.e. a part of him, that another can no longer have any right to it, before it can do him any good for the support of his life."[50] Without ownership, and the law that accompanies it, there could be no civilization. The distinction between cultivated land and wasteland ultimately became the basis, during the eighteenth and nineteenth centuries, upon which European colonial powers justified their legal doctrines of *terra nullius* and discovery.[51]

The basis, according to both Locke and Blackstone, for exclusive ownership derived from the sustained occupation and use of the land.[52] While the earth was given to all mankind by God to enjoy, "there must of necessity be a means to appropriate [lands] some way or other, before they can be of any use, or at all beneficial to any particular man."[53] Because man, in the state of nature, has property only in his body, he also owns the "labour of his body," "the work of his hands."[54] This principle, according to Locke, is one of natural justice. As the continuation of the God-given dominion over the earth's territory, it was the God-given, natural right of men to appropriate land that was needed for sustenance as populations grew and land became scarce.[55] In this way, Locke and Blackstone naturalize the ideology of improvement as the foundation of private property ownership, casting it as a matter of nothing less than natural justice.

The last matter of interest to draw from Locke and Blackstone is the fictitious time of property and civilization that shapes their narrative of linear improvement. For Locke, as explored more fully in chapter 4, the secularization of the divine origins of property ownership to meet the needs of agrarian capitalism and commerce requires a fictive time of the premodern and prelegal world of uncultivated, wild lands, inhabited by uncivilized Indians. For Blackstone, the fiction that underlies his attempt to rationalize the laws of property into a science is, in a proto-Malthusian vein, that of scarcity and overpopulation. As the "earth would not produce her fruits in sufficient quantities without the assistance of tillage," property ownership became necessary to human survival. "As the world grew more populous, it daily became more difficult to find out new spots to inhabit, without encroaching upon former occupants," and thus the art of agriculture developed.[56]

The uncultivated wilds that threaten human existence, the time before the emergence of laws of property upon which civilization depends, are mapped onto the space of the settler colony. As we will see in the next section, the ideology of improvement, with its roots firmly embedded in both rationales for property ownership and the racial superiority of Europeans, will come to define the legal response to struggles for the recognition of aboriginal title to land.[57] Whereas for Petty, Ireland became a laboratory for new methods of valuing and producing national wealth, Locke and Blackstone naturalize these new concepts of value as the basis for legal categories and justifications for ownership based on specific notions of use, rather than possession. The racial regime of ownership that interpellated indigenous populations as lacking the requisite attachment to land and practices of cultivation to be owners of their land continues to operate as a juridical stranglehold over movements for justice and restitution.

WAYS OF SURVEYING

On Sunday, October 26, 2014, the premier of British Columbia took part in a ceremony in Quesnel, a small town in the interior of British Columbia, in Tsilhqot'in territory. The ceremony was held to mark the premier's apology for the hanging of five Tsilhqot'in chiefs in 1864. Acknowledging that the hangings were wrongful, premier Christy Clark marked the 150th anniversary of the hangings with an apology that was part of a larger reconciliation effort that followed the Supreme Court of Canada's judgment in *Tsilhqot'in v. British Columbia* ([2014] 2 S.C.R. 256), discussed at length below.[58] While the apology from a provincial government whose arguments at the Supreme Court appeal reflected a mentality deeply rooted in a colonial worldview, and for that reason alone is notable, it remains to be seen to what extent the provincial government will honor the letter and spirit of the Supreme Court of Canada's judgment on the Tsilhqot'in land claim that recognized aboriginal title to 1,750 square kilometers of their traditional territory.

In 1864, Judge Matthew Begbie sentenced the five Tsilhqot'in chiefs to be hanged because, in his words, "the blood of 21 white men calls for retribution."[59] The Tsilhqot'in warriors had allegedly killed twenty-one white men in what Begbie described as the "first thing approaching to a war" since the formation of the colony of British Columbia in 1858.[60] The Tsilhqot'in had been defending their land from increasing encroachment of settlers since the early nineteenth century, when the Hudson's Bay Company attempted to establish a trading fort on Tsilhqot'in lands. Resistance to white settlement on their lands led to the fort being completely abandoned by 1844, a mere fourteen years after it had been established.[61] As Fisher notes, unlike many other First Nations, the Tsilhqot'in had "opted out of the fur trade."[62] As the fur-trading era transitioned to one of outright colonial settlement, the threat of encroachment became ever more present.

The appropriation of land by colonists that put the Tsilhqot'in in the position of having to defend their land through military means was typical of what was happening throughout the province. While the legal foundations of the settlement of British Columbia have been carefully recounted by scores of historians, I focus here on the twin legal devices of preemption and homesteading, which were the means through which aboriginal lands were appropriated and given their legal veneer. The enactment of legislation was accompanied by that indispensable and necessary practice that precedes nearly every colonial appropriation of land in the settler colonial context—the land survey. As Nicholas Blomley has argued, official representations of land have the power to "remake worlds." Quoting from the work of James Scott, Blomley notes that a state cadastral map "'does not merely describe a system of land tenure; it creates such a system through its ability to give its categories the force of law.'"[63] Here, I am interested in the survey not only for its power in redefining relations of ownership (also explored in chapter 2), but also to emphasize how it was a key device of measurement, not only in terms of mapping land in a quantitative sense, but as a key method of valuing land and people. Second, I aim to expose how individual surveyors such as Trutch, like Petty before him, exploited their offices to amass huge personal fortunes.

The proprietary colony of Vancouver Island was created in 1849, the Crown colony of British Columbia in 1858, and the two colonies were amalgamated into one in 1861.[64] James Douglas, chief factor for Hudson's Bay Company, became the governor of the colony in 1851 and remained in this position until 1864.[65] Douglas created and followed his own land policies, which included making treaties and purchasing land in some instances, while circumventing the issue of native title.[66]

In the early part of his tenure as governor of the colony of Vancouver Island, James Douglas recognized the proprietary interest of the native bands in their lands, and thus, in order to avoid justifiable anger against the settlers that might be engendered by the nonconsensual appropriation of those lands, he had a policy of purchasing the native rights in the land prior to the settlement of any district.[67] In mainland British Columbia, however, no such uniform policy was followed. Unlike in the rest of the colonial territories that would come to constitute Canada, no treaties were negotiated in mainland British Columbia.[68] Douglas's policies on the mainland had the twin objectives of creating reserves for aboriginal communities before settlement and, also, of facilitating the assimilation of aboriginal people into the mainstream in order that they would eventually be treated and recognized as equal with white settlers.[69] Douglas believed that native peoples should be able to preempt land in the same manner as white settlers.[70] And until 1866, native people were entitled to preempt land, although, as Cole Harris points out, due to the arduous conditions "for most Native people, pre-emption was still an unimaginable option."[71]

In keeping with the idea that settlement was integrally tied to civilization, the colonial authorities believed that it was in the best interests of the Indians to settle them in villages.[72] This strategy had been adopted by Sir George Grey in the Cape (of South Africa), and it was hoped that the "thoughtful policy of that vigorous and accomplished Governor" would enable the "long barbarous populations" to "[enter] into the pale of civilized life."[73] Settling the natives on reserve land was for their own protection from "oppression and rapid decay" in relation to the white settler population.[74] Governor Douglas was thoroughly convinced of the benefit that would accrue to the native subjects through settlement; Indians were not to be simply cast out of the colony, and through their confinement to reserves and leasing the remaining land allotted to them, they would be beneficiaries of the rent proceeds arising from the leases.[75]

In terms of reserving the land for First Nations, disputes were ongoing over the appropriate quality and quantity of land to be reserved for Indian bands, leading to successive land surveys. The commissioners for land, colonial governors, and colonial secretaries attempted to find a balance between appropriating the best and most fertile land for colonial settlers while reserving sufficient lands for First Nations to avoid violent disputes between aboriginal communities and the settlers. However, after the Douglas era, it became more and more clear that colonial administrators restricted the allocation of reserve lands to sizes that were not acceptable to many aboriginal communities. The fact that they were unacceptable was marked by ongoing disputes over boundaries of the reserves and native protests against the attempted settlement of foreigners on their lands.[76] At the same time, some colonial administrators also perceived a need to redraw the boundaries of the reserves, which were deemed to be too generous for the needs of aboriginal people.[77] The most strident of the colonial surveyors to diminish Indian reserve lands was Joseph Trutch.[78]

While the views and policies of Edward Bulwer-Lytton, who became secretary of state for the colonies in 1858, or Frederick Seymour, the man who replaced James Douglas as governor of the province of British Columbia, would no doubt offer insight into the prevailing colonial attitudes toward land use, ownership, and perceived English superiority over First Nations, I choose to focus on Joseph Trutch for two reasons. To begin with, he was responsible for significantly diminishing the reserve land base on the basis of a worldview that was thoroughly Lockean in nature. The sole criteria for the redrawing of reserve boundaries, effectively expropriating native lands twice over, were whether they were being cultivated and the manner in which this cultivation was occurring. Coupled with this notion of use was a view of First Nations as savages, who lacked, in Trutch's view, the capacities for improvement, including the capacity for abstract thought.

Joseph Trutch forged a successful career as a colonial administrator, amassing a personal fortune along the way.[79] Born into a middle-class English family whose various members were, like many such families of the time, spread throughout the empire in various capacities, Trutch began his career as a surveyor south of the U.S.-Canada border.[80] In 1859, after his father had intervened on his behalf with government ministers, arranging a meeting between Trutch and colonial secretary Edward B. Lytton, Lord Carnarvon, and others, Trutch arrived in British Columbia without a colonial appointment secured.[81] Between 1859 and 1864, when Trutch was appointed chief commissioner of lands and works, he availed himself of private contracts to engage in road and bridge construction. In 1864, however, his new appointment afforded him the opportunity to make long-lasting and devastating changes to Indian land policy.

Trutch's actions were symptomatic of the worst excesses and abuses of colonial authority. As Robin Fisher has detailed, once he became lieutenant governor of the province, Trutch falsified records and misled his colleagues and superiors as to the policies followed by James Douglas, and the rationales upon which they were based.[82] Trutch was systematic in his denial of First Nations' land interests and his objective of reducing their land base down to a level that would not, in some cases, even support bare subsistence.

It is undeniable that Trutch held racist views of the aboriginal people he encountered and would eventually govern. Robin Fisher argues that Trutch's racism determined his attitude toward the question of Indian land. He writes, "It was these views regarding colonial development and the total inferiority of the Indian that governed Trutch's attitude to the question of Indian land. His attitudes coalesced to produce something of an obsession with the idea that the Indians were standing in the way of the development of the colony by Europeans. The absolute superiority of English culture implied an obligation to colonize new areas."[83]

Here, however, I offer a different interpretation of Trutch's policies concerning First Nations' land. In my view, the governing ideology, if there was one, of Trutch's approach to land and aboriginal people was that of improvement. Improvement was to be measured by agricultural production and the capacity to engage in rational—that is to say abstract—thought as an economic actor. For Trutch, First Nations people lacked both these qualities (despite overwhelming evidence to the contrary, on both counts). Even after attaining his appointment as the chief commissioner for lands and works, his attitude was determined by a view of what constituted the proper use of land, by proper subjects, in conjunction with one another. The Englishness that Trutch held up as superior was both racial in nature and based on a particular cultural and economic ideal of how to live as a rational, productive economic actor, which had a specific valence in the settler colony in relation to land use.

It is also clear from his voluminous correspondence with family members that Trutch was primarily concerned with his own financial interests. Colonial settlement was above all a business opportunity, and any religious imperatives that may have driven Trutch to civilize the natives (and I see no evidence of this in his case) came a distant second to personal profit. For instance, in the two years leading up to his move to British Columbia in 1859, Trutch wrote several letters to his brother John while working as a surveyor in Oregon and, before that, Illinois. In nearly every letter, in addition to his brotherly concern for John, who apparently was a less than adequate letter writer, Joseph remarks on his financial interests. The value of contracts for surveying services rendered, the "safe and profitable" opportunities for surveying work in British Columbia, the value of Trutch's land speculation in Chicago, potential business ventures, the amount of money to be earned in the burgeoning settler colony of British Columbia, and other financial concerns mark nearly all of his correspondence with his brother.[84]

On July 27, 1858, Joseph was feeling particularly communicative and wrote a long letter to John, which is not only exemplary of much of his personal correspondence but captures the concerns of a private contractor, traveling throughout the colonies with the sole objective of making money. Why else would an Englishman leave his beloved homeland? As Trutch notes with emphasis, "*We can't live in England* for some years yet, that I *have satisfied myself* about, and a few weeks experience would equally satisfy you that it was not our destiny to live there now."[85] While he expresses disappointment about being in Canada, a temporary home for him, he is consoled by the fact that he (and his brother) will be able to "live as Englishmen under [their] own laws and flag."[86]

The letter begins in typical fashion, Joseph admonishing his brother for not writing with his news. Joseph then informs John of the travels of his family members between England, Madras, and Bombay, and the fevers and ailments they contracted in the colonies.[87] In addition to documenting the imperial trajectories of the family, the letter consists entirely of information regarding personal financial interests. He writes of having had "to pay another instalment to this RRd [railroad] stock as I anticipated, making now $4000 paid in. I shall have no chance of any dividend for a twelvemonth, so wait in patience. . . . Business is dull as ditchwater all over the U.S. and we do not now hope for any improvement until next Spring."[88] He continues to encourage his brother to consider moving to Vancouver Island or the mainland, as property values will rise, and to buy a farm there. He reassures his brother, "you will have money—now is the time to get a chance in."[89] In concluding, Joseph wrote, "My investments in this country although not readily convertible into money, are not by any means in a discouraging state, and if you thought it advisable I could obtain money on them, although it is now a most unfavourable period to undertake to sell or mortgage."[90] Clearly, Joseph knew he would have to be patient to realize a profit on his investments in the young colony. Accumulating wealth was the primary motivation for Trutch, surely as it was for many other private agents and state actors involved in the appropriation and settling of First Nations' lands. The divide between the private, personal interests of agents and those of the state on whose behalf they were working was porous indeed.

His personal correspondence includes few if any remarks on Indians, even when recounting his surveying work. In a letter to his sister Charlotte in 1850, however, his virulently racist views emerge when he wrote from Oregon, "We have plenty of Indians in the neighbourhood but of course they are friendly, indeed we get all our fish etc., through them, & they are also useful in carrying letters & parcels up & down the river. I think they are the ugliest & laziest creatures I ever saw, & we should as soon think of being afraid of our dogs as of them."[91] Trutch's views of Indians come to the fore after he takes on his official position as commissioner for land and works and, subsequently, lieutenant-governor for the province of British Columbia. At the same time, it is also very clear that the rationale for reducing reserve lands has as much to do with his perception that First Nations people were not using the land (i.e., cultivating it) and therefore had no use or, more significantly perhaps, no right to this land. Seeing aboriginal peoples as savages and incapable of improvement is a consequence of how they use the land and, relatedly, their perceived cognitive capacities. The racial regime of ownership that emerges during this period of colonization in British Columbia is constituted through the desire for personal profit, the views of British colonial agents moving through imperial circuits, surveying and mapping as techniques of appropriation, and, ultimately, the fabrication of racial subjectivity that was tied to the ideology of improvement.

In 1867, three years after becoming commissioner of lands and works in British Columbia, Trutch authored a report titled "Lower Fraser River Indian Reserves." In this report, Trutch falsified the historical record when he wrote that the process of reserving lands for native use "does not appear to have been dealt with on any established system during Sir James Douglas' administration. The rights of Indians to hold lands were totally undefined."[92] This report is written in the context of a dramatic reduction of Indian reserves in the Lower Fraser region. After rewriting the historical record to assert that Governor Douglas had given no "written instructions" as to how reserve lands should be determined, he asserted that Mr. Brew instructed Mr. McColl to mark out Indian reserves around existing Indian villages and "to mark out as Indian reserves any ground which had been cleared and tilled for years by Indians."[93] When Trutch makes his argument for a dramatic reduction of the Lower Fraser Indian reserves, his rationale is clear: "The Indians regard these extensive tracts of land as their individual property but of by far the greater portion thereof they make no use whatever, and are not likely to do so; and thus the land, much of which is either rich pasture, or available for cultivation and greatly desired for immediate settlement, remains in an unproductive condition, is of no real value to the Indians, and utterly unprofitable to the public interests."[94]

For Trutch, Indians had no rights to the land because they made no use of the lands, which were not "of any actual value or utility" to Indians.[95] Such lands could only serve the public interest if they were thrown open for pre-emption. He had taken the same approach two years earlier in regard to the reduction of reserves in the Kamloops region and claims made by the Shuswap First Nation. Trutch concurred with the view of Philip Henry Nind, gold commissioner for the Cariboo region of the interior, that the Shuswap Indians' claims to land were baseless as "they made no real use" of the land. As these claims were "very materially" preventing "settlement and cultivation," Trutch urged Colonial Secretary Lytton to authorize an enquiry into the true extent of Indian land interests throughout the province.[96]

Improvement, of both land and people, was the reigning idea governing Trutch's attitude toward First Nations and their entitlement to ever-diminishing tracts of reserve land. Responding to concerns voiced by the bishop of British Columbia and the Aborigines Protection Society in 1871, he noted in his letter to the secretary of state for the provinces that despite the benefits accorded to Indians by white settlement, he had yet to meet "a single Indian of pure blood [who had] attained to even the most glimmering perception of the Christian creed." Despite their concerted efforts to "advance the material and moral condition" and to "change their habit of mind," the "idiosyncras[ies] of the Indians . . . appear to incapacitate them from appreciating any abstract idea, nor do their languages contain words by which such a conception could be expressed."[97]

The language of savagery was deployed by Trutch to express what First Nations lacked in a racial and anthropological sense: the capacity for abstract thought, which consequentially made it impossible for them to relate practices of cultivation to a general settler economy of agricultural production. For Trutch, the lack of homesteads in the English model provided evidence for his conclusion that aboriginal people lacked the "habit of mind" required for civilization. In either case, in Trutch's view, aboriginal people lacked the very capacities defined by Locke as the conditions for proper human subjectivity (explored in depth in chapter 4). We can recall Fanon's acute description of a related tautology: "In the colonies the economic infrastructure is also a superstructure. The cause is effect: you are rich because you are white, you are white because you are rich."[98] Here, and as we will see in chapter 4 in relation to the racial assessment of Palestinians by early Zionist settlers, the alleged lack of mental capacity for abstract thought explains the absence of legible forms of ownership, and the apparent absence of ownership justifies the conclusion that these racial subjects lack the capacity for abstract thought.

As outlined above, Trutch redrew the boundaries of reserves because he deemed them to be too generous for the needs of First Nations.[99] The amount of land determined to be suitable for their needs in the Lower Fraser amounted to "the villages and spots where they have been in the habit of cultivating potatoes, as would amount in the aggregate to ten acres of tillable land to each adult male in the tribe, together with a moderate amount of grazing land for those tribes which possess cattle and horses."[100] As the "Indians of Snatt Village," situated at the Burrard Inlet (of Vancouver) wrote to Joseph W. Trutch in 1869, a mere ten acres per Indian family was a "very small portion indeed" compared to the 160 acres allotted to each white family.[101]

One of the primary devices utilized to endow white settlers with vast tracts of land was preemption. The law of preemption allowed white settlers to stake out territory and, upon improving the land by cultivation, to obtain ownership of that land. The first preemption act in 1860 was proclaimed by Governor Douglas and marked the definitive transition from the fur-trading era to one of formal colonial settlement. During Douglas's tenure as governor of Vancouver Island, he provided that each couple would be given two hundred acres, with an additional ten acres provided for every child. In mainland British Columbia, a settler could preempt 160 acres and buy adjoining land at twenty-five pence an acre, as established by the Pre-Emption Consolidation Act in 1861.

Subsequent to Douglas's policies, as set out in section 33 of An Act to Amend and Consolidate the Laws Affecting Crown Lands in British Columbia, 1875, settlers had to prove that after two years they had made permanent improvements on the land to the value of $2.50 per acre in order to be granted letters patent for the land. It was not until a certificate of improvement had been granted to the homestead settler that the fee simple title to the land would be executed in favor of the individual (s.36). Similarly, An Act Further to Amend the "Dominion Lands Act, 1883," 1886 R.S.C. ch.27, amended clause 29 of the 1883 act to stipulate that in order to fulfill the conditions of cultivation, the settler had to break the land and prepare a certain number of crops in order to secure patent to the land (see clause 38(d)). Consistent with Locke's philosophy of ownership, a settler could preempt land (i.e., appropriate it) and come to own it by mixing his labor with the land and cultivating it to a degree deemed sufficient by the colonial administration.

By 1908, the homestead was one of the key methods of settling the land entrenched in federal legislation. A "homestead" was defined as "land entered for under the provisions of this Act or of any previous Act relating to Dominion lands for which a grant from the Crown may be secured through compliance with conditions in that respect prescribed at the time the land was entered for."[102] The land that was available for homestead entry or for sale had been surveyed in accordance with the provisions of the Dominion Lands Surveys Act (along with other conditions), unlike the initial preemption of land in British Columbia in the 1850s, where unsurveyed land was also available for preemption.

Homesteading was a heavily racialized and gendered phenomenon. A man who was eighteen years of age could apply for a homestead. A woman, however, could make such an application only if she was the sole head of a family. Any doubt as to whether she was the sole head of a family was grounds for refusal of her application (Dominion Lands Surveys Act, sections 9(1) and (2)). A woman could make an application to homestead only if she was a single mother; if she was involved in a relationship with a man who was resident in her home, then her right to application could be refused. Legislation passed in 1911 by the province of British Columbia delineated similar conditions under which a white woman could preempt land to include a woman who was a widow, a woman over the age of eighteen who was self-supporting, a woman deserted by her husband, or a woman whose husband had not contributed to her support for two years.[103] The ability of white women to preempt land was informed by a Victorian morality that made their ability to own land conditional on their status as abandoned or widowed women.

Under An Act Respecting the Land of the Crown, RSBC, 1911, vol. 2, ch.128, the right to preempt land did not extend to "aborigines" except to such as shall have obtained special permission.[104] The dominion land legislation was the same as the provincial legislation in the paucity of references to aboriginal peoples. In An Act Further to Amend the "Dominion Lands Act, 1883," referred to above, there were only two references to aboriginal people. Section 39(2) stipulated that no lands were to be set aside for the purpose of an Indian or other public reserve, until other lands had been selected in lieu of these lands.

What emerges from an examination of the land legislation enabling colonial settlement is the creation of two separate economies of land and identity, the Indian reserve and the private market of individual ownership. The near-total absence of any mention of First Nations people in land legislation that secured their dispossession is symptomatic of this separation. Aboriginal people were written out of this new economy of property relations that was being mapped onto the province, relegated to a time and space that was set apart, and, as we will see in the next section, in a time prior to the instantiation of modern law in the settler colony.

One exception to the general absence of provision for First Nations in land legislation is section 76 of An Act Further to Amend the "Dominion Lands Act, 1883," which provides for the powers of the governor in council. Under this section, he could "withdraw from the operation of this Act, subject to existing rights as defined or created thereunder, such lands as have been or may be reserved for Indians." Section 76 also enables the governor in council to grant lands in satisfaction of claims of "half-breeds" arising out of the extinguishment of their Indian title. Third, the section enables the governor to make free grants of land to people. Such grants would effectively extinguish Indian title if the settlers could "satisfactorily establish undisturbed occupation of any lands within the said territory or tract." Indian lands, assumed to be free or vacant lands, were transformed into private property for settlers through the mere fact of their occupation and cultivation.

The early proclamations dealing with preemption and the granting of homesteads to British subjects and aliens made no mention of the rights of aboriginal people to maintain their rights over their lands or indeed to preempt land.[105] As mentioned above, James Douglas had allowed for the preemption of land by First Nations so long as they fulfilled certain requirements with respect to its agricultural cultivation. Those who preempted land were expected to assimilate; in order to gain the same rights as British subjects they had to live in a nuclear family, cultivate the land and produce crops, and forego their cultural practices and traditional ways of living, which included any notion of aboriginal title.[106] (Another aspect of this racial regime of ownership, explored in greater depth in chapter 4, was an acutely gendered notion of racial difference.) These provisions foreshadowed similar aspects of the Indian Act, 1886, which had as its objective the civilization and assimilation of aboriginal peoples.

CONSTITUTING AND CAPTURING THE SUBJECT OF RIGHT

Nearly 120 years after the hanging of the Tsilhqot'in warriors and struggles waged for the recognition of aboriginal ownership of land and resources in the courts, the incorporation of section 35 of the newly patriated Constitution would be hailed as a legal and political victory. The patriation of the Constitution signified a putative break with Canada's colonial history. Putative because, as constitutional theorist Peter Hogg has written, the Canada Act 1982, which included as Schedule B the Constitution Act, 1982, was in fact an imperial statute, enacted by the U.K. Parliament.[107] Canada's Constitution was not the result of a revolution, nor was it an act internal to the state.[108] Rather, the Canada Act 1982 was an imperial statute that proclaimed that "the Constitution of Canada is the supreme law of Canada, and any law that is inconsistent with the provisions of the Constitution is, to the extent of the inconsistency, of no force and effect."[109] The Canada

Act 1982 expressly abdicated the authority of the British legislature over Canada.

In yet another imperial gesture, this was done without any consultation or agreement by First Nations, many of whom still hold the view that the British Crown remains their partner in treaties signed during the nineteenth century, despite British conclusions to the contrary. Thus, in 2013, members of the Federation of Saskatchewan Indian Nations and other First Nations elders traveled to London to mark the 250th anniversary of the Royal Proclamation of 1763. Issued by King George III at the conclusion of the Seven Years' War, the proclamation recognized that all unceded lands of Indians would be left as such until they were ceded by way of treaty with the British Crown.[110] While the unilateral decision to transmute its treaty obligations to the Canadian Crown seems legally tenuous (at best), the British Crown has resolutely denied that it has any continued obligations whatsoever to the First Nations of Canada. In yet another instance of the fractured temporality that characterizes legal modernity in the settler colonial context, the colonial sovereign imposes a new postcolonial temporal order on First Nations, who remain subject to a colonial sovereign power that has changed in persona but not, fundamentally, in substance.

The constitutional reforms and the patriation of the Constitution in 1982 can be understood as a break with Canada's colonial past only in terms of the settler society's relationship to the imperial power. Along with this significant movement toward establishing an independent, postcolonial nation was the introduction of a Charter of Rights and Freedoms, provisions for the protection and enhancement of multiculturalism, and section 35. The constitutionalization of fundamental rights and freedoms has become an iconic dimension of Canada's identity as a nation, both within its own borders and internationally.

Section 35, which was lauded as a major political and legal shift in the status of aboriginal rights in Canada, provides the following:

(1) The existing aboriginal and treaty rights of the aboriginal peoples of Canada are hereby recognized and affirmed.
(2) In this Act, "aboriginal peoples of Canada" includes the Indian, Inuit and Métis peoples of Canada.

(3) For greater certainty, in subsection (1) "treaty rights" includes rights that now exist by way of land claims agreements or may be so acquired.

(4) Notwithstanding any other provision of this Act, the aboriginal and treaty rights referred to in subsection (1) are guaranteed equally to male and female persons.

Although aboriginal rights had been recognized at common law, section 35(1) elevated those rights, affording them constitutional status and protection. While governments may regulate aboriginal and treaty rights where justified, they cannot abolish these rights. Section 35(1) ensures that constitutional amendments to the provisions of the Constitution Act that "apply directly" to aboriginal peoples will not be undertaken without a constitutional conference to which representatives of the aboriginal peoples of Canada will be party. However, it is important to note that this section does not provide aboriginal peoples and their representatives with a veto power over potential amendments, which means that constitutional amendments can be made without their consent.[111]

Section 35 was a major milestone in First Nations' struggle for the recognition of their rights to their traditional territories and resources. However, the definition of the content of aboriginal title has been shaped by Anglo-Canadian common-law concepts of ownership, a reflection of the repeated insistence that the Crown holds underlying or radical title to the land. The historical weight of property logics that were used to dispossess First Nations overshadows the attempts to reconcile aboriginal and Canadian interests. Aboriginal title is rendered as a hybrid form of property, based on the prior occupation of the land by First Nations but defined according to Anglo-Canadian concepts of private property ownership. While the judgment of the Supreme Court of Canada in *Tsilhqot'in Nation* has gone some distance in incorporating First Nations' conceptions of use and ownership into the concept of aboriginal title, as we will see below, the court fails to fundamentally alter legal precedent that has continually reinscribed the primacy of Crown control over indigenous land in conjunction with the racialization of First Nations and their ways of life as inferior to settler society.[112]

In 1997, the Supreme Court of Canada handed down its long-awaited judgment in *Delgamuukw v. British Columbia*. The appellants were members of the Gitksan and Wet'suwet'en hereditary chiefs. Individually and on behalf of their Houses, they claimed separate portions of 58,000 square kilometers in British Columbia. Their claim before the Supreme Court of Canada was for aboriginal title over the land in question, and the government of British Columbia counterclaimed for a declaration that the appellants had no right or interest in and to the territory or, alternatively, that the appellants' cause of action ought to be for compensation from the Government of Canada.[113]

Delgamuukw v. British Columbia was the first judgment to deal with the "nature and scope of the constitutional protection afforded by section 35(1) to common law aboriginal title."[114] The power and imperturbable nature of colonial sovereignty preempted the determination of the substantive issues on appeal because of the court's formalistic approach to the pleadings. The court found that a new trial was required on two bases and left the factual issue of whether the appellants had aboriginal title unconsidered. The first ground for ordering a new trial was that the appellants tried to alter their pleadings on appeal so as to change the fifty-one claims brought by Gitksan and Wet'suwet'en Houses into two collective claims brought by the Gitksan and Wet'suwet'en Nations. The court found that such an amendment would prejudice the respondents because the pleadings had not been amended, and therefore the respondents had been denied the ability to address the issue of a collective claim at trial. John Borrows has persuasively argued that this finding was "rather formalistic and inflexible":

> It is interesting to note that the result of the *Delgamuukw* case, which considers the wholesale territorial dispossession of two entire Aboriginal peoples, turns on the court's finding that the province suffered prejudice in framing the pleadings. By imposing these technical requirements on the form of a grievance, the courts, like the legislatures before them, make an assertion of sovereignty. By relying on a defect in the pleadings to refuse to consider the claim, this Crown Court announces that disputes will be resolved on the settlers' terms. There is something deeply troubling about allowing Crown assertions of sovereignty to drive the

decision in a case that radically challenges these assertions and their effects.[115]

The other basis upon which the court found that a new trial was necessary was the misapprehension of oral history testimony by the trial judge, evidence that was crucial to the appellants' case. The court found that given the complexity and volume of the "factual issues at hand," the court would not do justice to either party by sifting through the evidence and coming to new factual findings.[116] As a result, the factual issues before the court in the first aboriginal title case brought under section 35(1) were left unsettled. As Borrows has written, "given the imbalance in the parties' financial and political resources, and the century-long denial of Aboriginal land and political rights in British Columbia, this sleight of hand is remarkable."[117] Despite the fact that the central factual issue before the court—whether the Gitksan and Wet'suwet'en had aboriginal title over their ancestral lands— was left undetermined, the court decided that when the factual issue went back to trial, the lower courts would need guidance as to the content of the right to aboriginal title itself. Accordingly, they proceeded to delineate the test for proving aboriginal title.

The court held that claimants must satisfy three criteria in order to prove the existence of aboriginal title:

(i) the land must have been occupied prior to sovereignty;
(ii) if present occupation is relied upon as proof of occupation presovereignty, there must be a continuity between present and presovereignty occupation; and
(iii) at sovereignty, that occupation must have been exclusive.[118]

In defining the criteria necessary to establish aboriginal title, the court imports one of the central features of Anglo-European private property ownership—exclusive possession—into the definition of aboriginal title. However, the definition of aboriginal title as being constituted by one of the central characteristics of Anglo-Canadian private property ownership exists alongside (and perhaps in conflict with) the temporal requirement that aboriginal nations must have enjoyed exclusive occupation prior to the assertion of colonial sovereignty and the imposition of Anglo-European private property relations. This points to the fundamental paradox that lies at the heart of aboriginal rights: they are based on aboriginal peoples' prior occupation of the land but defined in relation to Anglo-Canadian norms of private property ownership and colonial sovereign power. The fact that Peter R. Grant, lead counsel for the Gitksan and Wet'suwet'en chiefs in the *Delgamuukw* trials, has stated that the appellants argued for exclusive possession to be one of the defining characteristics of aboriginal title, so that the Crown could not interfere with First Nations' land held under aboriginal title, serves to emphasize the contradictory nature of aboriginal title. In this instance, protection from continued Crown interference even in the face of a (potential) legal declaration of aboriginal title had to be sought (perhaps unsurprisingly) through recourse to common-law concepts of private ownership.[119]

Questions of what constitutes exclusive possession are highly contextual and depend on the facts of each case. But it is here that we see the concept of use and the ideology of improvement determining what constitutes possession.

> The evidence at trial brought by the appellants was, as the majority judgment notes, "based on their historical use and 'ownership' of one or more of the territories." Recounting the trial judge's findings, they note that the proof of use and "ownership" [*sic*, placed in scare quotes by Chief Justice Lamer of the scc], were "physical and tangible indicators of their association with the territories . . . totem poles with the Houses' crests carved, or distinctive regalia" [para 13]. The Gitksan Houses had presented their adaawk at trial, the "sacred oral tradition about their ancestors, histories and territories. The Wet'suwet'en each have a 'kungax' which is a spiritual song or dance of performance which ties them to their land."[120]

In defining aboriginal title, the court noted that the source is the "prior occupation of Canada by aboriginal peoples."[121] The prior occupation of the land is relevant not only as the source of aboriginal title but as the physical fact of occupation derives from the common-law principle that occupation is proof of possession in law.[122] The characteristics of this sui generis form of title also include its being held communally: "Aboriginal title," notes the court, "cannot be held by individual aboriginal persons."[123] Further, the court noted that the uses to which the aboriginal claimants may put the land are not restricted to the customs, activities, or practices that are integral to the distinctive aboriginal culture of the claimant.[124] At the same time, the inherent limit on aboriginal title is defined by the "nature of the attachment to the land which forms the basis of the group's claim to aboriginal title."[125] Aboriginal title is sui generis and distinct from "'normal' proprietary interests" such as fee simple.[126]

This means, in practice, that "a group [who] claims a special bond with the land because of its ceremonial or cultural significance may not use the land in such a way as to destroy that relationship (e.g. by developing it in such a way that the bond is destroyed, perhaps by turning it into a parking lot)."[127] Of course, the court notes that this does not negate the right of a First Nation to surrender their lands to the Crown in exchange "for valuable consideration" were they to seek development of their land in a way deemed inconsistent with their cultural or spiritual relationship to that land.[128] The definition of aboriginal title was, at this point, clearly caught within the epistemological framework of the colonial legal system of property; fee simple ownership that allows for modern commercial relations of exchange and alienability exists in contradistinction to aboriginal title, which is defined overwhelmingly by a notion of culture firmly separated from modern economies of ownership. Race and racial difference are cast in the idiom of culture, which defines the specificity of the racial regime of ownership produced through aboriginal title litigation.

In *Delgamuukw*, the court found that both aboriginal perspectives and the common law are to be used as the basis for proving aboriginal title. How would aboriginal laws relating to ownership be translated into a legible form in Canadian courts? As the court notes, "if at the time of sovereignty, an aboriginal society had laws in relation to land, those laws would be relevant to establishing the occupation of lands which are the subject of a claim for aboriginal title. Relevant laws might include, but are not limited to, a land tenure system or laws governing land use."[129]

It is clear that in addition to identifying exclusive possession as a defining characteristic of aboriginal title, the criteria for establishing exclusive possession are only derived from aboriginal laws insofar as they mirror common-law concepts of use. How is factual possession to be established? Once again, the characteristics are those that are potentially legible to common-law concepts of private property ownership: "Physical occupation may be established in a variety of ways, ranging from the construction of dwellings through cultivation and enclosure of fields to regular use of definite tracts of land for hunting, fishing or otherwise exploiting its resources."[130] Occupation, which grounds the claim of possession, is defined on the basis of cultivation, enclosure, or regular use of the land claimed. Settled villages, as Trutch would have remarked upon in the course of surveying, provide proof of occupation.

While the court notes that the common-law concepts of exclusive possession must be "imported into the concept of aboriginal title with caution," the test remains "the intention and capacity to retain exclusive control."[131] Where two or more First Nations used or occupied the same territory, this would be translated into the common-law concept of "joint title."[132] First Nations' ways of owning and using land, assuming that they were indeed based on a completely different system of law, find no recognition in the law of aboriginal title as it was initially delineated, unless they were already compatible conceptually with the common law.

The emphasis on improvement reaches its apex in the justification test for the limitation of an aboriginal right. When an aboriginal right has been established, it can be justifiably limited if certain conditions are met. The test for a justifiable limitation on an aboriginal right was first established in *R. v. Sparrow* [1990] 1 S.C.R. 1075. In determining whether a right has been infringed, the court initially makes three inquiries: whether the limitation on the right is reasonable, whether the regulation at issue imposes undue hardship, and whether the regulation denies holders of the right their preferred means of exercising the right.[133] After determining whether there has been an infringement according to these three criteria, the court then inquires as to whether the infringement can be justified. In making this determination, the court must ask whether the government is acting pursuant to a valid legislative objective (conservation of fish, for example, was held to be a valid legislative objective in *R. v. Sparrow*). Second, the government must demonstrate that its actions are consistent with its fiduciary duty toward aboriginal peoples.[134]

The doctrine of limitation and the justification test developed in *Sparrow*, *Gladstone*, and *Van der Peet* are transposed to the context of an aboriginal title claim in *Delgamuukw*. The court reiterates the proposition that the objective of reconciliation underlying section 35 informs the limitation analysis and justification test. As established in *Gladstone*, the court notes that the objective of reconciliation (of aboriginal prior occupation with the assertion of the sovereignty of the Crown) will be the one most relevant to the justification test. This is because, just as aboriginal rights are central to the "reconciliation of aboriginal societies with the broader political community of which they are a part," "limits placed on those rights are, where the objectives furthered by those limits are of sufficient importance to the broader community as a whole," equally necessary.[135]

In the context of aboriginal title claims, the court finds that "the range of legislative objectives that can justify the infringement of aboriginal title is fairly broad."[136] In *Delgamuukw*, the court goes on to list any activities that further the improvement or development of the land: "In my opinion, the development of agriculture, forestry, mining, and hydroelectric power, the general economic development of the interior of British Columbia, protection of the environment or endangered species, the building of infrastructure and the settlement of foreign populations to support those aims are the kinds of objectives that are consistent with this purpose, and in principle, can justify the infringement of aboriginal title."[137] The development of industry and the improvement of the land in order to settle foreign populations continues, it seems, from the beginnings of formal settlement in the nineteenth century to the post-1982 realm of constitutional recognition, as a rationale for the dispossession of First Nations. Unlike the colonial administrators who oversaw the settlement of the province of British Columbia in the nineteenth century, contemporary courts recognize aboriginal title to land while justifying its limitation according to the same rationale used to justify the original dispossession of First Nations.

Similarly, the racial logic of improvement that emerges so blatantly in the legislative provisions and views of colonial administrators such as Trutch continues well into the present day. In *Dying from Improvement: Inquests and Inquiries into the Deaths of Aboriginal Deaths in Custody*, Sherene Razack explores in forensic detail the structural violence embedded in the public inquiries into the cause of death of aboriginal men in British Columbia and Saskatchewan. She argues that having been deemed to be "beyond improvement" by the settler state, aboriginal bodies become a site where settler violence is repeatedly enacted in order to secure and legitimate settler ownership over aboriginal land, particularly in the urban context.[138] The routine and often lethal violence that aboriginal people are subjected to at the hands of the police reveal the function of police power in enacting the violence of a settler legal regime, evidenced by the outcomes of the inquests, which rarely, if ever, result in police prosecution. At the same time, the inquest functions as a means of quelling settler anxieties about their dominant status, by allowing the settler regime to commit itself to "improving Aboriginal lives."[139] Improvement thus functions as both the ideological cause of systemic and structural violence against aboriginal bodies, and the proposed policy solution for settler crises of legitimacy.

While Razack points to the connection between land appropriation and racism as the twin forces of dispossession in the settler colony, her focus remains steadfastly on the racial dimensions of settler violence. Here, my aim is to elucidate the other side of the equation, that is, the modern concepts of property that subtend racial formations in the settler colony. Rationales for appropriation and private ownership emerging from the seventeenth century onward produced and reflected new conceptions of value, in relation to land, goods, commodities, and the value of human life. The racial logic that is continually reinforced in settler colonial spaces has economic roots among its origins, in that it emerges in conjunction with new forms of value and methods of evaluation used to classify land as available for particular kinds of use and ownership. As discussed throughout this chapter, the racial regime of ownership takes the notion of improvement as its primary mode of articulation.

The content of aboriginal title was reconfigured to some extent by the Supreme Court of Canada in *Tsilhqot'in Nation v. British Columbia*. The Tsilhqot'in First Nation challenged the blatantly Eurocentric nature of the legal criteria required to be fulfilled to establish occupation (and therefore possession) in their appeal to the Supreme Court of Canada. Among the issues on appeal in *Tsilhqot'in Nation* was the test for aboriginal title to land, the nature of that right, and the means of reconciling broader public interests with the rights conferred by aboriginal title (para. 1).

The court held that the Tsilhqot'in hold ownership rights "similar to those associated with fee simple."[140] This includes "the right to decide how the land will be used; the right of enjoyment and occupancy of the land; the right to possess the land; the right to the economic benefits of the land; and the right to pro-actively use and manage the land."[141] However, the court maintained that the nature of aboriginal title, as a collective form of title, means that it "cannot be developed or misused in a way that would substantially deprive future generations of the benefit of the land."[142]

It is clear in *Tsilhqot'in Nation* that the court goes further in this judgment than before, in recognizing what they refer to as "the aboriginal perspective." In fact, during the hearing, one of the justices interrupted counsel for one of the provinces, and asked, "Can't we just look at this from the aboriginal perspective?"[143] What would it mean to look at this case "from the aboriginal perspective" of the claimants? Where does the law of the Tsilhqot'in enter into the deliberations of the court, and, specifically, where do their laws relating to land appear in the judgment? To what extent did the court decenter the English common-law concept of improvement as the basis for an ownership right?

As to the content of aboriginal title, the court posed the issue in the following way: "How should the courts determine whether a semi-nomadic indigenous group has title to its lands?" They clarify the test as established in *Delgamuukw* to provide for the way of life and perspectives of First Nations who are characterized as "semi-nomadic." In the appellant's factum, counsel argues that Tsilhqot'in use of their territory was historically exclusive, and that the exclusive possession of their lands as an "occupying owner" bears "the very stamp of possession at common law."[144] At the same time, they argue that the standard applied by the Court of Appeal, that the test for aboriginal title requires proof of "intensive presence" at particular sites, "leaves no space to consider Aboriginal perspectives on land, including their systems of law."[145]

A perusal of the appellant's factum reveals that the aboriginal perspective on occupation differs from the common-law principles elucidated above, in that the Tsilhqot'in, among others, used and cultivated their lands in a seasonal fashion, and planted and harvested root plants, medicines, and berries for subsistence purposes, rather than commercial exchange.[146] In their judgment, the court extends the boundaries of recognition when they redefine "occupation" to include "the way of life of the Aboriginal people, including those who were nomadic or semi-nomadic."[147] They summarize the test as follows:

[W]hat is required is a culturally sensitive approach to sufficiency of occupation based on the dual perspectives of the Aboriginal group in question—its laws, practices, size, technological ability and the character of the land claimed—and the common law notion of possession as a basis for title. It is not possible to list every indicia of occupation that might apply in a particular case. The common law test for possession—which requires an intention to occupy or hold land for the purposes of the occupant—must be considered alongside the perspective of the Aboriginal group which, depending on its size and manner of living, might conceive of possession of land in a somewhat different manner than did the common law.[148]

They find that a "culturally sensitive approach" means that the regular, as opposed to the intensive, use of territories for "hunting, fishing, trapping and foraging is 'sufficient' use" to establish aboriginal title.[149] The test for occupation is augmented to include ways of living on the land that did not conform to the model of settlement outlined in the section "Ways of Surveying" in this chapter. To this extent, the judgment marks a dramatic improvement in the approach developed hitherto. Even though the basic principles as established in *Delgamuukw* and other section 35 jurisprudence (notably *Sparrow*, *Haida Nation*, and *Marshall*) are reaffirmed by the court, there is a clear shift in the emphasis placed on perspective of the Aboriginal claimant.

However, there remains an outstanding question regarding the status of aboriginal laws in the legal process through which the content of aboriginal title is defined. The Supreme Court affirmed the trial judge's findings, which were based on the acceptance of a great deal of evidence given by elders of the Tsilhqot'in, along with anthropologists and historians who testified as expert witnesses. Oral history testimony was accepted by the court as proof of historical occupation of the lands by the claimants. Tsilhqot'in collective memory and the passing down of history through an oral tradition was given due weight in the adjudication of the land claim.

In the appellant factum, counsel described the relationship between the landscape and the meaning it holds for the Tsilhqot'in people: "The landscape of the Claim Area resonates for Tsilhqot'in people with deep meaning: it is the physical expression of the legends that describe their origins, their laws, and their identity as Tsilhqot'in people. Some of the Claim Area's most distinctive features, such as the towering Ts'il?os (Mount Tatlow), are revered today as living persons with powerful personalities that must be respected."[150] The testimony of the elders demonstrated a long history of seasonal rounds that took place throughout the claimed territory. Tsilhqot'in forms of land use that did not, historically, conform to settled modes of cultivation and the laws and their identity as Tsilhqot'in are rendered in the archaeological and anthropological language of nomadism. It is arguable that the "aboriginal perspective" is taken into account only insofar as it can be rendered legible within an epistemological frame shaped by an anthropological discourse that has long been embedded within racialist discourses of human development.

Do the Tsilhqot'in see themselves as seminomadic? Do their laws, upon which their rights to land are grounded, recognize the language of nomadism? According to one journalist who interviewed chief Roger Williams, apparently not: "That's why the habit of government officials, of media and even of supreme court judges to call the Tsilhqot'in 'nomadic' bothers Williams so much: his people have lived on these lands for thousands of years, while it is non-natives who are constantly moving and resettling. And what could be more nomadic and transient than the extractive industry itself— grabbing what resources and profits it can before abandoning one area for another."[151] The nomad, and the more contemporary notion of the semi-nomad are terms devised within the fields of archaeology and anthropology to describe ancient modes of life that persist into the present in some parts of the world. However, historically, rendering indigenous people (and the nonindigenous poor and homeless) as "mobile and unfixed" has been used to "force a separation between a population and the space it occupies, rendering a collective claim to this space void, even invisible."[152] As Blomley has argued persuasively, mobility "compromises the telos of property," that improvement to land as a ground of legitimate ownership claims is utterly inconsistent with populations of people who are in transit and who move. As we will see in chapter 3, the Bedouin in southern Israel have been dispossessed of their lands on the basis that as nomads, they have no attachment to the land they claim as theirs.

What are we to make of the use of the term "seminomad" for progressive purposes by the Supreme Court of Canada? In *Delgamuukw*, the Supreme

Court ordered a new trial, in part on the basis that neither the trial judge nor the majority on the Court of Appeal had sufficiently taken into account the perspectives of the aboriginal claimants, and had failed to give adequate weight to the oral history testimony. As the majority held, "[A]lthough the doctrine of aboriginal rights is a common law doctrine, aboriginal rights are truly sui generis, and demand a unique approach to the treatment of evidence which accords due weight to the perspective of aboriginal peoples. However, that accommodation must be done in a manner which does not strain 'the Canadian legal and constitutional structure.'"[153]

Even where the court moves toward recognizing modes of land use that do not conform to an ideology of improvement as the basis for an aboriginal title claim, they have yet to do so on the basis of aboriginal concepts of land use and ownership. Furthermore, in not overturning the test for a justifiable infringement of aboriginal title established in *Delgamuukw*, the court refuses to address the constitutive violence that is repeated with every judgment that reiterates the fiction that the Crown maintains underlying sovereignty over First Nations lands. As John Borrows has pithily observed, with regard to the *Tsilhqot'in* judgment, "[The] assertion of Crown sovereignty leading to radical Crown title rests on an 'inanis iustificationem': an empty justification. It is a restatement of the doctrine of terra nullius despite protestations to the contrary. The assertion of radical title retroactively affirms the Crown's appropriation of Indigenous legal interests without their knowledge or consent. In some other contexts, this would be called stealing—at the least it would be considered dishonest to say you own something when it previously belonged to someone else."[154] Stealing, speculation, appropriation— all the corollaries of ownership in the settler colony, where the mystical foundation of colonial sovereignty is persistently and doggedly repeated by the highest legal authorities in the land. The racial regime of ownership that articulates improvement and use as rationales for ownership together with the figure of the native who requires civilizational uplift remains intact; here with the modification afforded by the racial-anthropological figure of the seminomad.

In chapter 2, I examine the shift to more abstract conceptualizations of property ownership reflected in the system of title by registration. Whereas the ideology of improvement was rooted in a turn to the quantification and measurement of land in relation to the labor of cultivation, the logic of abstraction deracinated land and its multiple usages even further, rendering its value in the form of a general equivalence with other commodities. The quantification and assessment of agricultural labor as a means of assigning racial and economic value to colonial populations is rearticulated in more abstract and putatively scientific terms as colonized peoples are taxonomized in a globalized schema of racial difference.

Chapter 2 / Propertied Abstractions

In *The Mystery of Capital*, neoliberal economist Hernando de Soto argues strenuously for the formalization of property rights through land titling programs as a key means of advancing a development agenda. For de Soto, the primary reason that countries outside of the monolithic entity he describes as "the West" continue to be rife with endemic poverty can be explained, for the most part, by the absence of abstract, formalized legal systems of property ownership. The key to improving economic development and social equality among the poor, whose houses are "built on land whose ownership rights are not adequately recorded," is to formalize their ownership through a representational process by which their homes could become assets and used as collateral for credit.[1] Writing before the seismic financial crash of 2008, de Soto identifies the ability of the poor to access mortgages as a necessary precondition for unleashing the wealth-creating potential of "dead capital" into a valuable, liquid asset.[2] To the contrary, studies have shown that in the aftermath of "a comprehensive urban titling programme in Lima and seven other cities [in Peru] . . . property titles had no significant effect on access among the poor to business credit."[3] Rashmi Dyal-Chand has noted how titling programs in many cities of the global South led to land speculation and a rise in the value of residential homes, but often at the expense of the original low-income owners.[4]

My aim, however, is not to assess whether the neoliberal promise of the potential benefits of formalizing title for the poor has thus far been borne out, or not, as the case may be. Rather, I argue that land titling programs such as those advocated by de Soto, the World Bank, and some governments are the contemporary manifestation of a legal device that has had a long and pivotal position in the appropriation and transformation of indigenous lands into individually held private property. The rational and abstract form of a system of title by registration, so admired by de Soto and his supporters, is exemplary in its signification of modern laws of property as the sine qua non of civilized life and progress. Placed within view of the historical development of systems of title by registration, de Soto's thorough disregard for the owners and users of land whose interests were covered over (and, in some cases, legally eliminated) by a system of title by registration appears as an inheritance from a long line of colonial property reformers, as explored throughout this chapter.

De Soto exhibits a tendency in *The Mystery of Capital* to dismiss cultural explanations for "Third World" poverty while at the same time relegating this Third World to a historically prior state of development. The Third World, to stick with de Soto's terminology, is what the United States was 150 years ago.[5] Writing against the grain of decades of postcolonial critique that has firmly refuted the notion that modern capitalist development in the colonies unfolded in a temporally linear manner, de Soto also seems to view the development of modern property law in England and the United States with a degree of Occidental romanticism that mirrors the Orientalist discourses of a previous era.[6] Furthermore, the discussion of the development of property law in the United States, his much-vaunted model, proceeds without any recognition of the effects of land titling on indigenous nations who occupied the land prior to settlement. Many critical engagements with de Soto seem to miss these dimensions of his work, with a few notable exceptions.[7]

In settler colonies and postcolonies alike, land titling systems have effectively diminished ways of relating to land that do not conform to capitalist property norms and, once imposed, have worked to the radical disadvantage of indigenous people who did not adopt the formalities of ownership as prescribed by settler laws. For instance, J. Kēhaulani Kauanui notes how in the mid-nineteenth century, foreign residents and missionaries believed that native Hawaiians could be "saved from extinction through the acqui-sition of land in fee simple, which would help them in re-establishing a life of farming."[8] Individual land titles were viewed as the panacea for the large-scale displacement and dispossession of indigenous Hawaiians, with small, individual farmholdings established as the most desirable model to follow.[9] However, after the large land division of 1848 (called the Māhele), which created three categories of landholder including the monarch, the govern-ment, and the chiefs, it became evident that common native Hawaiians had received a very small portion of their allotted acreage.[10] "Less than 1 percent of the total land acreage passed in fee simple to Hawaiian commoners, and little more than 8000 fee simple titles were allotted to them under the *Ku-leana Act* of 1850."[11] The rationale for why so few native Hawaiians formalized their ownership through fee simple title is strikingly similar to that used to explain why so few Bedouin in Palestine registered their land interests dur-ing the Ottoman period in the mid-nineteenth century: the costs involved (in procuring a survey of their land, which was a precondition for claiming title in fee simple) made it prohibitive; and with respect to native Hawai-ians, the "fraud, adverse possession, tax sales, and undervalued sales to spec-ulators" often rendered the formalization of their ownership irrelevant.[12]

The use of a system of individual fee simple titles to diminish or abolish indigenous systems of land tenure that do not conform to an economic sys-tem based on an ideology of the possessive individual (as was the case with First Nations of Hawai'i and parts of the continental United States, Brit-ish Columbia, and South Australia; and Palestinians throughout historic Palestine and the West Bank), and a juridical structure premised on private property ownership remains prevalent in both settler colonial and postco-lonial contexts. Attempts to transform land collectively held by First Na-tions and aboriginal communities in Canada and Australia have also been met with criticisms that this move will only serve to reduce the indigenous land base. In Australia, with regard to the Northern Territory specifically, proposals to convert land held communally (restored to its owners through the use of the Native Title Act, 1993) into property held in fee simple by in-dividuals has met with criticism on the grounds that it will not ameliorate social and economic conditions in aboriginal communities.[13]

The imposition of fee simple title was (and perhaps remains) the juridi-cal expression of an economic system and philosophical worldview that posits individual private property ownership as a necessary precondition for individual and national development and progress. Indeed, fee simple ownership interests, the strongest ownership interest within a common law system, and those parasitic on this right, such as leasehold interests, have consistently been privileged over aboriginal title. For instance, in British Columbia, where aboriginal rights to land have been constitutionally protected since 1982 (as discussed at length in chapter 1), there has not been a single successful claim on registered land that is privately held in fee simple. Aileen Moreton-Robinson notes how in Australia, the Native Title Act, 1993, delivered to pastoralist leaseholders "the guarantee that they would be able to renew their existing leases on identical terms and conditions without ever consulting with a native titleholder."[14] Private ownership interests, even that of a lessee, that are secured by a state guarantee of their certainty and trustworthiness appear to be insurmountable obstacles to the restitution of indigenous lands.

The drive to register land and impose a system of ownership rationalized through the bureaucratic function of the registry has a long and varied history. From the early nineteenth century in colonial Bengal, the British devised systems of registration for land as a means of increasing their revenue base; the formalization of land rights enabled them to more effectively tax the owners.[15] In addition to concerns about revenue, the rationalization of land holdings to suit the imperatives of a capitalist agrarianism by colonial authorities was also facilitated by a system of title by registration. In Mandate Palestine, as discussed below, the British authorities attempted to survey and register a great deal of rural land on the basis that civilizing the area required English property laws that would improve agricultural productivity.[16]

At the same time, however, the uneven application of this mode of ownership in settler colonial and neocolonial settings reveals fissures in the narrative of a linear and progressive movement to a system of ownership that, ostensibly at least, does not privilege possession as its basis. Maurer and Schwab, for instance, argue that the exigencies of accelerating ownership over natural resources in postinvasion Iraq meant that "establishing title to property was set behind the immediate push to allow Iraqis the freedom to contract with foreign trading companies and to grant foreign trading companies the right to Iraqi property—even before the latter could be appropriately registered and assessed."[17]

Maurer and Schwab argue that the usual trappings of the liberal political sphere in which the rights of individual citizens are recognized by a public sphere that upholds private law was bypassed in order to secure trade and property for foreign investors.[18] The neoimperial drive to exploit Iraqi resources privileged expediency over the type of administrative and legal regulation that would have created at least the appearance of a liberal legal order that protects formal property rights, a tendency that echoes colonial modes of appropriation from earlier times. In South Australia, for instance, colonization ventures were funded through the sale of lands to English investors before proper surveying of the land had even been carried out (discussed below). In Mandate Palestine, on the other hand, the drive to register land was halted in areas where political sensitivities might have jeopardized the political authority of the Mandate government.

The contradictory and uneven imposition of a system of title by registration in different settler colonial contexts challenges a developmental narrative of property law, in which possession as the basis of ownership has slowly been displaced by a system of title by registration. Rather, it seems evident that these two rationales for ownership coexist alongside one another. The fragmented and recombinant nature of property law in the settler colony reflects the reality of colonial modernity. The imperatives of settler colonialism, itself a capitalist formation, require the maintenance of noncapitalist rationales for the appropriation of indigenous lands. Dispossession achieved through ongoing forms of primitive accumulation requires a panoply of premodern and modern property logics that operate in conjunction with one another, reflecting the fragmented and contradictory nature of colonial modernity.

In this chapter, I argue that the progressive move toward a system of title by registration, first instituted in its most pervasive form in the colony of South Australia in 1858, reflects logics of abstraction that determine the nature of both the commodity form of landed property and the racial abstraction of the Savage. The colony was, in the minds of English land reformers, quite conveniently free of a population with recognizable preexisting ownership of the land. The transformation in prevailing conceptualizations of property and the drive to render land as fungible as possible, the desire to commod-itize land, which had been pursued in earnest since the seventeenth century, could be realized in this vacant land so much more easily than in England itself.[19] As such, the Torrens system of registration was inaugurated in South Australia some seventy years prior to its introduction on a national scale in England and Wales. After its successful trial in South Australia, it was next adopted in the colony of British Columbia, which was with the exception of approximately fourteen treaties (concluded during governor James Doug-las's tenure on Vancouver Island) treated as if it were terra nullius. Thus, I argue that the space of the settler colony was highly significant in the devel-opment of this particular system of ownership.

The fact that the Torrens system was first imposed in the colony of South Australia was no accident; the racial abstraction embodied in the figure of the Savage or Native, encoded in the doctrine of terra nullius, reflects a dual vision of property and race that colonists carried with them to South Aus-tralia. The land was understood as a commodity without any owners, to be claimed, partitioned, securitized, and cultivated. Indigenous peoples who had lived on the land for thousands of years prior to the arrival of Europe-ans were cast as a primitive race, which would vanish from the landscape or, failing that, could be salvaged through assimilation. The counterpart to the alchemical nature of conjuring fictitious value in land as a commodity was the burgeoning pseudoscientific classifications of race and racial differ-ence. Echoing earlier movements of enclosure in England and Wales, title by registration functioned during the nineteenth century as a technique of dispossession in the settler colony.

This chapter proceeds in three parts. In the first part, I examine the devel-opment of the Torrens system of title by registration in the colony of South Australia and argue that it gave expression to a "new grammar of property" that reflected an increasingly abstract concept of ownership.[20] In the United Kingdom, long-held justifications for and practices of ownership that were based on possession and use gave way to an affective grounding of owner-ship rooted in expectation and the desire for security.[21] Property ownership came to be defined by these abstract qualities and required different legal forms and techniques, such as title by registration, to structure and realize newly configured relations of exchange and modes of alienation. While the myriad factors involved in the history of land reform are inevitably complex and irreducible to any singular causal explanation, the logic of abstraction shaped a new grammar of property ownership and, consequently, the legal form of property that emerged during the nineteenth century in Britain and its colonial possessions.[22]

In the second part, I examine the racial logic of abstraction that enabled English colonial authorities to treat Australia as terra nullius. Focusing on the emergence in the mid-nineteenth century of racial science, it is clear that abstraction, as a mode of scientific thought, underpinned methods of measuring and evaluating human value based on anatomy and biology. I argue that racial formations in the settler colony, like modern property logics, do not adhere to a strictly teleological development; while the emergence of racial science marked a departure from natural history taxonomies of racial difference to a biologically grounded notion of race, they both rely on a logic of abstraction that situates whiteness at the apex of civilized human life.

In the third part, and by way of conclusion, I turn from the historical context of South Australia to the contemporary scene of Palestinian dispossession in East Jerusalem, to demonstrate how possession retains its importance to settler colonial control over indigenous land and urban spaces. In the context of East Jerusalem, the imperatives of Israeli ethnonationalism compete with and hamper the imposition of mechanisms that a rational market in land requires. In other words, the objective of Israeli settler nationalism to reduce the presence of Palestinians in the city of Jerusalem requires the frustration of the logical development of a land market in which formal title is a precondition. Many Palestinian homeowners, holders of Ottoman-era title deeds that exist in an "unsettled land registry," cannot formalize their title because of the state's aim to disenfranchise and dispossess Palestinians of their long-established presence in Jerusalem. The repeated attempts to evict Palestinian residents from East Jerusalem illustrate the importance of actual, physical possession, accompanied by a colonial animus to control the city, over formal and more abstract concepts of ownership. Ultimately, possession retains its status as a ruling concept with respect to ideologies of ownership that both maintain and exceed (the boundaries of) property law itself.

REGISTRATION AS A MEANS OF CREATING
SOCIAL AND LEGAL FACTS

Possibly, some . . . may concur with me in regarding it [English property law] as altogether too splendid and ingenious a work of art to suit either our means or our requirements in these colonies; that, like those exquisite carvings in ivory which we see marshalled in order in some recess or cabinet of a lady's boudoir, but never drawn out when the game of chess is really to be played, the proper place for this "*splendid code*" is the cabinet of the antiquary, where those who have leisure and a taste for that sort of thing, may admire this "*proof of the vast powers of the human intellect, however vainly or preposterously employed*" [quoting from Blackstone]. In playing out the game of life in this work-a-day part of the globe, we require something less costly, something less artificial, something which we may handle with more freedom and rapidity.

—Robert Richard Torrens, *Notes on a System of Conveyancing by Registration of Title*

Robert Richard Torrens, who would become the third premier of South Australia after campaigning largely on the basis of land reform, wrote confidently about the unsuitability of English land law for the colonies. Relegating the art (as opposed to the science) of English property law to a prior time that could find its proper place only in the vitrine of a bourgeois drawing room—or indeed, in Torrens's masculinist vision of land and law, the unattainable reaches of a lady's bedroom—he counterposes this image with that of the unencumbered and empty space of the settler colony where the everyday business of settlement demanded a more convenient mode of ownership.

Torrens was the primary architect of the land registration system that came to be known as the Torrens system, in which the ownership of property is registered on a title document and archived in a state-run registry.[23] The state thus becomes a guarantor of the indefeasible title of the owner, along with those who have lesser interests listed on the title document, by way of liens, easements, covenants, or mortgages. The land title document is intended to mirror ownership as well as any other legal interests that another person might have over that piece of real property, which is represented on the title document as a drawing indicating the boundaries of the property and a description of it in words. Of significance to the analysis pursued here is that the system of title by registration renders prior ownership interests irrelevant; that which is recorded on the document archived in the state registry becomes the proof of ownership, not the historical memory, social use, kinship ties, or other relations that were bound up with land use and ownership for centuries prior to becoming more fully commodified.[24] As I explore below, even English landowners had difficulty with a move toward what they viewed as a fictitious form of ownership. But the drive to render land as fungible as possible, pursued in earnest since the enclosures began, could be secured only with a system of conveyancing that made property ownership and its alienation as secure, predictable, and certain as possible.

In 1925, the United Kingdom enacted the Land Registration Act 1925 (15 Geo. V ch.21) and the Law of Property Act (15 Geo. V ch.20). This legislation imposed throughout England and Wales a compulsory system of title by registration, bringing to a close a series of failed attempts by land law reformers to rationalize the laws of property conveyancing, pursued from as early as the sixteenth century.[25] It is important to note that the system of title by registration implemented in 1925 was not introduced ex nihilo. A system of registration existed in Scotland as early as the seventeenth century.[26] However, the struggle to impose a system of title by registration in England and Wales was a long one, with key sites of resistance based in two quarters: one was the legal profession, who stood to profit from the continuation of a baroque system of conveyancing that required their expertise.[27] The other was an aristocracy who were not inclined to make the alienation of their vast estates any easier. As Torrens noted:

> The lands of England are held by a comparatively small number of proprietors, and are handed down in the same family from father to son for generations, so that transfers are rare, and when they do occur are for amounts so considerable that the costs of conveyancing, great though they be, amounting on the average to two and a-half per cent on the purchase-money (as shown by the evidence taken by the late Parliamentary Commission), does not constitute a very heavy percentage upon the value of the property transferred. The class immediately affected (the landed gentry of England) are proverbially averse to changes in existing institutions; the genius of conservatism is opposed to any such radical reform as would lead to diminish obstructions which tend to preserve the hereditary acres in the old lines of descent.[28]

The logic of registration begins to emerge, as noted above, with the shift to an increasingly commoditized vision of land. Local county registries and a fledgling one in London itself emerged in the 1860s, but it would take until 1925 for the system to be imposed in a definitive and compulsory manner throughout England and Wales.[29] Thus, the legal profession and other opponents of the system of registration were not abruptly defeated, but land law reformers won the day gradually and, notably, as I argue here, sometime after the Torrens system had been introduced in various British colonies.[30]

It is also clear, however, that the aristocracy and landed gentry were using their vast estates to engage in speculative financial ventures. The far-away plantations in the West Indies that served as the backdrop for much Georgian- and Victorian-era literature, such as Austen's *Mansfield Park* to name but one novel of many, and, indeed, for Bentham's own speculations on the nature of ownership in his *Theory of Legislation*, were emblematic of the enormous amounts of capital invested in the slave trade, plantations, and land speculation throughout the empire. The rise of a system of financial speculation premised on credit (see discussion of Baucom, below) required the use of landed property as collateral. At the same time, the social-cultural significance of land that developed during the feudal era did not diminish with the long transition to an agrarian capitalist economy. As Sugarman and Warrington note, "In the strange, half-timeless world of the traditional English landed estate, feudal concepts blissfully lingered long after feudal relations had been eradicated."[31] In a compelling analysis, the authors show how the equity of redemption, a core device in the law of mortgages, was utilized to protect the rights of landholders from the encroachments of capital, while at the same time "fostering the extension of commercial contracts sustained by credit."[32]

Prior to a system of registration, the sale of land was based on contractual principles.[33] The seller had to produce each and every deed of conveyance (going back as far as possible) to show the purchaser a good chain of title. Of course, one of the major defects with this system is that "not every interest in the land was created by or recorded in the deeds forming the chain of title"; the same held for interests created outside the frame of conveyancing (such as inheritance).[34] In other words, even the most thorough searching of the title deeds did not always provide sufficient security for prospective purchasers. In light of this, contracts for sale and purchase of land reflected an amalgam of title deeds and local knowledge of the land.

Given that the formal ideal of a good root of title was often unattainable, contract formation became a practical art, which referred only obliquely to the theory of conveyancing. In practice, conveyancing was an exercise in evaluating the plausibility of a paper title against practical senses of property that had arisen from land use, and which lay in local memory or in the memory of an estate inventory.[35]

Pottage explores in depth how the system of conveyancing that preceded the introduction of registration relied upon "a local sense of place and property."[36] Prior to the cartographic mapping of the country, which happened at different moments throughout the nineteenth century, boundaries were determined and identified by reference to natural or local landmarks, and what Pottage calls "a logic of localised practice."[37] This local knowledge was gradually codified with the emergence of mapping from the sixteenth century onward, and Pottage illuminates both the emergent techniques of cadastral mapping and the significance of the transposition of ownership signified by the memory of lived, social experience to ownership signified by paper held in an administrative archive, the registry.[38]

The defects with the contractual system of conveyancing were many, reiterated at length throughout the nineteenth century as members of the British Parliament repeatedly attempted to introduce local registries of titles and, ultimately, a national system of title by registration. As noted above, the greatest defect with the system was considered by many to be the insecurity of title.[39] As the commissioners stated, "In all civilized countries, the Title to Land depends in a great measure on written documents." They went on to detail all of the circumstances in which every material document might not be produced, and even in cases not involving fraud, as noted above, there might be interests that were not conveyed in a deed.

The resistance among the aristocracy to a system of title by registration that would render land more easily fungible was thus consistent with the paradoxical nature of the uses of landed property during this period: its value as social-cultural capital remained undiminished, while it was simultaneously retooled to facilitate emergent financial forms of capital investment and speculation. Moreover, archaic forms of entitlement attached to status property clearly did not disappear with the transition from feudal property relations to an agrarian capitalism. The possession of aristocratic, noble, or royal lineage was an indicator of the value of one's self and a prime determinant of one's life chances. The degree to which this type of inheritance has diminished in force in contemporary British society is an open question. The identity-property nexus encapsulated in the concept of status is explored in length in chapter 4.

In making the case for the adoption of a system of title by registration in the colony of South Australia, Torrens wrote with great conviction about the opportunity for property law reform presented by a place that was unencumbered by a landed English aristocracy and the remnants of a feudal property regime. Setting sail for South Australia in 1840, Torrens was elected to the Parliament of South Australia in April 1857, largely because he campaigned on a platform of conveyancing reform.[40] He was to become the third premier of South Australia in that same year, and worked tirelessly to promote the wholesale reform of the conveyancing system. Introduced as a private member's bill in 1858, the Real Property Act eventually came into force at the beginning of July that year.

Prior to moving to South Australia, Robert Richard Torrens worked as a landing waiter in the Port of London. Once he had arrived in Australia, he was appointed as a customs officer in the Port of Adelaide. It was at the Customs Department that he gained experience of the shipping system, where funded property was bought and sold within a system of registration. Working with a system of property that was funded rather than landed, Torrens was to gain an acute appreciation of the similarities in forms of moveable and fixed property. The system of registration for land title that was introduced into South Australia was in part modeled on the system of registration of the Hanseatic states of Germany, and Torrens relied upon the expertise of his German collaborator Hübbe in no small measure.

His formative experiences with the system of registration employed by the shipping industry influenced Torrens's vision of landed property as a commodity, abstracted from prior relations of ownership and, to whatever degree possible, from particular and individualized characteristics or traits. One of the many objections to a system of registration for land titles was that unlike funded property, landed property was subtended by the facts of occupation, possession, and individual characteristics that required special attention in the selling and purchasing of land. It was in response to these objections that Torrens elaborated on what he saw as the likenesses between funded property and landed property.[41]

The process by which property comes to be seen in abstract terms, both generally and specifically, is typified by Torrens's comments on the similitude between fixed and moveable property. Torrens wrote that "this objection on the score of difference in essential attributes disappears like a mirage upon investigating closely the nature of property in shipping."[42] He argued that a ship is even more indivisible than land and also bears the trait of individuality. He also argued that registration was even more suitable for immobile property as compared to that which is shipped, as the latter "may be removed beyond the ken and jurisdiction of the registering officer."[43] Torrens refuted the notion that there are material differences between land and funded property, and argued that land is essentially the same, for purposes of conveyancing, as intangible and/or mobile forms of property. He quotes from J. S. Mill, who remarked, "to make land as easily transferrable as stock would be one of the greatest economical improvements which could be bestowed upon the country."[44]

Registration was a necessity in the shipping trade because in order to be transferred, ships had to be identified by a long description in the register.[45] The shipping registers kept by customs officers reflect a system of recording that emerged as a form of writing as early as the thirteenth century. Entry books emerged as a form of record keeping that stood somewhere between the official rolls and the literary treatises connected to them:

> Here, as in other branches of record-making, the Exchequer was the pioneer. In the two Black Books and in the Red Book of the Exchequer we have perhaps the earliest instances of this kind of compilation. In later times the example of the Exchequer was extensively followed.... From the period of the Restoration the War Office possesses a series of entry books. Many corporate towns made similar collections; and the great landowners, lay and ecclesiastical, possessed registers and cartularies which were used for their possessions in the same manner as the official publication were used for the department of state to which they referred.[46]

The register as a form of record keeping emerges as one means of creating social and legal facts. Registers recorded surrenders of land to the Crown, along with copies of statutes, state papers, and other public documents that related to the activities and jurisdiction of the Exchequer. By the eighteenth century, registers recorded all manner of transactions that related to various state departments. Significantly for my purposes, it is interesting to note the primary place of registers in colonial governance. In registers produced by colonial administrators and customs officers, everything from each bushel of wheat that was produced in the British North American colonies and imported into Britain, to the number of tons of cotton exported from India, to parcels of land carved up for sale in the colony of Australia, were recorded in registers and thus became a crucial instrument in creating colonial taxonomies of productivity, income, and expenditure. The laws of customs, as they related to shipping, navigation, and revenue, are digested in successive tomes that detail in the form of a register the revenue collected from the importation of each and every item that was arriving by ship from the colonies and elsewhere.[47]

The registers for shipping, with which Torrens would have been well acquainted, first arose in order to make the national provenance of ships easily identifiable and legally verifiable.[48] As Thring points out, "Ships, by international law, are for the most purposes considered as a portion of the territory of the nation to which they belong," and thus the legal identity of the ship's paternity was essential to secure commerce and to determine "without difficulty which ships are subject to our municipal laws and regulations."[49] The system of registration for British ships became a precondition for enjoying the privileges afforded British seamen. Moreover, it also provided a means of making the title and transfer of ships much more efficient in an increasingly globalized system of trade.

Thring, writing a memorandum that was published in 1854, addressed the similarities between the two types of registry, that of shipping and those proposed for real property: "It is the more important to look at the law determining the rights to ships in this general point of view [the rights of owners as established by English law], as the registration of real property, now so much discussed, rests on precisely the same principles, and the same rules might, with certain modification of details, accommodate the migratory character of shipping and the fixity of land, be applied to both species of property."[50] The logic underlying this argument that property, whether fixed or mobile, landed or seaborne, could be governed by the same type of system of registration rests on the assumption that despite their differences, the realization and use of their value as commodities required a system that would allow for maximum amounts of security in trade and exchange. From the late sixteenth century, a variety of different mercantile and commercial devices such as double-entry bookkeeping, trade agreements, commercial sales contracts, and precise records of price and value were generalized across fields in order to produce a "general logic of contractual exchange."[51] Paraphrasing Alain Pottage, registration was a key device utilized to codify and rationalize the fictive and abstract quality of property.[52] This is evidenced by the use of registration across a range of fields during the nineteenth century, including life insurance and patent law.[53]

Pottage has persuasively shown how the system of title by registration, inaugurated with the 1925 Law of Property Act in the United Kingdom and, subsequent to that, the 1930 Land Registration Rules relating to conveyancing, embodied a "logic of registration" that replaced the property logic of contract and conveyance. Registration "superimposed" a new sequence onto practices of conveyancing, which essentially reordered primary elements of the old scheme "according to a new grammar of property."[54] This new grammar of property gave expression to an increasingly abstract concept of ownership. Property ownership came to be defined by these abstract qualities and required different legal forms and techniques, such as title by registration, to structure and realize newly configured relations of exchange and modes of alienation. Pottage has traced the rules and practices of conveyancing, and the cartographic techniques that were essential to the transformation in landholding that title by registration inaugurated. Significantly, he illuminates how the coexistence of two different forms of registration (in relation to mortgages, for instance) during a long transitional phase from one paradigm of ownership to another exposed property owners' distrust of this new logic of registration, which, in their eyes, created a form of ownership of real property that lacked reality. A registered owner of a mortgage charge was understood to be a "person with power" but bereft of a legal estate in the property. Actual possession of the title deeds by the mortgagee, deeds that signified ownership, was being displaced by a bureaucratic and abstract representation of ownership interests in an administrative archive. The coexistence of a system in which the mortgagee took the registered charge and also held the mortgage off register was "[c]onsistent with the idea that registration involved the construction of fictitious ownership."[55]

As explored above, the anxiety created by a space imagined to be empty and unpopulated by law was thus quieted through the use of land as financial collateral. Once propertized in this way however, land ownership still augured fear in relation to the insecurity of title. Torrens, in introducing the Real Property Bill in the South Australia legislature, was somewhat dramatic about the evils of insecurity accompanying conveyancing. After citing the pecuniary loss involved in procuring a good title, he said, "But the pecuniary loss is not the worst feature. The harassing, spirit-wearing perplexity in which the land-owner is too frequently involved is yet more distressing. . . . How many purchasers for *bona fide* consideration, having parted with their money, pass their days in anxiety and bitterness, dreading lawsuits, eviction and ruin."[56] The problems of conveyancing reiterated in the colonial context, which do not at any point acknowledge the presence of aboriginal communities on the land (which at a minimum may have at least constituted a problem for the security of title) reflect a degree of non-recognition that is truly revealing of the meaning of terra nullius.

The imposition of the Torrens system of registration was explicitly intended, like all registries, to provide greater security to title holders.[57] In order to identify the parcel of land represented on the title document with sufficient precision, surveying and cadastral techniques of mapping became indispensable. However, as many others have noted, the surveying and mapping of territory, "when allied with state power, enable much of the reality they depict to be remade."[58]

A great deal of scholarly work has been done on mapping, examining its emergence as a technique of appropriation and a mode of knowledge production. The cadastral map was, for James Scott, "the crowning artifact" of the process of simplification of land tenure that modern property law has had as its objective.[59] This simplified representation was a means of creating a very narrow and partial vision of land as fungible, taxable property. As discussed in chapter 1, Nicholas Blomley has written cogently of the role that the cadastral survey and map making played in the reconceptualization of land (and their attenuating rights) as commodity property during the enclosure movement and during colonial settlement.[60] Maps based on the cadastral survey "help make possible the very idea of 'space' as an abstract category" and, as Blomley continues, "If space can be imagined as abstract, perhaps, it begins to be possible to treat it as the reified and alienable 'object' of property."[61]

The surveying and mapping of land rearticulated it in entirely different terms (temporally, spatially, and materially) from what existed prior to the mapping exercise. In the specific context of land titling, Pottage argues that the move to registration effectively reduces land to paper, and surveying and mapmaking are the means through which this reduction happens. "Registration extracted land from the network of relations and understandings which formed the 'local knowledge' of different communities, relocated it on an abstract geometric map, and deciphered it according to a highly conventionalised topographic code."[62]

The surveying and mapping of territory was certainly an integral dimension of implementing a system of title by registration and, more significantly, effacing preexisting ways of knowing and using the land.[63] Surveying and mapping of territory had particular force in relation to agricultural laborers in the English context, and indigenous communities in the settler colonial context whose relationships to land were to be dramatically suppressed, literally buried under the vision of colonial surveyors.[64] In South Australia, however, Torrens argued that mapping was not a necessary precursor to the registration of title, because in new colonies the size and boundaries of new estates were constantly changing and being created. Quoting from the Real Property Commissioners' reports, he noted that "[o]ne of the witnesses has observed in his evidence that 'A map is a good servant but a bad master; very useful as an auxiliary, but very mischievous if made indispensable.' "[65] The necessity of procuring maps as a prerequisite for a system of registration was thus a contested issue in South Australia. "The grant or certificate of lands contained a diagram of the land, drawn accurately and to scale, and a verbal description of the parcels and of the parties entitled."[66] And as I have outlined above, surveying and mapping was not carried out on a large scale prior to a vast number of sales of parcels of land being sold prior to settlement.

In fact, the mode of settlement of the colony of South Australia illuminates both the financial dimension of colonization and the centrality of the operation of terra nullius to colonial settlement, two factors that were, I argue, quite intimately related to one another. The land, infamously claimed by the Crown on the basis that it was uninhabited, was sold to settlers before their arrival. The colonization commissioners for South Australia note that by 1839 (three years after the first settlers had landed on the coast of St. Vincent's Gulf), 250,320 acres of public land had been sold for the sum of 229,756 pounds. The customs and license duties added a further yield in revenue of 20,000 pounds per year.[67] The enabling legislation that established the Colonization Commission provided that the surveying of the land was to be funded by a combination of the advanced purchase of public lands in South Australia (35,000 pounds) and a further 20,000 pounds raised "on the security of its future revenues and un-appropriated lands."[68]

Thus the survey of land was funded not by the British colonial government but by private individuals and the South Australian Company, who bought "unexplored land" that was intended for settlement. After much exertion by the commissioners, 437 preliminary land orders for 135 acres each (composed of 134 acres of rural land and one acre of town land) were sold at the fixed price of twelve shillings per acre.[69] Moreover, the legislation required the commissioners to raise a guarantee fund "by raising a loan upon the security of the probable revenues of a proposed settlement, the site of which was yet unknown."[70] They were authorized to raise a loan for up to 200,000 pounds at an interest rate not exceeding 10 percent per annum. The money borrowed was to be a charge upon the revenue or the monies received from duties and taxes levied in the colony with the unsold lands as collateral.[71] A portion of this loan would be invested in government securities, to protect the metropole from any liabilities that might result in the course of colonization.

Colonial settlement was thus privatized from the very beginning, with the techniques of finance capitalism, such as speculative investment on futures, funding the colonial venture. What is also very clear from the enabling legislation is that the land was viewed, even prior to settlement, as a fungible commodity to be used both to finance settlement through its sale and speculatively, as collateral for securities. This mode of colonization reflected a concept of property imbued with the characteristics of the commodity form, abstracted from any preexisting social relations or use, even before the arrival of the settlers. It also reflects the spatialization of capital; South Australia was produced as a space of colonial settlement through the use of land for financial speculation.[72]

For Torrens, the colony of Australia was a space unencumbered by the social relations of aristocracy, by history, by a past. The colony of Australia as a terra nullius provides a space for a radical break with the political and legal inheritance of England. "Here feudal tenures—the source of all the complication—never had existence."[73] Contrary to the assertion made by Elizabeth Povinelli that the English carried the "prior" with them in the very substance of English property law, it is clear that the primary objective in the reforms sought by Torrens and his supporters was to begin anew, and the doctrine of terra nullius provided the means and justification for creating this new system of ownership in the colony.[74]

Aboriginal communities in Australia were not consigned to a time of the prior; and, significantly, nor were English property owners. The specific concept of ownership that was imposed had as its primary objective to displace the concept of the prior, and prior ownership, from the juridical sphere. Perhaps the most radical aspect of a system of title by registration is that it renders all prior ownership claims irrelevant. Title by registration precludes any consideration of what was there before. This is more akin to a logic of elimination, radically negating what was there before, based on the doctrine of terra nullius. Coupled with this erasure of indigenous interests was the desire to shed the weight of English land conveyancing and the aristocratic stranglehold over forms of land ownership, in order to implement a new system of registration of title. The retrospective recognition of aboriginal communities' prior presence on the land comes much later; but to assert that a governance of the prior arrives in Australia with the colonists is to mischaracterize the nature of property ownership that was imposed in South Australia in the form of the Torrens system.

Torrens, like Bentham, rejected Blackstone's rather more romanticized vision of English property law, as evidenced by the quotation that opens this section. Blackstone's concern with how colonists ought to deal with the existence of prior legal relations among indigenous communities at the point of colonial encounter reflects his overarching preoccupation with how to theorize the transition from natural law conceptualizations of ownership to a more rational scientific basis, which he attempted to construct in the *Commentaries*. In other words, the existence of prior legal relations in the state of nature presents a logical problem for Blackstone's objective of creating a rational science of law, more than an ideological concern with modes of governance or the legitimacy of colonial sovereignty.

The bifurcation of issues relating to aboriginal peoples from considerations of property law in several different archival sources (Reports of the Colonization Commissioners, legislative debates of the South Australian Parliament, and colonial correspondence) make it clear that the land was viewed as a commodity entirely divorced from the people living on it. Aboriginal peoples were an inferior race, racialized as black, to be displaced and corralled into reservations, educated, civilized, and protected by the Crown. It is often argued that because the land was viewed as terra nullius, the colonists were able to impose a system of private property ownership in Australia. However, it seems that this misses the significance of how the land was viewed and the prevailing concept of property held by the colonists even prior to settlement. The discourse of savagery makes aboriginal rights to their land a nonquestion, and the doctrine of terra nullius facilitates the materialization of this vision of the land as free and fungible.

Armed with a battery of new concepts grounded in the political philosophy of the Utilitarians, an English government desirous of colonization, and deep-rooted resistance to a transformation in the existing modes of land ownership and conveyancing in England, the colonists were able to push forward radical reforms in land law. The ultimate violence of abstraction that lay at the basis of the proposed rationales for the imposition of the Torrens system was that land was deemed to be vacant, a tabula rasa. The relationship between a colonial ontology (based on a racial taxonomy) and property ownership was thus central to this process of transformation. Abstraction as a central modality of propertization was based not just on changing justifications and conceptualizations of ownership, as I have explored above, but on an abstract fiction that posed a continual threat to civilization and security: the figure of the Savage.

LOGICS OF ABSTRACTION AND THE LEGAL FORM OF PROPERTY

The transition to more abstract concepts of ownership that characterized the commodification of land required new legal forms to express, in the form of a general equivalence, a singular property value. As many others have observed, title by registration was a legal device that reflected and facilitated more abstract conceptualizations of property.[75] This logic of abstraction effectively transformed the idea of property (in land) as a socially embedded set of relations premised on use, political hierarchies, and exchange, to a commodity vision of land that rendered it fungible in the same way as any other commodity.[76] This is qualitatively different from the ideology of improvement explored in chapter 1, where Petty's notion of a general equivalence between the value of land and labor was still shaped by the belief in the specific significance of cultivation (and productive agricultural labor) as the source of national wealth. However, the method for quantifying value devised by Petty, the general emphasis on measuring the value of populations, and his concept of the racial inferiority of the Irish remain as traces in the growing predominance of racial science in the nineteenth century. The commodity logic of abstraction reflected in a system of title by registration emerged in conjunction with a racial science that reified taxonomies of human value.

The logic of abstraction, in a basic, Marxian sense, reflects the separation of the material and ideal from one another. As Derek Sayer argues in *The Violence of Abstraction*, Marx's radical challenge to the presuppositions of Hegel's dialectic of consciousness was to reject the validity of separating the material conditions in which consciousness is formed from its ideal concept.[77] When the material (world) and the ideal are separated, it comes "at the cost of the 'abstraction' or reification of both."[78] Laws, to take another example, cannot be separated from the material conditions in which they are produced, and the social relations that particular modes of production sustain. To posit property as a general category is thus to render historically bound social relations in the form of an abstract category: "In each historical epoch, property has developed differently and under a set of entirely different social relations. Thus to define bourgeois property is nothing else than to give an exposition of all the social relations of bourgeois production. To try and give a definition of property as an independent relation, a category apart, an abstract and eternal idea, can be nothing but an illusion of metaphysics or jurisprudence."[79]

Of course, property laws effectively materialize just such a jurisprudential illusion, much like the commodity form itself. However, the violence of abstraction does not simply lie in the creation of a false distinction between the material world and ideal notions of property, and the reification of concepts that are divorced from the social and political realities from which they emerge. Marx's notion of "real abstraction" reflects a passage, as Toscano writes, "from [a] fundamentally intellectualist notion of abstraction ... to a vision of abstraction that, rather than depicting it as a structure of illusion, recognizes it as a social, historical, and trans-individual phenomenon."[80] The legal device of title by registration reflects the culmination of a long transformation to a commodity form of property (and law) that was forged in both England and its colonies, and significantly in relation to the latter, embedded in social relations of race and racial domination.

Property law, as noted in the introduction, was central to the appropriative objectives of colonialism. A theory of legal form, offered by Soviet Marxist legal theorist Pashukanis, is useful (to some extent) for understanding the legal changes that accompanied the commoditization of land from the seventeenth century onward. Pashukanis's theory of law as a form is derived from the actual, real operation of law and legal relations, challenging the empty formalism of neo-Kantians such as Kelsen.[81] Pashukanis analyzed the central role that law plays in structuring and facilitating relations of exchange and the regulation of labor, resulting in a theory of law as a form rather than as a system of norms and rules or, conversely, as ideology.

A legal form analysis helps to orient our attention toward the mechanisms, in this case, title by registration, that were developed in order to transform land into private property in its modern, commodity form. Modern landed property becomes the "basis of the legal form only when it becomes something which can be freely disposed of in the market."[82] Property, in the hands of legal subjects defined through their self-ownership, provides the fertile soil for a world to be made through the logics of ownership, alienability, and exchange. The Marxist critique of the cunning of abstraction reveals how the commodity form congeals multiple forms of use value, the various types of labor involved in producing, cultivating, and tending to the land (or scientific invention, or coats, or hats for that matter), into a "material shell of the abstract property of value."[83] In masking these different forms of labor and use, the commodity logic of abstraction obliterates preexisting relations to the land, and preexisting conceptualizations of land as something other than a commodity. The legal form renders invisible (and severely constrains) the ways in which people live, act, (re)produce the conditions of their existence, and relate to one another in ways not confined to commodity relations of ownership and exchange.[84] Echoing the words of Marx, Pashukanis notes that the general "concept of property loses any living meaning and renounces its own prejuridical history."[85] The legal form of property imposes its homogenous time on the title document held in the registry, or the patent registered in the Patent Office, and condenses multiplicity into a singular figure of the owner.

Of central significance to the theory of legal form elucidated by Pashukanis is the relationship between the subject of law and property. While anything that approaches a satisfying or fully fleshed out theorization of property in Marx's *Capital* eludes us, Pashukanis's focus on the close relationship between the legal subject and the commodity form places property at its center. The transition from feudal to capitalist social relations brought into being an abstract legal subject who was defined by his capacity for self-ownership.[86] Whereas possession in the broadest sense, including relations of subservience and dominance, was "inextricably bound up" with property, perhaps especially prior to the emergence of modern forms of property, the legal subject of capitalist relations of exchange and ownership assumes the illusory mantle of equality in its status as an abstract legal subject.[87]

So far, this rendition of Pashukanis may seem familiar to anyone with a passing acquaintance with the commodity-form theory of law, one that has been subject to sustained critique by successive generations of political theorists and legal scholars. Paul Hirst, for instance, criticizes Pashukanis for reducing the figure of the legal subject to that of the "archetypical capitalist . . . who engages in economic calculation" or alternately the independent laborer, united with all other individuals through exchange.[88] Hirst also points to the limits of conceiving of property law solely in its strictly capitalist forms, thus ignoring what were once emergent and new forms of economic organization in capitalism, such as the joint stock company. This, in his view, radically and unjustifiably limits the purview of a Marxist theorization of property and, consequently, capitalism itself. He also criticized Pashukanis for devising a concept of law that, in his view, "mirrors that of the idealist legal philosophies he opposes. In defining law as form he seeks a common defining essence of the legal sphere." The problem with what he sees as a mistaken form of idealism is ultimately that this concept of the legal form "is naively apolitical: law becomes an 'expression,' a recognition of what is, rather than an arena of struggle, a form with potential political and economic effects."[89]

Hirst's criticisms of Pashukanis's theory of the legal form are helpful insofar as he points to the limits of what was understood as germane to a critique of property relations, that is, the limits of a Marxist purview that excluded juridical and economic forms of ownership that did not fall within the triumvirate relation of "property, possession and calculation."[90] Similarly, the figure of the legal subject in the work of Pashukanis presumes a near-Lockean subject who is defined by his capacity to alienate his labor and constituted through his capacity to know and reason. While a more thorough deconstruction of the self-possessive individual is undertaken in chapter 4, it is clear that the imposition of private property relations in the colony of South Australia (as elsewhere) presumed not only the existence of the abstract individual proprietor but an abstract figure of the Native whose lands were open for appropriation.

While we approach Pashukanis's theory of the legal form with a recognition of its limitations, the attempt to denaturalize and to reveal the masking of economic and social relations that occurs in the consolidation and articulation of the legal form of property is crucial to the argument presented here, which emphasizes the importance of the colony in the development of the legal techniques that facilitated this transition to modern landed forms of property. From Ireland in the seventeenth century to South Australia in the nineteenth or Mandate Palestine in the twentieth century, the abstractions of property as a legal form are best understood by grasping the social and historical processes through which they are brought into being, a point that Marx makes in the first pages of the *Grundrisse*. The legal form of property works to naturalize modern private property relations, rendering illegible all preexisting relations of use and ownership; this is more easily realized in places where the inhabitants are deemed by the force of law to be something less than civilized (defined, of course, in spectacularly circular reasoning, by the absence of private property). The treatment of the landless during the long period of enclosure in Britain, premised on a similar logic, if not habit of mind, as the racialization (and criminalization) of indigenous peoples in the colonies, may certainly be viewed as having established the ideological grounding for what followed elsewhere.

Beyond the Marxist critique of abstraction, the practices of abstraction find their philosophical ground in the work of Locke, Bentham, J. S. Mill, and others, who had reconceived of land ownership as based not on hereditary titles and inheritance (birthright), but on labor, expectation, and security. In the work of Bentham, we see an abstract notion of ownership not based on physical possession or occupation. Primary to the property relation is law, which secures the property relation, or guards and protects the expectation.[91] Title by registration can be seen, then, as an ideal form for articulating and representing this abstract notion of ownership.

In addition to emphasizing the essence of ownership as being, for Bentham, rooted in expectation, it is equally important to understand the centrality of security to this notion of ownership. Law's raison d'être, for Bentham, is security. The expectation of being able to use and exploit one's property hinges on this ability to be free from the imposition of others' interests, be it the state authorities or arbitrary powers. Further, the law must protect the owner from the needs of others and work to diminish the fear of loss by any other means. The fear of losing one's property arguably functions as an expression of a fear of losing civilization altogether. Savagery, defined by the lack of respect for property law, is that which property law must guard itself against.[92] In another instance of tautological reasoning, the "beneficent genius" that civilizes savagery is security.[93]

The figure of the Savage runs throughout Bentham's theorization of property. He extols the acts of William Penn, who, landing upon "the savage coasts," established a colony with other "men of peace," avoiding bloodshed.[94] North America is a place of savage nature prior to its colonization and cultivation, the rulers of the Ottoman Empire a bunch of "barbarous conquerors," and governments of the east inflicted with "oriental despotism."[95] The language of primitivism conflates with a racial discourse of savagery and tribal life, both defined by the absence of property.[96]

RACIAL ABSTRACTIONS

As I have argued, the commoditization of land required a system of ownership that would facilitate exchange without the bothersome encumbrances of the past and of preexisting relationships to the land, and with the maximum possible amount of security for owners. The settler colony of South

Australia afforded English settlers a place where they could experiment with a system of registration that had been resisted in England and would not be fully implemented at home for another sixty years.

The concept of terra nullius, or vacant land, was based on a racist discourse of the civilized and noncivilized, with civilization being signified by private property ownership, the cultivation of land, modes of governance, and social organization.[97] Ironically, while the racist underpinnings of the doctrine of terra nullius have been repeatedly disavowed by contemporary courts in the context of aboriginal rights litigation, aboriginal title is persistently defined in relation to the same Anglo-European norms and concepts of property ownership that were the basis of indigenous dispossession. However, dispossession was not, as I have been arguing thus far, simply a matter of racist notions of civilized and barbaric peoples. Dispossession was both a prerequisite and a consequence of the coproduction of racial value and property ownership, rendered possible by a logic of abstraction that was central to emergent capitalist forms of property and the racial subjugation of indigenous peoples and their lands and resources.

The emergence of a capitalist economy that was based on the exploitation of colonies required new forms of knowledge. Baucom has referred to the novel forms of knowledge that accompanied the economy of exchange and trade in slaves as a new episteme. The eighteenth and nineteenth centuries mark a moment when human life and property are imbricated in relations of exchange to the extent that one stands in for the other. This is a moment when the meaning of the word "stock" is rendered ambiguous, referring to cargo that is inanimate, slaves that become property like any other, and animal livestock. It is a time when the term "specie" refers to both money and slaves, a species of property that is utilized as a stand-in for currency.[98] While the histories of the transatlantic slave trade are clearly germane to the formation of property and racialized indigenous subjects in the United States, they are somewhat less directly of import to the colonial settler contexts of Australia and Canada.

Nonetheless, the fact of blackness certainly was a live and material concern in the Australian context. Indigenous communities, referred to as blackfellas from the time of colonial settlement onward, were marked and identified as a vanishing race. Certainly this racial identification was related to a myriad of radical differences between them and the colonists, and blackness no doubt was among them. While aboriginal bodies were not commoditized in the same way as those of African slaves, I argue that the logic of abstraction was a formative influence on the racialization of aboriginal populations; racial difference was quantified and measured as a property that could be bred out. The pseudoscience of blood quantum figured significantly in colonial policies on aboriginal peoples in Australia.[99]

By the mid-nineteenth century, racial science emerged in both Europe and the United States, and it would exert a lasting influence on racial formations for the next hundred years.[100] Racial science marked a departure from earlier conceptualizations of racial difference, based on visible differences and similarities to a concept of race based on putatively scientific methods of measurement and quantification. At the same time, however, it is also apparent that like property logics themselves, modern concepts of race and racial difference did not develop in a linear fashion. For instance, early modern anatomists sought explanations for black racial difference through the analysis of tissues, organs, and blood extracted from black bodies in the first part of the eighteenth century, long before the emergence of a fully biologized concept of race.[101] The emphasis on blood as being the carrier and determinant of racial difference in the eighteenth century persists alongside the development of both craniometry and phrenology.

With respect to Australia specifically, Anderson and Perrin argue that the shift to scientific racism in the nineteenth century (and the attendant assertion that indigenous people were biologically and innately inferior to whites) provided a resolution to the failed attempts to civilize indigenous peoples through the imposition of practices of cultivation and settlement. Modern racial science, then, despite its putative epistemic differences from theological and natural history accounts of racial difference, added evidence to a consistent narrative of racial inferiority. As discussed in the introduction, the production of racial subjects, like foundational rationales for ownership in modern property, does not adhere to a coherent, linear narrative of development that sees a clear departure from one epistemic framework to another, but rather uses different concepts of race recombinantly to buttress theories of racial inferiority.

The modern discourse of race that emerged during the seventeenth century in political and philosophical discourses laid some of the groundwork for the anthropological history of humanity that followed.[102] The modern discourse of racial science was to a great extent influenced by the inauguration of the science of natural history and, subsequent to that, the shift to the modern science of biology.[103] The development of measurement and quantification as the primary techniques utilized to taxonomize and classify life forms was globalized, in the making of what Mary Louise Pratt has termed a "planetary consciousness."[104] Abstraction as a modality of thinking and as central to modern scientific method underlay the reification of ethereal concepts such as intelligence for the purposes of measurement and taxonomization.[105] In the words of Nancy Stepan:

> The goal of science was to extract regularities from variation in nature and to discover the laws behind variation. The model for the human sciences was Newtonian science, or perhaps the geological sciences, which had undergone their own "revolution" between 1770 and 1840. Travellers who visited Africa or the New World in the eighteenth century knew at first hand the range of variation in the colour, physical structure, languages and customs of the various people they encountered. The tendency in science was, however, to abstract general notions from the mass of information, ideas and suggestions about human groups collected by explorers—to transform travel literature into scientific text.[106]

Whereas racial difference was in the period prior to the eighteenth century defined primarily in relation to visible physical traits and differences (evident in Petty's observations of the Irish, as discussed in chapter 1), this framework shifts from the eighteenth century onward with the development of a racial discourse that is based in both anatomy and biology. Race (and the racial superiority of white Europeans) came to be grounded in something other than theological precepts of the God-given sovereignty of the Christian races over others; rather, the measurement of skull size and, subsequently, the segregation and displacement of peoples based on the measurement of the quantum of black or aboriginal blood that bodies carried as a result of their biological and ancestral inheritance served to justify dispossession in settler colonial contexts.[107]

Linnaeus and Cuvier in the eighteenth century questioned the basis for classification that had preceded the classical age, namely, resemblance, similarity, and difference.[108] Linnaeus first classified human beings according to a racial taxonomy divided into four categories, determined by geography: Americanus, Europaeus, Asiaticus, and Africanus.[109] Gould notes that Linnaeus "mixed character with anatomy"; African men were described as "indolent" while *Homo sapiens europaeus* was "ruled by customs."[110] None of the foremost naturalists of the eighteenth and nineteenth centuries "held black people in high esteem," as Gould puts it, in a rather understated fashion.[111] Cuvier, as he notes, referred to native Africans as "the most degraded of human races, whose form approaches that of the beast and whose intelligence is nowhere great enough to arrive at regular government."[112]

However, the obscene degrees of racism evident in the attributes ascribed to the various taxonomic categorizations of Africans and Asians is in some ways beside the point I emphasize here; it's the logic of the taxonomy and the drive to categorize and to measure that render racial thinking part of an articulation with modern property logics. We cannot, in other words, understand the emergence of modern concepts of race without understanding their imbrication with modern ideologies of ownership and property logics, as is the case vice versa. Pratt argues that Linnaeus's project of classification extended to the colonial world in a way that relied upon the same navigational mapping utilized to "search for commercially exploitable resources, markets, and lands to colonize."[113] It shored up and produced a "world historical subject" who was "European, male . . . and lettered."[114] The logic of abstraction serves the interests of commerce and colonization, with a natural history of humanity that charts racial difference in a taxonomy that standardizes notions of white European superiority.

The naturalists of the eighteenth century eventually gave way to evolutionary theory, which was accompanied by what Gould describes as a trend that reached all corners of the human sciences, a near-religious faith in the idea that "rigorous measurement could guarantee irrefutable precision."[115]

Evolution and quantification formed an unholy alliance; in a sense, their union forged the first powerful theory of "scientific" racism. By the end of Darwin's century, standardized procedures and a developing body of statistical knowledge had generated a deluge of more trustworthy numerical data.[116]

While the measurement of the human body becomes a key site in the production of scientific racism, the role of measurement in assessing human value emerged much earlier, as we observed in the work of William Petty. Petty, as noted above, was heavily influenced by the work of Francis Bacon, who in the sixteenth century transformed prevailing ideas of nature, setting the scene for changes in predominant understandings of how "newly discovered people" inherited their observable physical and mental traits.[117]

If the emergence of racial science in the nineteenth century was reliant upon larger scientific developments in philosophies of life itself, one might well speculate about the ways in which prevailing notions of race as biologically grounded come to bear on forms of knowledge central to capitalist relations of exchange. This is precisely the point that O'Malley makes when he argues that racial knowledge was used to fix value in relation to currencies, which, during the late eighteenth and early nineteenth centuries, lacked any fixity of value. Abstracted from the actual lives of non-European peoples, blackness and indigeneity came to signify a lesser value not only in relation to white European settlers but with respect to relations of ownership.

In Australia specifically, racial science emerged in the nineteenth century, and the measurement of aboriginal skulls marked them as a "distinct and degraded type."[118] Warwick Anderson remarks that Adelaide, South Australia, would become the center for the scientific study of indigenous people in Australia for much of the twentieth century.[119] Prevalent uses of racial science in the nineteenth century were combined with well-entrenched ideas about racial status and biological difference being determined by climactic and environmental factors. This was the case as much for the construction of whiteness and white identity as it was for race science studies of indigenous people. The monogenist and polygenist theories of the human species, in contestation throughout the nineteenth century, took on a particular valence for white scientists in Australia, where the tropical climate and physical environment were at the center of scientific study of the capacity of white immigrants to adapt to their new surroundings. In other words, even if indigenous people were part of a single human species, climatic and environmental factors were far from irrelevant in accounting for racial difference. With the advent of Darwinian evolutionary theories, indigenous people were cast as remnants of an earlier historical period. By the 1890s, leading biologists "regarded Aboriginal Australians as predominantly a form of archaic Caucasian."[120]

In the settler colony of South Australia, racial science produced a scene of violent dispossession and displacement.[121] The taxonomy of racial classification that accompanied the imposition of the systems of land ownership across various types of colonies becomes clear by contrasting the way in which aboriginal communities and Indians were viewed by the Australian colonists, evidenced by a short but lively debate that took place in the South Australian Legislative Council on Wednesday, January 27, 1858. Moved by the Honourable Mr. Morphett was a motion to present to Her Majesty the "sympathy and feelings of this Council in reference to the insurrection in India." They were referring to, of course, the Indian Mutiny of 1857, which is often understood as symbolizing the beginnings of the nationalist, anti-colonial movement. The members of the Legislative Council duly noted their upset and quibbled over whether their sentiment ought to be backed up by something more material, such as horses for the British cavalry or financial support. The other affect that is expressed, and more significant for my purposes here, is disappointment and vicarious shame at the "disgrace which [the Sepoys] had heaped upon themselves, knowing how gallantly those regiments had formerly fought when under the command of British officers."[122]

The Sepoys were rebellious colonial subjects, but were more in need of stronger authority and discipline, which their British colonial masters would undoubtedly provide, than anything else. This horrid warfare was to be roundly condemned, and, with perceptible melancholia, some members of the Legislative Council lamented that during the time they had served as British officers in India, it was evident that very few of the native soldiers could be depended upon for loyalty.

This is in stark contrast to the way in which aboriginal communities are described in correspondence between Lieutenant-Governor Arthur and Her Majesty's secretary of state for the colonies relating to aboriginal communities living on Van Diemen's Land (today known as Tasmania). Although the correspondence covers an earlier period, around 1831, the contrast is dramatic. Aboriginal communities are described as "predatory hordes," as "partially civilised," and as "abject beings" (Dispatch No. 1). The "tribes of savages" (Dispatch No. 2) are described as though they are another species altogether, driven by an insatiable "love of plunder" (Dispatch No. 7). The only remedy for those with an inherently "savage spirit" is expulsion from settled areas and, eventually, extermination. While the history and settlement of South Australia are vastly different from those of the penal colony of Van Diemen's Land, the discourse of the vanishing race of aborigines was certainly pervasive throughout Australian colonies. What I am gesturing toward is the racial taxonomy that marked black aboriginal bodies as abject and capable of expulsion. This abstract notion of the irredeemable Savage accompanied the vision of their lands as free of encumbrance, malleable and capable of being shaped into a new commodity form that embraced the mercantile and marine logic of registration as the most expedient and future-oriented means of ownership.

The long transition from feudal to capitalist property relations in land and the gradual transformation in concepts of ownership and systems of land tenure can appear as a linear, developmental process. Possession became an irrelevance; ownership under a system of title by registration displaced older property logics with the primacy of the paper title. However, as noted at the outset, there are many historical and contemporary instances of land titling systems either postponed (see discussion of Maurer and Schwab, above), rendered unnecessary by local practices, or, in the case considered below, cast aside at the expense of an ethnoracial nationalism that requires the physical dispossession and displacement of Palestinian residents of East Jerusalem.[123] In the final section of the chapter, I explore how possession, as a juridical concept, remains central to settler colonial control over land despite the diminution of possession as a basis for ownership in most common-law jurisdictions.

UNSETTLED REGISTRATION

During the British Mandate in Palestine, colonial authorities, with Sir Ernest Dowson at the helm, surveyed and registered approximately 20 percent of rural Palestine. As Forman notes, Dowson's firm belief in the superiority of English property law (and Western civilization more generally), coupled with an interest in improving agricultural productivity along capitalist agrarian lines, was among the primary rationales for land reform undertaken during the Mandate.[124] Dowson was enthralled with the success of the Torrens system elsewhere and was eager to spread this rationalized system of landholding throughout Palestine.[125]

While the protection of the fellahin's land interests was another ostensible motivation for land settlement in Palestine, Ghandour argues that the primary concern of the Mandate government "and its agents and experts was not the improvement of the natives' agricultural practices, but the requisition of as much land as possible."[126] And certainly, after 1948, land registration came to be a primary tactic in the expropriation of Arab land in various parts of the newly established Israeli state.[127] However, it is questionable to what extent the British drive for registration was influenced by political Zionism rather than colonial land policy as it had taken shape elsewhere. As Bunton notes, Ernest Dowson's detailed records "paid very little attention to Zionism."[128]

Given that the Torrens system of registration effectively renders all prior relationships to the land legally null and void, its utility in the colonial setting becomes quite evident. The name that appears on title in the registry designates the owner, regardless of the prior claims of those who cultivated, occupied, and possessed the land prior to the moment of registration. However (as I discuss in chapter 3) one of the things that distinguishes Palestine from other settler colonial jurisdictions is the fact that the British, and subsequently the Israelis, did not treat Palestine as if it did not already have a system of property law. In fact, the Ottoman administration could not impose its own reforms at the village level by pretending they were operating on a legal tabula rasa.[129] The Ottoman legal system, unlike indigenous legal systems in other colonies, was legible to Europeans, the history of the Ottoman Empire being enmeshed with that of Europe in a way that subject populations of lands "discovered" by European explorers were not. Through the land reforms of 1858, the Ottomans had also attempted to impose the *tapu* registration system.[130] In the Palestinian context, therefore, it is necessary to employ a more flexible periodization in characterizing land reform, and to acknowledge the persuasive argument that in some areas at least (such as the West Bank), a cadastral survey and the allotment of titles to Arab landowners could provide some protection, in theory at least, against the colonial appropriation of their land.[131] The relevance of the Ottoman land titling reforms becomes apparent when considering the types of evidence that some Palestinian landowners have proffered, usually to no avail, in their attempts to protect their property from misappropriation.

The drive to survey, map, and register land undertaken by the British was slow and time consuming; after 1929 the rise in political unrest and resistance also impeded those efforts. One place that was relatively untouched by the registration process that the British undertook was Jerusalem. In East Jerusalem specifically, much residential property is held as unsettled land. The deed registry exists separately from the "rights registry."[132] This rather sui generis form of unsettled title contributes to the relative lack of security of tenure that Palestinian residents and property owners of East Jerusalem have faced for decades.[133] Ownership for many Palestinian residents of East Jerusalem is reflected in title deeds and fiscal records held in Ottoman registries. Not based on modern surveys of the land, this title is deemed less trustworthy than title established under the Torrens system of registration, which the British attempted to impose throughout Palestine.[134] It is also important to note the historic resistance on the part of many Palestinians to registering their land; whether it was due to a reluctance to pay the taxes associated with registered land or to move to a system of landholding that would dispense with the kinship relations and social, communal memory in which older forms of ownership are embedded, this reluctance did not help matters.[135] For under Israeli law, only registered title gives owners full proprietary rights over their land; rights held within the unsettled registry are merely contractual. Thus, Palestinian property rights are rendered insecure and inconclusive for the purposes of establishing property boundaries, inheritance, or duration (unregistered title deeds are subject to statutes of limitations).[136]

For Palestinians in other parts of Israel who want to register their property interests in the rights registry, the process is often expensive, complicated, and burdensome.[137] In Jerusalem, the situation is somewhat different. To begin with, much Palestinian land was appropriated prior to 1967 through the abuse of the Absentee Property Law. In East Jerusalem, 30 to 35 percent of the land was appropriated through the use of a Mandate-era law, the Land Ordinance (Acquisition for Public Purposes Law) of 1943.[138] Of the remaining land in East Jerusalem owned by Palestinians, as advocate Elias Khoury explains, more than 70 percent remains unsettled and unregistered.[139] In Jerusalem, the settlement process itself has been frozen since the 1967 war, and Israel did not continue with land registration in Palestinian areas. In East Jerusalem, Palestinian owners have thus been unable to utilize their property as other owners would, for instance, as leverage for raising capital for other investments or, indeed, to make improvements on their own homes.

As Khoury notes, ownership remains legally unclear, while life somehow continues.

As noted above, the practical realities of land registration rules in Jerusalem make it virtually impossible for Palestinians to formalize their rights. Unless a settlement commissioner gives permission for settlement and registration—and the holder of this office does not usually give any such permission—it remains impossible for Palestinians to shift the title they hold to one that is registered. Palestinian owners can make a claim in the settlement office; however, as noted above, the process of land settlement (the precondition for registration) has been frozen since 1967 in Palestinian areas. Palestinians have thus been making claims for settlement and registration for nearly half a century with no hope of having their ownership rights formalized.[140] It is difficult to square Israel's claims of being the only democracy in the Middle East when the basic tenets of a liberal democracy— the protection of private property rights—are denied some of its own citizens on the basis of a racialized national identity.

The uneven application of the land settlement process in Jerusalem after 1967 is consistent with land policies followed elsewhere: the registration of title for land owned by Jewish Israelis to secure ownership and the use of land laws to weaken Arab ownership.[141] Land registration in contemporary Israel/Palestine is a vastly complicated issue in some ways; but the refusal of the Israeli courts to recognize preexisting ownership evidenced by Ottoman-era title deeds reflects the blatantly ideological treatment of property law rules in the Israeli context. It also, however, challenges the idea that the global drive to title and register land has displaced possession as a central part of ownership in settler colonies. In Palestine, title to land in the older form of deeds that should provide the basis for the settling and registration of title, which is in turn meant to provide the highest form of security of ownership, is often rendered meaningless in the face of physical dispossession.

In historic Palestine/Israel, and Jerusalem specifically, one does risk stating a banal and obvious fact in noting that the primary objective behind Israeli infrastructure projects, land use planning and property laws, archaeological and heritage projects, and control over the legal status of Palestinian Jerusalemites is to radically diminish (if not wipe out) the Palestinian presence in the city.[142] The strategic plan for Jerusalem, set out in the Israel 2020 Master Plan for Jerusalem, is understood by some to have the aim of reducing the Palestinian population to approximately 8 to 12 percent of the city's population.[143] Possession, in this instance, reflects and is effected through property laws that render Palestinian ownership insecure, but also describes the larger colonial animus to appropriate the city as an Israeli capital. It is this nexus between property law concepts and the sovereign imperatives of settler colonial regimes that I continue to explore below.

We can recall here Edward Said's poetic analysis of one of the final scenes in Michel Khleifi's film *Fertile Memory*. The film, released in 1980, depicts the lives of two Palestinian women, one living in the West Bank and the other in Nazareth. Farah Hatoum, an elderly widow, was dispossessed of her land through the Absentee Property Law. As she is still in possession of her title deeds, her children beseech her to make a deal, to sell the land, to exchange it for another piece of land being offered by the Israeli state. She steadfastly refuses. In one of the last scenes of the film, Farah is taken to her land for the first time in her life; she had been dispossessed of it already when her late husband bequeathed the deeds to her. In Said's words, "Somehow Khleifi has managed to record Farah's first visit to her land. We see her step tentatively onto a field; then she turns around slowly with arms outstretched. A look of puzzled serenity comes over her face. There is little hint on it of pride in ownership. The film unobtrusively registers the fact that she is there on her land, which is also there; as for the circumstances intervening between these two facts, we remember the useless title deed and Israeli possession, neither of which is actually visible."[144]

Possession, despite having been surpassed by the modern grammar of property that is built on a logic of abstraction, remains central to the reality of property relations in the settler colony. In chapter 3, we will examine the nature of possession and its corollary, use, which remain at the forefront of indigenous struggles over land in Israel/Palestine. I will analyze the ideology of improvement as it traveled to Palestine in the late nineteenth and early twentieth centuries with Zionist settlers. The notion that existing modes of cultivation by Palestinian peasantry reflected an inferior intellectual capacity and less developed culture bears a remarkable resemblance to the racial regime of ownership explored throughout chapter 1. Land that required improvement was the result of its stewardship by people who required improvement; the colonial authority had the technology, vision, and, most importantly, the cultural habits and intellectual capacity to modernize spaces that had yet to become modern. Modern property laws defined according to particular types of cultivation and use emerged in conjunction with racial thinking that relegated indigenous people to the margins of civility and deprived them of the status required to be owners of their land.

Chapter 3 / Improvement

On a warm spring day in April 2014, we visited Al-Sira,[1] an unrecognized Bedouin village several kilometers away from the small outpost city of Bir Al Sabe, or Be'er Sheva as it's known in Hebrew. Khalil Al-Amour was our host. Khalil is head of Al-Sira's village council, representing his community and the Bedouin more widely at national and international forums. He explained to us the problem of the unrecognized Bedouin villages, took us on a tour of his house, and described to us the workings of the small village.[2] The large number of unrecognized Bedouin villages in the Naqab desert of southern Israel are denied the basic municipal services, including running water, electricity, sewage, health care, and education, enjoyed by Israeli citizens, even though the Bedouin hold Israeli citizenship.[3] Approximately 84,000 Bedouin reside in unrecognized villages, under crushing levels of poverty, denied the resources that they are entitled to. These villages, which bear the literal designation of nonrecognition, provide a near-transparent instance of the perilous effects of the state's refusal to recognize the legal and historically based rights of the Bedouin to their land.

We sat on the terrace of Khalil's house, listening to him summarize a long history of the ongoing struggles of the Bedouin for recognition of their land rights in a short span of time. It was his second meeting of the day, and it became clear that this meeting was one stop on a tour of sites in the Naqab, surrounding Bir Al Sabe, designed to educate foreigners (journalists, politicians, nongovernmental organization [NGO] workers, academics, and diplomats for the most part) on the plight of the Bedouin. The brief conversations that we had with Khalil at this first meeting were confined to a well-honed discourse of advocacy that addressed the illegality of Bedouin dispossession, their rights, and environmental and economic concerns. This was traditional Bedouin territory, misappropriated under an abuse of the Ottoman doctrine of *mewat* land, as well as through the seizure of territory for military purposes, along with outright misappropriation. Legal precedent had established that the withholding of basic services such as water and electricity was a violation of their rights; they were actively fighting this long-standing dispossession in the courts and through political activism; and the Bedouin had environmentally sound economic plans for development of their villages, were their autonomy and land rights to be given their due recognition.

Later that afternoon, the confines of this well-rehearsed tour would be shattered by another kind of ritual, the destruction of Bedouin tents by the Israel Land Authority. Driving around the desert, grappling with the extreme differences in wealth and the standard of living between the unrecognized Bedouin villages and the neighboring suburban gated Israeli settlements, camouflaged by colorful bougainvillea and small saplings courtesy of God TV, a Christian Zionist evangelical television channel in the United States (whose billboards were yet another blight on the landscape), our party received a call from an activist about an impending demolition. We drove to the village of Al-Araqib, which has received a lot of international focus in media coverage of the Bedouin and the Prawer Plan.[4] While there, we witnessed a type of violence that had both ritualistic and performative dimensions, a display of brutal destruction characteristic of the Israeli settler colonial regime. The vehicles rolled up to several tentlike structures on the land outside of a cemetery. (Inside the cemetery, dozens of residents had taken shelter for weeks, thinking that the security forces would not destroy homes located on consecrated ground. In June 2014, however, the Israel Land Authority would order the demolition of even these homes.)[5] Bulldozers and a small pickup truck drove right onto the land adjacent to the cemetery-cum-village. After destroying the Bedouin tents, they planted their yellow flags, indicating their intention to evict and claiming the land as state property. After they drove off, several young boys from the village immediately went up to the piles of rubble, extracted the flags, and helped each other to tear them up.

The destruction was ritualistic in the sense that what we witnessed was the seventieth such event since 2010.[6] The village has now been razed, at the time of writing, ninety-one times.[7] After the destruction, the community rebuilds. The repetition made it no less violent and, if anything, reflects the persistent harassment and oppression of the Bedouin in the Naqab region of southern Israel. As Hanna Nakkarah documented, the destruction of Bedouin homes and crops began in the 1970s, notably after the creation of the Green Patrol (discussed below) under Ariel Sharon's tenure as the minister of agriculture, which began in 1977.[8] Today, some Bedouin construct their homes out of makeshift materials not only due to high levels of poverty but because their pliable nature makes reconstruction somewhat easier after such demolitions. Atheel Athameen, committee chairman of the Khasham Zaneh unrecognized village near Bir Al Sabe, stated that several residents of the unrecognized villages demolish their own homes, to avoid the costs charged to the residents of the house when it is demolished by the state authority. He explained that if you are taken to court in the process of having an eviction order executed against you, you will be criminalized and will also have to pay the court costs. He paid for someone to build his house and paid the same person to destroy it.[9] The state's determination to deny the historic and contemporary presence of Bedouin on their land requires the constant and repeated destruction of the very evidence of their ownership rights—settlement in the form of homes, villages, and crops.

While the Bedouin had some interaction with early Zionist settlers in the first half of the twentieth century, the history of their displacement begins in earnest with the establishment of Israel in 1948. The expulsion of approximately 80 percent of the Bedouin population from their traditional territory began a struggle for reclamation that doesn't appear to have any end in sight, with every single land claim to reach the Israeli courts having, at the time of writing, been defeated. The legal claims, one of which I discuss in some detail below, focus on the facts of Bedouin ownership of their land, as evidenced by their cultivation of the land for centuries prior to the establishment of the state of Israel. Other forms of evidence, such as records relating to the payment of tax on agricultural produce during the period of Ottoman rule, and tax receipts relating to land transactions, are used to establish proof of Bedouin settlement on their lands and to support the claim that they did indeed own and cultivate their lands. Cultivation plays a central role in defining who is entitled to own land in Israel/Palestine legally, but also, ideologically. In ways that are similar to the colonial settlement of indigenous lands in British Columbia, a lack of cultivation or, indeed, land cultivated according to traditional methods by non-Europeans, was the basis upon which early Zionists justified their encroachment on Palestinian lands. In keeping with the European colonial worldview of the nineteenth century, subsistence agriculture (or even agriculture bound for internal markets) was a sign of cultural and intellectual inferiority, a prime indicator of a backward, premodern people. Modern civilization meant modernizing agriculture, which was central to the early Zionist settlement mission in Palestine during the late nineteenth and early twentieth centuries. Cultivation became the prime basis for establishing a moral and legal right to land in Palestine, in the eyes of political Zionists.

However, cultivation in the context of Israel/Palestine is a primary legal determinant of ownership in indigenous land claims because of its imputed quality as a defining characteristic of ownership and, indeed, modernity itself, as explored in chapter 1. In the decades prior to the establishment of the state of Israel, cultivation figured prominently in many political Zionists' vision of how Jews ought to return to their primordial territory. It was through the mixing of his sweat with the soil of Palestine that the exiled Jew would redeem himself, re-forming his attachment to the land of Zion, while at the same time creating a viable and sustainable Jewish economy in Palestine.

Thus, when the Bedouin attempt to prove that they have been cultivating their lands as a means of establishing a legal ownership interest, they are not only confronting a racially inflected concept of ownership that is based on modern European forms of cultivation, but they are challenging the ideological basis of their dispossession as embedded in a very particular form of nationalism. For the founders of modern political Zionism, such as Theodor Herzl and Arthur Ruppin, Jews needed to reestablish themselves as the people of the land of Palestine, and this could only be accomplished, practically speaking, through an attachment to the soil through acts of cultivation. Moreover, the people who were already there, and who had indeed been cultivating the land for generations, needed to be cast as mere tenants of the land, unable to "make the desert bloom," as the hackneyed Zionist slogan goes.

In this chapter, I explore the place of cultivation in early Zionist thought, primarily through the writings of Arthur Ruppin, then examine the state of Jewish cultivation in Palestine leading up to 1948, and note the somewhat rapid decline of actual agricultural production in Israel in the first few decades of the state's existence. I argue that cultivation retains its force largely as an ideological bulwark against challenges to political Zionism that seek to expose its primary claims as recent historiographical inventions. In other words, the history of agricultural settlements of the late nineteenth and early twentieth centuries provides a basis (however thin) for the Zionist narrative of a successful return to the land, a negation of exile that was realized through working the land. Through the ideal of agricultural colonization, Zionist political claims came to have a territorial reality. Despite the fact that cultivation remains a heavily ideological phenomenon rather than a reflection of actual economic and social realities on the ground, its status as a flashpoint for contestations over proving entitlement to land remains undiminished. The Bedouin, who inhabited the lands of the Naqab for hundreds of years prior to the establishment of Israel in 1948, are reduced to claiming recognition of their land rights on the basis that they cultivated their land in a manner cognizable to what is in essence a European settler colonial project.

THE IDEOLOGY OF IMPROVEMENT IN ZIONIST THOUGHT

Zionism, as a modern political, cultural, and theological ideology, has always contained within it many different schools of thought. Here, my focus is on the brand of political Zionism that had, from its beginning, explicit territorial aspirations, which clearly prevailed in the mode of colonization pursued in Palestine. As Amnon Raz-Krakotzkin, Maxime Rodinson, Gershon Shafir, and Gabriel Piterberg, among others, have argued, the Zionism of Theodor Herzl, Arthur Ruppin, Chaim Arlosoroff, and other founding fathers of settlement was heavily influenced by, or indeed modeled upon, European colonialism. Furthermore, Herzl argued repeatedly that Britain should support the establishment of a Jewish homeland in Palestine because of its strategic location on the imperial map. As the crow flies from England to India, Palestine was located, geopolitically, in a position of prime importance to British colonial interests.[10]

As such, the notion that land that was not being cultivated according to European models of agriculture was waste, and capable of being legitimately appropriated, was certainly a formative notion in early Zionist thought. What is of significance, however, is that the early Zionists were influenced not primarily by Lockean property rationales based on the imperatives of a burgeoning agrarian capitalism, but by German idealism. The notion of the *volk* as being of the land, rooted in the soil of their national homeland, forms the basis for entitlement to a state based on their natural ties to that territory. Zionism was a political, spiritual, and territorial nationalist project.

Gabriel Piterberg has stressed the continuity between European colonial thought and early political Zionism. Herzl's novel *Altneuland* is analyzed by Piterberg as an example of utopian colonialism.[11] The aspirations of creating a territorial homeland for the people who had been hitherto spiritually defined by exile could be realized in Palestine, the utopian dimension of settlement rendered possible by acting as if Palestinians were not already there, on the land. Whether the early settlers were socialists or believed that collective forms of agricultural settlement were more feasible and efficient, at least initially (as with Ruppin, discussed below), they based their modes of colonization on European (first French and then English and German) colonization projects.[12] In the early twentieth century, Ruppin sought out expert advice from the American agriculturalist Professor Mead on how best to proceed with agricultural development based on the perceived similarity between the colonization of California and that of Palestine. It is difficult to understand how anyone can object to contemporary characterizations of Israel as a settler colony; the early founders and advocates of the Jewish colonization of Palestine had absolutely no difficulty in using the term "colonization" to describe their intentions and actions in Palestine. To differentiate the founding of Israel in 1948 from the early Zionist project to colonize Palestine is to engage in a revisionism that doesn't warrant further comment. Israel, like Canada, Australia, and a multitude of other places, remains a colonial project.

However, as noted above, the Zionist colonization project was not primarily driven by economic or financial considerations of profit and resource exploitation, and herein lies one of the differences between the founding of Israel and other settler colonies. As I argued in chapter 2, the ethnonational imperatives of Zionism, which have as their primary objective populating the land with Jewish settlers and diminishing the Arab presence, have precluded markets in land that are organized according to a capitalist rationality from taking hold. Ownership of land was a necessary precondition for the establishment of a homeland for the Jewish people, not, as with other settler colonies, a precondition for creating and growing a productive, capitalist economy that would enrich both individuals and the coffers of the imperial state. The collective nature of ownership pursued by settler organizations such as the Jewish Colonization Association during the Mandate and after 1948 attest to the primary objective of acquiring land for the Jewish people, as a collective national entity. Indeed, the Jewish National Fund, established in 1901, had the mandate of purchasing lands to be held in trust for the metaphysical entity called the Jewish people. Arlosoroff pointed out the explicit differences between European and Zionist colonial aspirations: "Contrary to the European colonial experience, in the case of Palestine, the land itself which is to be settled is not of any appreciable economic value, nor has the specific territory—Palestine—been chosen for economic reasons as the most profitable or potentially bountiful land. The choice was determined by considerations transcending economics—historical memory, national identity—and consequently the means required to carry out such a project cannot be articulated in purely economic terms."[13] However, despite the higher spiritual principles involved in Zionist colonization, the rationales devised to justify colonization, and, specifically, an idea of cultivation that was heavily inflected with a racial discourse of superiority, bear great similarity to European colonial models.

While early Zionists such as Arlosoroff were committed to Jewish socialism, Piterberg argues that "in terms of ideational flows from Europe to Palestine, ideas of colonization and race rather than socialism" were the ones that prevailed. Indeed, in examining the writings of Arthur Ruppin, one of the primary architects of the agricultural colonization of Palestine in the early twentieth century, it becomes quite apparent that his primary concerns lay with the economic viability of settlement, successful models of colonization that could prove useful to Jewish settlers, and the particular challenges of establishing a permanent presence on the land for European Jews who had a higher standard of life and greater intellectual capacities than the Arab fellahin. The primary economic concerns of Ruppin are thoroughly immersed in racial thinking about European Jews, Yemeni

Jews, and Arabs; these economic concerns and racial thinking produce, in dialectical fashion, a vision of the most appropriate mode of colonization that fuses together the value of land and the racially differentiated labor of the people living on it.

Arthur Ruppin grew up in a small town on the Prussian-Polish border and would later move with his family to Magdeburg, Germany. He describes a family life consumed by a crushing and persistent poverty. It seems that Ruppin's first experiments in political economy took place in the family household, where he attempted to master the provision of nourishing meals for a family of seven on a meager income.[14] Ruppin would go on to complete a law degree in Berlin and then a doctorate in philosophy (political economy) at Halle, and eventually find success as a businessman.[15] Ruppin writes in his memoirs of moving away from the strictly religious practices of his youth as a university student, while he faced increasing levels of anti-Semitism.[16]

In 1904, after he spent several weeks in the Whitechapel area of London, England, Ruppin published *The Jews of Today*, a book that was warmly received by Zionists. At this juncture, Ruppin recounts traveling to Berlin to acquaint himself with "practical Zionists," Martin Buber among them. He rejected the "diplomatic Zionism of Herzl" as "hopeless and unrealistic" and eventually joined the Zionist Organisation in 1905.[17] In his own words, he had by 1907 become "such an ardent Zionist" that he left for Palestine to study the conditions of the Jewish settlers in Palestine. He accepted the invitation of the Zionist Action Committee to emigrate to Palestine as the representative of the Zionist Organisation.[18] From that time onward, Ruppin devoted himself to analyzing, documenting, and advocating for the agricultural colonization of Palestine, based on European and American models of colonization.

In *The Agricultural Colonisation of the Zionist Organisation in Palestine*, published in 1926, Ruppin presents an analysis of the successes, failures, and future directions for Jewish settlers based on seventeen years of experience in the field. He remarks on the failure of the plantation-style settlements established in the years before the twentieth century, an initiative that was largely funded by Baron de Rothschild. These settlements of the "1st Aliyah" failed, in Ruppin's view, for a number of reasons. The plantations failed because the owners relied on "cheap Arab labour."[19] When Jewish settlers hired Arab workers who knew more about agricultural production than the settlers, this prevented those settlers from developing a genuine and organic attachment to the land.[20] Attempts to cultivate extensive tracts of wheat also failed, because, in Ruppin's view, "the Jewish mentality cannot conform to its monotony, and the small produce is not enough for a European minimum of existence."[21] Right from the beginning of his analysis, the racial difference of Jews from Arabs is put forward as a rationale for why particular modes of cultivation could not succeed, and shapes his advocacy of particular modes of agricultural settlement. The formation of the racial regime of ownership in Palestine during colonial settlement encapsulated cultural, social, and scientific rationales that took specific economic and legal form.

The primary challenge for Jewish settlers, in Ruppin's view, lay in the fact that European standards of living were superior to those of the Arab fellahin, and were thus more costly. As such, Jewish settlers were at a distinct disadvantage; they could not compete with the low wages paid to Arab laborers, for whom such wages were perfectly adequate given their low standard of living.[22] What followed the observation that Jews would be competing with people who required less income, given their backwardness, was an indictment not only of Palestinians but of the entire geohistorical space that was imagined as the Orient:

> The whole Orient is characterised by a frightful exploitation of human labour, especially that of women and children. The woman, who in Anatolia or Persia sits in front of the carpet-loom from her childhood till her last days, and all the time scarcely earns a crust of dry bread; the fellah woman in Egypt, who, when but thirty years old, is turned into an old woman through a combination of the poorest of foodstuffs and the heaviest of labour; the Egyptian and Syrian children who work in factories then and twelve hours daily for 2–3 piastres (half gold-franc) a day, these are all examples of this terrible exploitation. Thus Palestine only shares the fate of the whole Near East if the standard of the life of its native population is wretched in the extreme, and if wages are at the lowest possible level.[23]

In this passage, the echoes of the well-worn European image of Oriental culture rife with despotism in which women and children in particular are oppressed and exploited forms a core part of Ruppin's political anatomy of Palestine.[24] The wretched conditions he observes are then cast in historical-civilizational terms, with European Jewry belonging to modernity: "Even in Palestine, the Jew wishes to remain a product of the twentieth century."[25] As such, only those modes of colonization that could support the European standard of living that Jews were accustomed to would be pursued.

The racial typologies that Ruppin relied upon in assessing the viability of the agricultural colonization produced a racialized vision of labor. In turn, it is through agricultural labor and the act of cultivation that the European Jew—as an exilic figure with a higher intellectual aptitude than the Arabs, and also a European subject who had been rejected and cast out of Europe—would redeem himself in Palestine. The mistake that the earlier colonists made was precisely to ignore the spiritual imperative of agricultural labor, the basis of the Jewish future in Palestine:

> The present-day settlers are no less intelligent than the earlier colonists, and they have the same Jewish mentality, i.e. that same mental mobility and the same esteem for learning and the cultivation of the mind. This mentality is inseparable from the life and soul of the Jew. But it can be guided into another channel, namely that of an elevation and hallowing of agricultural work. . . . The new settlers look upon agriculture not only as the means of existence, but as the source of new national life. They feel that they are laying the foundations of a new Jewish community in Palestine, and that an immense responsibility rests on them, the founders and creators. The monotonous labour behind the plough is connected by many fine-spun threads with the distant future, in which the work will be continued by new generations of free Jewish peasants, increased a hundred times in number, continuing on the lines on which their fathers . . . have started.[26]

Unlike the backward styles of cultivation of the fellahin, the agricultural labor of the European Jewish settler was of a rather more elevated quality.

Mere ownership would not suffice. Ruppin viewed Palestine as a place of redemption for Jews who had labored under the accusation that as landless "middlemen and parasites" they had never produced and contributed to the economic and social life of European states.[27] For this reason, he emphasized that mere ownership of land in Palestine was not enough to overcome this age-old prejudice. Ruppin took Lockean rationales for the moral legitimacy of ownership into the field of German idealism, and argued that only by mixing one's sweat with the soil of Palestine could an authentic possessive nationalism be borne: "We must not only own the land, but also till it in the sweat of our brow, and thus show the world that there are mighty forces latent in us, which only need suitable conditions in order to spring again to new life."[28] Mere investment in the land of Palestine could not sustain a genuine claim to the national home of the Jewish people, and while Ruppin emphasized the necessity for Jews in America and Europe to invest in the colonization effort, he did not think this was a sufficient criterion for establishing an authentic national home in Palestine.[29]

Ruppin had clearly adopted the racial-scientific thinking of his time. He had a firm belief in a racial difference that was biologically grounded in physical traits, appearance, and variations that were hereditary. Morris-Reich has noted that in the English edition of Ruppin's diary, a crucial entry is omitted, from August 16, 1933, which recorded a meeting between Ruppin and Hans F. K. Günther, who was none other than Himmler's mentor.[30] Ruppin accepted without question a deterministic racial theory that led him to warn against the pitfalls of interracial marriages, which would dilute the Jewish racial type. Exposing his Darwinist roots, Ruppin's views on how to manage immigration to Palestine is expressed in the article "The Selection of the Fittest":

> Since it is our desire to develop in Palestine our Jewish side, it would naturally be desirable to have only "race" Jews come to Palestine. But a direct influence on the process, via the selection of such immigrants as most closely approach the racial type, is not practically possible. On the whole, however, it is likely that the general type in Palestine will be more strongly Jewish than the general type in Europe, for it is to be expected that the more strongly Jewish types will be the ones which are most generally discriminated against in Europe, and it is they who will feel themselves most strongly drawn towards a Jewish community in Palestine.[31]

How are we to interpret the distinction that Ruppin makes between "racial Jews" and "Jewish types"? His concern here is whether it is possible to keep the "Jewish racial stock pure" in Palestine.[32] We know that Ruppin distinguished between those who were racially Jews, and those who were not racially Jewish but part of the Jewish national body (such as the Falashas in Ethiopia, and converts to Judaism in Russia).[33] We also know that Ruppin held a firm belief in a Jewish racial difference that was internally differentiated according to metaracial categories of "white, yellow and black" as depicted in a "Diagram of Jewish Racial Populations" contained in his *Sociology of the Jews*.[34]

Ruppin's theory fit with the racial thinking of the time, as noted above, but also reflects the development and use of full-blown racial scientific thinking in determining the types of labor and modes of colonization that were appropriate for particular racial groups. For instance, the Yemeni Jews, who, facing persecution in Yemen circa 1910, immigrated to Israel, are viewed by Ruppin as incapable of performing the same types of labor as their superior Ashkenazi Jewish brethren. He writes that "[c]ompared with the Ashkenazic Jews, they [the Yemeni Jews] possess smaller powers of insight and organisation. It would thus be extremely difficult for them to undertake independent work."[35] Ella Shohat has argued that seeing Sephardic Jews as "'natural workers' with 'minimal needs' ... came to play a crucial ideological role, a concept subtextually linked to color."[36]

Given the particular nature and needs of Jewish settlers to form an organic attachment to the land of Palestine, and given their modern and civilized standards of living as compared to the native inhabitants, what modes of colonization would be most expedient and profitable for Zionist aspirations? Ruppin compared the agricultural settlements in Palestine to the ones that had been established during the Rothschild administration, the German colonies in Prussia, and the American colonization of California. On the basis of these comparisons, he advocated strongly for mixed farms over plantations, emphasized the need for the formalization of land rights for Jewish settlers, and believed that collective agricultural work required much more private capital investment than had hitherto been afforded the settlers. Collective forms of organizing agricultural settlement were understood to be the most expedient, but this form of colonization required, as in various British colonial contexts, a great deal of private investment.[37]

Thus the influence of European colonial endeavors on the founding fathers of modern political Zionism, such as Herzl and Ruppin, was not solely in regard to racial ideologies of European superiority, but was also about the legal and economic form that colonization would take. Arrangements for private investment to fund settlement, backed by legal pronouncements as to the legitimacy of investment schemes and settler land ownership, were central to the Zionist vision. In what can now be read as an ironic twist of history, given the repeated violations of international law by the state of Israel since its founding, Herzl's address to the first Zionist Congress, held in Basel, Switzerland, in 1897, proclaimed that "[t]he Aim of Zionism is to create for the Jewish people a home in Palestine secured by Public [International] Law."[38] Herzl emphasized the need for any Jewish settlement to be recognized by the laws and legal structures that govern relations between sovereign states, for the political protection that this would afford.[39]

Herzl emphasized, as Ruppin would after his death, the necessity to establish a bank that would fund the establishment of colonies, whether they were to be held collectively or individually. In his pamphlet *The Jewish State*, published in 1896 (shortly after Herzl had attended the Dreyfus trial in Paris), he outlines in some detail a proposal for a Jewish Company that would, like its precursors, be a joint stock company subject to English jurisdiction. Partially modeled "on the lines of a great land-acquisition company," this Jewish chartered company would be "strictly a business undertaking" that was to facilitate the private acquisition of land in Palestine for settlers.[40] The company would raise capital through appeal to big banks, small banks, and public subscriptions, would acquire large areas of land in Palestine, and through this centralized mode of purchase the Jewish Company would facilitate settlement and receive "an indefinite premium" when selling the land onward to its officials.[41] At the same time, this arrangement would avoid the perils of excessive land speculation to which many settler societies fell prey.

Subsequent to the proposals set out in *The Jewish State*, Herzl would author a charter that he believed ought to be the basis of an agreement between the World Zionist Organization and the Ottoman government.[42] The charter, and specifically the proposed entitlements and jurisdiction of the Jewish-Ottoman Land Company (JOLC), was modeled, like the Jewish chartered company described above, on the colonial charters that had hitherto empowered joint-stock companies, such as the East India Company and the Dutch East India Company, to inaugurate European colonial endeavors in the eighteenth and nineteenth centuries.[43] Herzl's proposal provided that the JOLC would have varying degrees of property rights over land that it acquired: ownership and usage of land that it purchased outright from private landholders; ownership of land belonging to the sultan for a yearly payment; and the right to occupy land to which there was no legal title, also in return for a yearly payment.[44] With the right of ownership in article 1 came the entitlement to use the land for purposes of settlement, including the building of roads, bridges, houses, and industry and having the right to use the lands for agriculture, forestry, mining, and horticulture. The JOLC would also have powers of taxation over its areas of jurisdiction. Walid Khalidi has commented on the "impressively extensive" powers that the JOLC would attain through such a charter, pointing out that population transfer was perhaps the "most crucial right requested by the JOLC." Colonization was to happen through private investment structured according to English laws of contract, property, and company law.[45]

A number of different companies were established at the turn of the twentieth century in order to finance settlement, both for individuals and for collective associations. Herzl's blueprint as set out in his pamphlet would be realized with the establishment of the Jewish Colonial Trust Fund, brought into being at the second Zionist Congress in 1898. The trust's primary aim was to finance settlement. The Anglo-Palestine Bank was formed in 1902 as a subsidiary of the trust, to carry out its activities in Palestine. The trust would operate with mixed success until 1934, when it was dissolved and became a holding company for shares of the Anglo-Palestine Bank.[46] The Jewish National Fund would be established at the fifth Zionist Congress in 1901. The purpose of the Jewish National Fund was, as it is today, to buy land in Palestine as "the permanent possession of the Jewish people."[47] The Palestine Land Development Company, an institution established under the auspices of the Zionist Organization, had as its purpose "systematic land purchases" in Palestine, in order to resell these purchases without profit to private persons.[48] The need for private investment to colonize Palestine, wherein land would be held collectively, distinguished the Zionist project from other European colonial endeavors.[49]

One complicating factor for the Zionist Organization was existing laws that would determine to a large extent the legal forms that settlement could take. Unlike colonists in British Columbia or South Australia, the Jewish colonists could not impose a legal tabula rasa that allowed for blanket experimentation in legal form. There was the Ottoman legal system to contend with, and then the application of British common laws under the Mandate. Shafir has argued that changes in the Ottoman Land Code (OLC) of 1858 facilitated the Jewish purchase of Arab lands in Palestine from the late nineteenth century. The "centralising and modernising reforms" inaugurated by a significant period of reform changed both the social strata and the laws governing ownership that subtended it, in ways that made it easier for large landowners to sell their land.[50] "The Tanzimat, a grand movement of top-down internal reforms between 1839 and 1878, reformed taxation, land tenure, public administration, and many other facets of life and concomitantly transformed the social hierarchy in the Empire and, within it, in Palestine. By so doing the Tanzimat created the specific legal and economic preconditions that served as the backdrop to Jewish colonisation."[51] Specific to land reforms and taxation, Shafir describes how reforms in 1867 liberalized rights of succession, encouraged land improvement, and increased the freedom of landowners to rent their land.[52] These changes were one aspect of the attempt to reform the agricultural sector to increase cash crops and exports to Europe. Wheat and oranges in particular were integrated into an international market and "gave rise to a capitalist industry."[53] The gradual rise in land values (and, accordingly, revenue for the Ottoman administration) and the increasing commodification of land made the sale of land by notables and large landowners an attractive option. As Shafir notes, between 1878 and 1936, only 9.4 percent of the land sold to Jewish settlers and settlement companies was sold by fellahin; over 75 percent was sold by big landowners, "most of whom had acquired their land in the last half of the nineteenth century."[54]

Ultimately, despite the complexities, the model of colonization was, as discussed above, similar to other settler colonies in its use of private investment in property ownership facilitated by companies and associations to establish a colonial presence on the land, and to lay the scaffolding for a future state. In addition to the land being held collectively, the other striking difference was that unlike other settler colonial contexts, profit was not the driving motivation; in the words of Patrick Wolfe, Zionists had "freedom from the discipline of the bottom line."[55]

Territorial acquisition was the means through which the Jewish Question could finally be settled. And of course, settling the land of Palestine and creating a homeland for the Jewish people is what differentiates political Zionism from other forms of settler nationalism. While settler colonial nationalisms in Canada, the United States, and Australia were also racial formations, it would be a mistake, as Raz-Krakotzkin has argued, to fail to account for the theological dimension of political Zionism. Indeed, in the writings of Herzl one sees precisely the collapsing of theological and political treatments of exile, resolved through the ideal of territorial acquisition. This is distinct from the civilizational imperatives of white settlers in Canada and Australia, which while cast in indisputably Christian terms, did not purport to carry with them the biblical burden of a return to history through the appropriation of lands to which they had a divine right.

Raz-Krakotzkin invites us to reject the distinction between the religious and secular and, instead, identifies a secularized messianism of political Zionists.[56] The settlement of Palestine becomes the return to their ancient homeland but, more than that, signifies the return to history of the Jewish peoples, cast out of history after the destruction of the Second Temple. This return to history, argues Raz-Krakotskin, is premised upon a "Christian attitude concerning Jews and their destiny."[57] While I cannot engage with Raz-Krakotzkin's arguments in much depth here, I want to emphasize one of his insights. The concept of history that is deployed by the Zionists is one that emerges from Enlightenment thought, based on a linear-teleological model that emphasizes human progress.[58] The Zionist return to Palestine incorporated both Christian theological and Enlightenment perspectives on history that posited the Jews on the side of modernity in opposition to the Orientalist world of the Arab, who became for the Jewish, as for Christian Europeans, a backward, inferior people. The ideology of improvement and progress, informed entirely by a European episteme, was an inherent part of modern political Zionist ideology.

The return to history has a companion concept, the negation of exile, which was effected through the territorial acquisition of Palestinian lands. Ruppin's writings on the agricultural colonization of Palestine exemplify the Zionist desire to negate the physical and spiritual exile of Jews through settlement.[59] The Jew was "unable to feel 'at home' anywhere and at any time" because of political persecutions that kept the East European Jew on the move. The only thing that could create an attachment "to a locality, a house, a garden, property in general" was "long-lasting possession."[60] In keeping with a Lockean rationale for (land) ownership premised on labor, and a German romanticism that posited an ideal of ethnonationalism rooted in the possession of land, the Zionists believed that an organic attachment to the land of Palestine could be cultivated, literally and metaphorically. This aspect of Zionist thought also involved a transformation in the self-conception of the Jewish subject as a strong, masculinized farmer, as opposed to the effeminate Jewish figure of the Diaspora, who was unable to sufficiently defend himself from anti-Semitism.[61]

But to what extent did agricultural settlement prevail in the decades leading up to 1948 and in the first decades of Israel's existence? It is clear that today, agricultural production accounts for a very small proportion of the Israeli economy. In fact, in 2010, total agricultural produce in Israel accounted for a mere 1.9 percent of Israel's GDP.[62] The agricultural kibbutzim that were at the center of Zionist attempts to establish a landed presence in Palestine from the late nineteenth century suffered a sharp decline from the 1960s onward.[63] Scholars mapping the social, cultural, and economic changes in the kibbutzim after 1948 have identified a number of different causal factors. The shortage of water for cultivation and the inability of kibbutz members to meet the demands of the quotas for the production of various crops produced a labor crisis, which led to the need to hire laborers from surrounding immigrant and refugee camps, something which contravened the social and cultural objectives of the kibbutzim movement. As Vallier noted, as early as 1962, "The concept of self-labor was so important to the whole of Zionist objectives that it had visibly dominated the land settlement and colonization program for fifty years. To hire laborers was tantamount to rejecting the very core of the kibbutz social order."[64] Necessity, however, required just such a rejection. Vallier documented how, on one particular kibbutz, the "hirelings" who were mainly migrants from Eastern Europe and North Africa were excluded from the social life of the community and assigned "subordinate occupational roles" throughout the kibbutz economy.[65]

Other challenges included government support for industrialization, the desires of older kibbutz members for alternative and less taxing forms of work, and those of well-educated Jewish immigrants for types of labor suited to their work experience.[66] Some scholars have noted that the early emphasis on "productive work" in the kibbutzim movement facilitated the transition from agricultural to industrial activity.[67] By the 1980s, crisis in the agricultural sector led to an economic restructuring that increased the amount of private ownership in the kibbutzim. Today, many kibbutzim are home to private enterprises that are run like any other business. Twenty-two kibbutzim were, as of 2010, listed on the stock exchanges in Tel Aviv, London, and New York.[68] While agriculture and cultivation remain important to Israeli nationalist ideals, it is clear that the model of communal landholding and collective agricultural labor began to diminish not too long after the founding of the state in 1948.

The legal scaffolding of the kibbutzim has also undergone radical transformations since the early 1990s, whereby collectively held land designated specifically for agricultural use has been rezoned to allow for private land ownership. As Oren Yiftachel writes:

> [I]n the beginning of the 1990s a profound change occurred in the status of agricultural landholders. Starting in 1992, the ILA [Israel Land Authority] passed a number of resolutions allowing rezoning and redevelopment of agricultural land, thus greatly increasing the property rights of agricultural landholders. Contrary to the contract and ILA Resolution 1, landholders would now be able to rezone their land and acquire ownership over part of the redeveloped land. This increased the transfer of funds to the farmers by a thousand-fold, as compared with the previous regulation, and granted control over a large portion of Israel's land reserves to a small group.[69]

Israel embarked on further land privatizations in 2009.

The Naqab has become a focal point for Israeli agribusiness. The Ministry of Agriculture and Rural Development, in a booklet produced for "Overseas Visitors" presumably engaged in the agro-biotechnology industries, describes the presence of Israeli agricultural settlement in the Naqab as follows: "Population dispersion and a national economic and development policy made it necessary to inhabit this region, while simultaneously meeting challenges posed by the desert conditions."[70] "Population dispersal," a bureaucratically rendered euphemism for the Nakba, belies the nature of Israeli settlement in the area in the aftermath of 1948. The laws that were used to dispossess Palestinians of their land from 1948 onward have been detailed by many scholars, and it is not my intention to reiterate them here.[71] However, a brief overview of the legal regime imposed on the Naqab is essential prior to analyzing the Israeli Supreme Court's rejection of the al-Uqbi family's claim to their land in *el-Okbi v. the State of Israel* (June 2, 2014, Case 4220/12).

The Bir Al Sabe (Be'er Sheva) district in Southern Israel currently makes up about 62 percent of Israel's territory.[72] The Naqab, an arid desert that stretches from the Gulf of Aqaba in the south to the city of Bir Al Sabe in the north, has been inhabited by the Bedouin for centuries, and evidence of their presence on and cultivation of the land has been noted over the course of centuries by travel writers, geologists, archaeologists, and eventually colonial administrators during the Mandate. As Abu Sitta writes, the British Mandate records of the area document the presence of seventy-seven "official Arab clans (ashiras) grouped into 7 major tribes in the district," in addition to the Bedouin presence in the town of Bir Al Sabe.[73] Throughout the Ottoman period, Bedouin customary law prevailed, determining the way in which land was owned, sold, inherited, mortgaged, or divided.[74]

While some Jewish settlements had been established in the Naqab prior to 1948, Jewish ownership of land that was registered, at the time of the UN recommendation to partition Palestine in 1947, did not amount to more than 0.5 percent of the Bir Al Sabe district.[75] The mass expropriation of Bedouin lands occurred during 1948 and its aftermath, when Israeli forces occupied the entire area, expelling most of the Bedouin inhabitants of the Naqab to Gaza, Jordan, and the Sinai, and imposed military rule on those who remained, about 12 percent of the original population. The military zone, or *siyag*, to which the Bedouin were confined, operated much like a reserve. The siyag constituted a very small proportion of the total area of the Bir Al Sabe district, approximately 7 percent.[76] The Bedouin required permits to leave the siyag, making it extremely difficult for them to maintain a presence on their land. The Israeli authorities leased a small amount of land to Bedouin to cultivate, in the amount of approximately 250,000 *dunams*. Military rule, imposed upon all Palestinian villages, was not lifted until 1966.[77]

The legal architecture of Bedouin dispossession, as noted at the outset, has been well documented by others. However, three aspects of the legal devices used to dispossess the Bedouin are germane to the contours of the legal claims explored in the third section of this chapter. The first relates to the role of title registration in the dispossession of the Bedouin; the second is the creation of the Green Patrol, a paramilitary force that was established to displace the Bedouin under the pretense of nature preservation and environmental protection; and the third is the manipulation of the mewat land doctrine.

As noted above, the Ottoman regime recognized Bedouin ownership and customary laws of property ownership. The 1858 OLC initiated reforms that were intended to increase revenues for the Ottoman administration and, relatedly, to modernize landholding so as to render land more fungible.[78] The Land Code divided all lands into five different categories of ownership: (1) *miri* land, which was owned by the state but vested a usufruct right in the individual holder; (2) *waqf* land, which was controlled by the Supreme Muslim Council and reserved for pious or religious purposes; (3) *mulk* land, which was privately owned by individuals; (4) *matruka* land, "owned by the state but preserved for public use"; and (5) mewat, uncultivated land that was owned by the state but could be claimed by individuals for cultivation and use under certain conditions.[79] In 1913, the Ottoman government reformed the law to allow a much wider range of uses to holders of miri land, which is translated as a right to possess state land and is likened to the common-law concept of a usufruct, including the right to lease, lend, and mortgage the land as security for a debt.[80] This was accompanied by the requirement that miri land be registered by individual titles in newly established Land Registry offices.[81] As Bisharat and others have noted, many Palestinians did not register their lands in order to avoid tax liability.[82] Kedar notes that "only 5% of the land in Palestine had been registered by the end of the Ottoman period."[83]

However, in the Naqab, such land reforms did not take hold. The Ottoman land registers were not based on cadastral surveys, and Hadawi asserts that the Naqab was never surveyed by the Ottomans.[84] In any case, the Ottoman administration did not require the Bedouin to register title to their lands as a precondition for recognition of their ownership. The British also recognized Bedouin ownership of the land, implicitly at least, as evidenced by two ordinances that encouraged the Bedouin to register their title in the Land Registry. The Mewat Land Ordinance of 1921 provided for the registration of Arab land that had been claimed and cultivated according to the Ottoman land doctrine of mewat (discussed in detail below). Hanna Nakkarah has written that this law was designed to "curtail Arab ownership and increase state lands with a view to implementing Article 6 of the British Mandate."[85] Article 6 of the Mandate provided that the British administration of Palestine would encourage "close settlement by Jews on the land, including State lands and waste lands not required for public purpose" (Mandate for Palestine, 1922, article 6). The 1928 Land (Settlement of Title) Ordinance required residents to register their land claims, but promised those holding land under customary law would not be affected.[86]

The British would again provide for the registration of Arab ownership under the auspices of the Land Acquisition for Public Purposes Ordinance of 1943. The drive to survey and register land title, as discussed in chapter 2, has been interpreted as one means through which the British acquired as much land as possible in order to facilitate Jewish settlement in Palestine.[87] Prior to the 1943 ordinance, the British land reforms during the Mandate were premised on the belief in the superiority of the English common law of property, a civilizational imperative to modernize the natives, and the desire to fulfill their promises under the Mandate to facilitate Jewish settlement in Palestine. Despite the fact that Palestine was designated as an A mandate by the League of Nations, meaning it was to be administered by Britain as a trustee until such time as it was ready for self-government, in practice, notes Martin Bunton, it was treated like a Crown colony.[88]

During the period of Mandate rule, the Bedouin did not, as a general matter, register their title pursuant to the ordinances of 1921 or 1943. The cost of registering their title, the failure of authorities to adequately inform the Bedouin of the registration provisions (such as the two-month time limit on registrations after the publication of the 1921 ordinance in the Official Gazette, which, as Abu Sitta notes, few Bedouins read), and the fact that the Bedouin, who had lived according to their own laws for centuries, saw little need to prove their ownership in a foreign system of registration, have all been cited as the reasons why the Bedouin did not register their land for the most part.[89] The failure of the Bedouin to register their ownership in the British registry is now, as we will see below, used by the state to deny their land rights, with the additional irony that Jewish purchases of land prior to 1948 from Bedouin have been honored as legitimate on the basis of title documents held in "old defective registers."[90]

However, the use of registration as a means of dispossessing the Bedouin has happened in conjunction with two other notorious laws, as in many other parts of Palestine. In 1948, as mentioned above, the Israeli state declared that tribal lands in the Bir Al Sabe district were mewat, according to article 103 of the OLC, and therefore state land. The 12 percent of the Bedouin population that remained in the area after the Nakba were relegated to the category of landless nomads.[91] In 1953, the Land Acquisition (Validation of Acts and Compensation) Law allowed the state to endorse expropriations undertaken directly after 1948 and, crucially, "allowed the state the right to register previously confiscated land in its name if various conditions were met, including that the owner was not in possession of the property on April 1, 1952."[92] This effectively formalized the expropriation of the Bedouin, who had been captive in the military zone and were unable to meaningfully access their lands until 1966.

Here, two modern property logics work in concert to foreclose Bedouin land rights. In the face of a long history of political autonomy and ownership that was recognized by both the Ottomans and the British, the Israeli state renders the type of cultivation and land use of the Bedouin, so clearly marked on the terrain and documented in photographs, travel literature, and Ottoman legal instruments, as illegible. Upon treating Bedouin lands as unsettled, inhabited only by transient nomads, the system of land registration is used to formalize this expropriation. As explored in chapter 2, the system of title by registration renders prior ownership claims legally irrelevant.

The second technique that was utilized to harass and dispossess the Bedouin was the Green Patrol, which was established in 1976–77 as a "paramilitary unit to pressure the Bedouin to move into urban settlements."[93] While the unit is located within the Ministry of Environmental Affairs, its directors include representatives from the Jewish National Fund, the Israeli military, the Ministry of Agriculture, the Ministry of the Interior, and the Israel Land Authority.[94] The creation of the Green Patrol (Amara, Abu-Saad, and Yiftachel note that the Bedouins refer to the unit as the Black Patrol) reflects a perverse and cynical use of environmental concerns as a means of expelling the Bedouin.[95] Echoing the colonial tendency toward putting the welfare of flora and fauna above that of colonized human beings, the Green Patrol remains a constant threat to the Bedouin of the Naqab.

Finally, perhaps the most significant means of appropriating Bedouin land in southern Israel (as in the West Bank) is the manipulation of the legal doctrine of mewat land. Alexandre (Sandy) Kedar, Oren Yiftachel, and Ahmad Amara have written extensively on what they term the "Dead Negev Doctrine," which is their term for the persistent and erroneous use of the mewat land doctrine by the Israeli state to dispossess the Bedouin in the Naqab. They have examined, in forensic levels of detail, the Israeli state's abuse of this doctrine on historical-geographical and legal bases. The mewat category of land, as noted above, was defined in articles 6 and 103 of the 1858 OLC as having the following characteristics: it is vacant; it is grazing land not possessed by anybody; it was not assigned to the use of inhabitants *ab antique* (from ancient times); and it is land where no human voice can be heard from the edge of habitation, estimated to be a distance of approximately 1.5 miles.[96] Bedouin land in the Naqab was never deemed by the Ottoman administrators to be mewat, the implication being that Bedouin ownership and cultivation of their lands was not challenged or in question. Nor was the land deemed by the Mandate Authorities to be mewat. The Mewat Land Ordinance of 1921 modified Ottoman law in two respects: first, it required individuals who had cultivated mewat land to register title to their land within two months of the publication of the ordinance in the Official Gazette of Palestine (as noted above); second, it stipulated that occupiers of mewat lands who had not sought permission would be deemed illegal trespassers.[97] The Mandate law thus changed the nature and character of the concept of mewat land in important ways. During the Ottoman period, the category of "trespasser" did not exist as such; creating the legal category and idea of illegality pertaining to occupiers of mewat who did not register their interests clearly had devastating consequences for autonomous Bedouin populations who did not see the need or, perhaps in a gesture that reflected their sovereignty, preferred not to register their lands in the Land Registry.

As Kedar, Yiftachel, and Amara note, the Israeli state deemed in 1953 that all mewat land was state land and defined mewat in contradistinction to land that was "permanently settled."[98] Much of the critical literature on the Dead Negev Doctrine focuses on conflicting accounts of whether the land was cultivated during the nineteenth century, in the years prior to the establishment of the Mandate and then the state of Israel. Both Palestinian and Israeli historians, geographers, sociologists, and lawyers have somewhat exhaustively proven that indeed, the Bedouins cultivated their lands, belying the Israeli narrative that the land was dead, barren, and vacant.[99] Uncovering evidence of travel writers' accounts, maps created by foreign missionaries and explorers, Royal Air Force aerial photographs, tax records, records of land sales, and other material, they have roundly demonstrated that the Israeli appropriation of Bedouin land is based not only on a refusal to accept reams of recorded evidence—in both written and visual forms— proving Bedouin ownership and use of their land, but also on a rather antiquated and cynical refusal to acknowledge that the Bedouin had forms of ownership and land use that were significantly different from European legal norms of ownership and settlement. Differences in economic systems and forms of cultivation, and a mode of life that required movement across and through desert territories, have led successive foreign observers to conclude that tents, unlike houses, do not constitute a sign of settlement. What is seen as at best an encampment has enabled the Israeli state to act as if the Naqab was literally uninhabited, even though early Zionists knew better.[100] As Ronen Shamir has noted to the contrary, the tents of the Bedouin in fact operate as a "rigid structure that orders social life according to strict spatial rules."[101]

Unlike other jurisdictions, such as Canada and Australia, where deeply flawed forms of recognition have at the same time acknowledged that First Nations had different systems of law and landholding that do not conform to Anglo-European ideas of property ownership, the Israeli courts have rejected over two hundred Bedouin claims, without even the promise, it seems, that a strong dissenting judgment can leave open for future change.[102] In this respect, the Israeli settler colonial regime does seem to differ from others, which can perhaps be explained by the difference that demographic factors make to the settler colonial project. The Bedouin, along with Orthodox Jewish communities, have the highest birthrate in Israel. Beyond the demographic factors, however, to conclude that the recognition of indigenous rights to land and resources in jurisdictions such as Canada and Australia are politically more advanced, or more liberatory, belies the cunning of recognition evident in aboriginal rights jurisprudence, as many scholars have argued.[103] Aboriginal rights jurisprudence in Canada, as noted in chapter 1, has developed on the basis of denying First Nations sovereignty and reaffirming Crown (colonial) sovereignty. In the Australian context, this amounts to recognizing the "radical underlying title" of the Crown. The "jurisprudence of regret" that characterized the Australian High Court's decision in *Mabo* has developed into a "regrettable jurisprudence," as Alex Reilly argues, with the political potential of native title increasingly limited by subsequent judgments.[104] It took decades of litigation and political struggle before First Nations and their advocates achieved an actual declaration of aboriginal title; only in 2014 was the Tsilhqot'in First Nation in British Columbia recognized as holding aboriginal title to a portion of their traditional territory. As I argued in chapter 1, while not diminishing this important political and legal victory, the Canadian Supreme Court recognized aboriginal title based on forms of customary land use within the world of the somewhat suspect anthropological category of the seminomad.[105]

"NOMADS AGAINST THEIR WILL"

Resistance against the appropriation of Bedouin lands has a long history.[106] Right from the establishment of the state of Israel in 1948, the Bedouin and their supporters have attempted repeatedly to enforce their legal and political rights to their lands. The struggle of the Bedouin came to have greater international prominence recently with the very effective international advocacy of organizations such as Adalah, the Arab Centre for Minority Rights, based in Haifa, Israel; the Association for Civil Rights in Israel; and Zochrot, the latter of which are both Israeli NGOs. Adalah and other lawyers have undertaken countless cases for Bedouin clients, to defend them from being criminalized due to their presence on their land, enforcing their right to water and other basic services, and to halt house demolitions and evictions.

The precedents relevant to the determination of the al-Uqbi land claims generally revolve around the question of whether the land being claimed is mewat; and as early as 1962, the Israeli Supreme Court shaped and changed the legal criteria for establishing what is mewat in order to maximize the appropriation of Palestinian land by the state. The transformations of the content of the legal doctrine of mewat were based on a conception of property ownership that privileged cartographic measurement over oral practices of determining what is sufficiently isolated land to be deemed to be vacant, and a vision of what constitutes a settlement that ran counter to Bedouin modes of land use and ownership.

In *Badaran*, Bedouin claimants (respondents at the Supreme Court) argued that two parcels of land were not mewat but miri according to article 78 of the OLC, having been possessed and cultivated for longer than the period of prescription.[107] At trial, they were successfully awarded two parcels of land, and the state appealed this ruling. They counterclaimed against the registration of a third disputed parcel of land in the name of the state. The Israeli Supreme Court overturned the trial division's ruling and rejected the counterclaim, awarding all of the disputed land to the state. At issue was whether or not the disputed land was in fact mewat.

As noted above, article 6 of the OLC provides for two ways of measuring the distance of a parcel of land from the nearest settlement, for the purposes of determining whether a piece of land can be considered mewat. The Israeli Supreme Court, in *Badaran* (1962), eschews part of the original definition of mewat land on the basis that the oral/aural basis for determining whether a parcel of land is sufficiently distant from a settlement lacks the precision of units of measurement cognizable to a putatively more modern, scientific worldview.[108] Justice Berenson concludes, "in the contest between distance by measurement and distance by hearing, distance by measurement wins and is the determining one."[109] The denigration of oral cultures as inferior and also in some contexts as subversive, as they could not be controlled or regulated, finds expression in a range of British settler colonial regimes, including both Ireland and Canada. For instance, as David Lloyd has persuasively argued in *Irish Culture and Colonial Modernity, 1800–2000*, the transformation of oral space in Ireland was intimately connected to the dispossession of land and the creation of colonial subjectivities. "Orality," writes Lloyd, "has been understood as a stage antecedent to literacy in the gradual evolution of increasingly sophisticated human civilisations."[110] However, Lloyd argues that the focus on temporality (and the developmental telos of oral cultures to literate ones) occludes the "spatial formations" that both underpin oral cultures and are also transformed by the advent of literacy.[111] If literacy is the precondition for the interior life of the civilized subject, it also occasions affective, spatial, and material enclosures characteristic of modernity and modern law.

In Canada, as discussed in chapter 4, the colonial authorities made traditional indigenous ceremonies of dance, of which song was an integral dimension, illegal. The significance of indigenous oral histories for determining legal relationships of ownership and use, some of which are transmitted through song, was only recognized in 1997 in *Delgamuukw v. British Columbia* by the Supreme Court of Canada, who confirmed the importance of oral history testimony to indigenous rights claims. At trial, which stretched over a four-year period, the claimants had presented oral history testimony only to be told, in what would become an infamous dismissal of such testimony by Chief Justice McEachern, that "the songs would do no good" as he had a "tin ear." In step with the late chief justice, the oral history testimony of Nuri al-Uqbi was dismissed outright at trial in *El-Uqbi v. State of Israel* (2009) on the basis that the collective memory of settling the land in Al-Araqib, to which Nuri al-Uqbi testified, was inadmissible as witnesses could only testify to "what they had experienced first-hand."[112]

In *Badaran*, counsel for the appellants, Hanna Nakkarah, argued that the land was not more than one and a half miles away from the village of Arab al-Suweid. The disputed land had been determined to be more than that distance away from Bi'na village. In rejecting Nakkarah's argument, the court concluded that the buildings constructed in Arab al-Suweid were wool tents, and that the presence of only seven families in such dwellings could not possibly constitute a permanent settlement.[113] In addition to imposing a vision of what constitutes a permanent settlement that does not account for the landholding practices of the Bedouin, Justice Berenson imposed a new condition relating to the "legal point of measurement," which was that the place of settlement needed to be established before the enactment of the OLC.[114] Kedar argues that the imposition of this condition was not based on legislation or any other legal precedent, and constituted a very heavy burden on the Bedouin claimants because it "curtailed those categories of settlement that demarcated inner (non-*Mewat*) and outer (*Mewat*) lands."[115] This also had the effect of disqualifying Bedouin who had "gradually moved into permanent dwellings at the end of the nineteenth and the beginning of the twentieth century."[116] By refusing to recognize Bedouin settlements that consisted of very few buildings and/or tents, or indeed settlements that contained cemeteries or mud houses, the state authorized itself to declare much more land as mewat.[117] Here, it is also apparent how different rationales for ownership work recombinantly to dispossess indigenous communities—land that was not registered, and was deemed to be more than a mile and a half from permanent settlements, could be appropriated by the state.

The court also noted that the Mandate Ordinance of 1921 "completely changed the situation" regarding mewat land by introducing the charge of trespass for anyone reviving and cultivating dead land without receiving government permission. On this basis, the court concluded that the respondents lost their right to claim ownership as they failed to follow the instructions of the ordinance. Property rights could not be claimed for land that was revived without permission from the British authorities after 1921, and as the respondents had failed to provide sufficient evidence, in the judge's view, that their ancestors had cultivated the land from 1858, he upheld the state's appeal and denied the counterappeal of the respondents. Unlike later claims that were to follow, the court at least refrained from awarding costs to the state.

The *Badaran* ruling set an immovable precedent for Bedouin claims and was reaffirmed in the *al-Huashela* ruling that followed in 1984. In *al-Huashela*, the Israeli Supreme Court heard an appeal from a 1972 ruling of the Bir Al Sabe District Court, in which thirteen members of the al-Huashela tribe claimed ownership of several parcels of land pursuant to the provisions of the Land Settlement Ordinance (New Version) 1969. The relevant provisions of this act provided that any land belonging to the mewat category would be registered in the name of the state, and that where a person had received a title deed for mewat land pursuant to article 103 of the OLC, he would be entitled to have his ownership of property registered in his name (s. 155). Their claim was rejected on the basis that the parcels of land were deemed to be mewat according to articles 6 and 103 of the OLC. At trial, the appellants had claimed ownership of the disputed plots of land on the basis of possession and cultivation. They did not hold title deeds, and their claim was based on "unregistered rights which had been passed down by many generations." They also claimed that the land was not mewat but was cultivable from "the outset."[118]

When the court reiterated the definition of article 3, the definition of mewat did not include the alternate measurement for the requisite degree of isolation of the dead land. In the words of Aharon Ben-Shemesh, whom the court quoted, the land must lie "at such a distance from towns and villages from which a human voice cannot be heard at the nearest inhabited place."[119] Similarly, legal commentator Moshe Doukhan, whom the court also cited, notes that mewat lands are "one and a half miles or one half an hour's walk from an inhabited area."[120] Despite the emphasis on the aural means of establishing the relative isolation of mewat lands, the court reaffirmed *Badaran* and the primacy of establishing distance by a standardized imperial measurement.

As with *Badaran*, the court dismissed arguments by the claimants about the nearest relevant settlement for the purposes of establishing whether or not the disputed lands were sufficiently isolated to constitute mewat. A settlement claimed by the appellants to be close to the disputed lands was deemed irrelevant as it was "only a police station standing next to a Bedouin encampment, and nothing else."[121] In the course of rejecting the appeal, the court created an image and narrative of Bedouin lands as terra nullius. Emphasizing the term "vacant" to describe the concept of mewat lands, the court concluded that the disputed land was "desolate for ages"; and based on the observations of British scholar Palmer from the 1870s along with the arid nature of the climate, juxtaposed the Bedouin "preference" for nomadism with the "orderly and profitable cultivation of land" that the Bedouin apparently rejected. Mandate-era legal judgments redefining cultivation to mean permanent improvement of the land are noted, only to reaffirm the trial court's rejection of the oral testimony of Bedouin elders attesting to the cultivation of their lands.[122]

In many ways, the al-Uqbi claim is unremarkable, similar in nature to many other Bedouin land claims that came before it. What is novel, however, are some of the legal arguments that were put to the courts, including the claim that the Bedouin have rights as an indigenous minority to their ancestral lands. The decades-long activism of the Bedouin, their persistence in fighting the appropriation of their lands, their displacement and impoverishment, bears obvious similarities to the struggles for land and autonomy of other indigenous communities around the world. The growing prominence of international indigenous activism, including the United Nations Declaration on the Rights of Indigenous Peoples (2007) and the Standing Committee on Indigenous Rights have shaped recent land claims brought forth by the al-Uqbi family in particular.

Nuri al-Uqbi was born in Al-Araqib, as were several generations of his family before him. At trial, he gave evidence of his family's presence on their ancestral lands in Al-Araqib, testifying to their gradual settlement of the area from the eighteenth century onward. He recalled in some detail the crops that were grown, the methods of cultivation employed, and the conditions of village life for his family.[123] In 1948, the majority of Bedouin living in the Naqab were violently expelled, leaving only 12 percent of the original population in the area.[124] The al-Uqbi tribe were ordered by the military governor to leave their land in 1951 for military training exercises, a common mechanism that has been continually used to remove Palestinians from their land. They were transferred to the town of Hura, which was established by the Israeli state for resettlement of the Bedouin, and were continually refused permission to return to their land. In the 1970s, Nuri al-Uqbi founded an NGO, the Association for the Defense of Bedouin Rights, to consolidate and collectivize their ongoing resistance to the dispossession of their lands.[125]

Indigenous struggles for land have often been articulated by scholars and activists as a struggle for recognition. The legal recognition of aboriginal rights in jurisdictions such as Canada and Australia has failed, for the most part, to diminish the power of the colonial settler state to define the legal subject of aboriginal rights according to the figure of the possessive individual, subtended by the common law of property. That is, as discussed in chapter 1, even in the moment of recognizing aboriginal rights to land and resources, there is simultaneously a capturing of the rights claim into a juridical framework that denies First Nations sovereignty, laws, and concepts of ownership and use.

In the al-Uqbi judgment of the Israeli Supreme Court, and as a reflection of the larger political context, there is a degree of nonrecognition of Bedouin rights that is truly striking. To begin with, there is virtually no background discussion of the claimants, their history, and what has brought them to the court. There is, in other words, a peculiar lack of narrativization by the court. Compared with their colleagues in other settler colonial jurisdictions, the Israeli Supreme Court justices display a profound lack of interest in the claimants' situation. While this could, of course, simply be a matter of style, it is also arguable that this indifference is reflected in the wholesale dismissal of the claims, the evidence presented, and the argument pertaining to the land rights of the Bedouin in Israel.

As laid out by the court, the al-Uqbi claim revolves around a process of land settlement that began in 1971, pursuant to the 1969 Land (Settlement of Title) Ordinance (discussed above). The al-Uqbi claimants (six different lawsuits had been combined before the district court) argued that the confiscation of their land by the state in 1954, under the Land Acquisition (Validation of Acts and Compensation) Law, was invalid. Drawing on a wide range of evidence, they argued that they had cultivated their lands between 1858 and 1921, and that according to Ottoman land law and the Mandate mewat doctrine, the lands were miri and not wasteland. The main issue before the court was what constitutes a settlement for the purposes of establishing ownership.

Before ruling on the issue of whether or not the disputed lands were miri or mewat, the court addressed itself to the "unique characteristics" of the Acquisition Law of 1952.[126] In a mode of legal reasoning that can only be described as astonishingly conservative, the court held that despite the "constitutional difficulty" that arises from the blatant violation of the right to property enshrined in the Basic Law, there is no possibility of reinterpreting the Acquisition Law in light of the fact that it is grossly out of step with contemporary provisions for constitutionally protected rights. The historical imperative of Israeli settlement on Bedouin lands was rendered in the language of "unique historical circumstances" that led to the execution of the Acquisition Law.[127] By refusing to entertain the argument that such a blatantly unjust law ought to be reinterpreted, or at least amended with more flexible tests for interpreting the necessary conditions for confiscation, the court dramatically closed off legal avenues for a just resolution to Bedouin dispossession.

Analysis of the court's ruling on the issue of whether or not the land was cultivated and settled can be summarized by stating that the court unequivocally reinforced a notion of settlement based on the idea of permanence, rooted in the English common law of property and Ottoman law (arguably refracted through an English legal consciousness). The appellants argued that the "restrictive definition of the term 'settlement' in the Ottoman Land Law . . . according to which only a permanent settlement with stone houses is a settlement whose surrounding lands are miri lands, causes grave harm to the Bedouin and discriminates against them due to their culture and nomadic way of life."[128] This is precisely the argument put forth by the appellants in *Tsilhqot'in Nation v. British Columbia* ([2014] 2 S.C.R. 256), which, after thirty-two years of litigation under section 35 of the Canadian Constitution Act, the court accepted. However, it is clear from the discussion above that the Bedouin have been seeking remedies before the Israeli courts since 1948. The temporality of dispossession and the legal recognition of this dispossession is certainly not linear; while one could argue that settler colonialism in Canada began hundreds of years prior to 1948, this does not account for or explain the contemporary refusal of Israeli courts to adhere to norms of legal reasoning that account for constitutionally enshrined human rights, as well as international legal norms pertaining to the rights of indigenous peoples.

The forms of evidence put forth by the claimants to prove that the land was miri oscillate between written acknowledgment of Bedouin ownership and other media, particularly photographic evidence that demonstrates the existence of cultivation. The court rejected the spectrum of evidence provided, whether it was in the form of records of taxes paid on agricultural produce, registration documents kept within an internal Bedouin system of land ownership, or photographs showing evidence of cultivation, mainly on the basis that they deemed the records to be untrustworthy in their physical form (one document was excluded because it was poorly photocopied, for instance) or relevant to the general area but lacking sufficient specificity to prove ownership over the areas claimed.[129]

Of relevance to the arguments pursued in this book about the recombinant and fractured nature of how legal rationales for ownership are used to dispossess indigenous peoples of their land is the sleight of hand used to dismiss the evidence of sales transactions to Zionist bodies by the Bedouin. The appellants argued that many Bedouins registered great swaths of land in the Naqab in the Tabu, the Ottoman registry that was recognized by the Mandate government as the official land registry, proving Bedouin ownership of their lands.[130] Furthermore, land transactions between the Bedouin and Zionist settlers were recorded in the Mandate "transaction registry."[131] The court proceeded, however, to conclude that a purchase for sale of lands does not necessarily prove ownership, and that the reason why Zionist settlers paid for the lands was because they were aware that the "Bedouins' rights in Negev lands had not yet been clarified and that this could pose difficulties when they asked to be registered as the owners of the land."[132] One of the sources for this finding is a book titled *From Wilderness to an Inhabited Land*, authored by one C. Porat.

The court found that the Mandate government itself recognized that Bedouins had certain rights in the Naqab, but that these were of an indeterminate nature, mirroring the indefinite character of the use of land itself. As quoted by the court, the Simpson Report of 1930 stated, "Their [the Bedouins'] rights have never been determined. They claim rights of cultivation and grazing of an indefinite character and over indefinite areas."[133] These "attractive" and "picturesque" fixtures in the countryside were "an anachronism" in the onward march of development. Sir John Hope-Simpson emphasized the need to recognize Bedouin rights, but their mode of land use and ownership was uncognizable within an English common-law paradigm in which property interests had to be of a definite, bounded nature in both physical parameters and time.

It is difficult to reconcile the purchase and sale of land with the conclusion of the court, that the Bedouin had no recognized ownership rights over the land. Essentially, the court inferred that Zionist settlers paid for the land in order to indemnify themselves against potential future claims by the original inhabitants of the land. However, it is clear that even the Mandate government recognized Bedouin rights in the land, a fact that disappears in the outright rejection of any Bedouin interests by the court.[134] Bedouin cultivation and occupation of land was deemed to be lacking in both permanence and the requisite signs of permanent improvement, reinscribing Anglo and European notions of civilization that have informed Zionist settlement from the late nineteenth century. There is continuity in the primary place that agricultural improvement occupies in settler colonial law in Palestine.

Improvement of the land through types of cultivation that mimicked European (and American) agricultural practices was a central part of early Zionist ideology. Improving the land was the means of redemption for the Jewish people, a return to history. The profound significance of cultivation and improvement to Zionist nationalism occupies central ground in Palestinian claims for the restitution of their land. As explored throughout this chapter, the ideology of improvement in the context of Israel/Palestine is constituted through Lockean notions of wasteland, which were legally encoded by the British during the Mandate, as well as a German idealism that posited a connection to the soil as the organic foundation of a people's nationalism. Nationalist and ethnoreligious identities were bound to land,

and this land accordingly had to be as cultivated as the people whose civilization was rooted within it.

The ideological weight of the equation that renders cultivation, civilization, and Israeli national identity each to be the necessary precondition of the other means that Palestinian cultivation must be denied, ignored, or erased in order to sustain the Zionist fantasy of making the desert bloom. Between 2000 and 2001, Aziz Alturi's crops in al-Araqib were sprayed with Roundup two to three times by Israeli crop-dusting planes. The pesticide killed hundreds of livestock, and the al-Turi tribe attributed the death of one man and several miscarriages to the toxicity of the spray.[135] In the West Bank, the decades-long uprooting of Palestinian olive groves and crop destruction has been a mechanism routinely deployed by settlers to harass Palestinians and initiate a process of displacement.[136] The Israeli courts' insistence in defining what cultivation is and what constitutes evidence of the same, according to their own cultural norms and Zionist imperatives, is a central feature of the attempt to create a relationship between Zionist nationalist identity and the land.

The more general connection between land and identity, as I explore in chapter 4, is bound together from the nineteenth century in British North America through the juridical concept of status. Rendering indigenous peoples' access to reserve land contingent upon their status, as determined by the colonial government, became a primary mechanism of controlling the lives, livelihood, and relations to land of First Nations. The notion that one's legal status could determine one's mobility and ability to reside upon and use one's land marks a specific development in modern law. Status was no longer a mutable legal designation that was contingent upon time, place, and one's circumstances, but became a somewhat more rigid juridical instrument used to discipline and control racialized populations. Identity and property relations become fused in the concept of status, and status, as we will see in chapter 4, comes to function as a form of property in and of itself.

STATUS AND STATUS (AS) PROPERTY

In 2007, Sharon McIvor, a First Nations woman and member of the Lower Nicola Lake Indian band, successfully argued before the British Columbia Supreme Court (BCSC) that the registration provisions in section 6 of the Indian Act, R.S.C. 1985, c.I-5 (aka the 1985 Indian Act), were discriminatory on the basis of sex and marital status. The amendments to section 6 in the 1985 Indian Act were intended to ameliorate the profound inequalities embedded in the registration provisions for Indian status since the mid-nineteenth century. However, as McIvor's case before the BCSC established, the provisions brought into force with the 1985 amendments to the Indian Act had effectively continued the preferential treatment of "descendants who trace their Indian ancestry along the paternal line over those who trace their Indian ancestry along the maternal line."[1] This judgment at the BCSC (discussed in more detail below) reflected a resounding legal victory, with Madam Justice Ross concluding that section 6 of the 1985 Indian Act was discriminatory on the basis of sex and marital status, and was not a justifiable infringement of McIvor's rights. Regrettably, the British Columbia Court of Appeal would, in 2010, dramatically narrow the basis upon which these provisions were deemed to be discriminatory, and the Supreme Court of Canada denied leave to appeal.[2] As it currently stands, the full array of injustices leveled against First Nations women who were denied Indian status on the basis of marriages to nonstatus men, and the inheritance of this particular type of dispossession suffered by their children and grandchildren, remains without remedy.

Indian status is a colonial invention of the mid-nineteenth century. As English and French settlers were in the process of consolidating their colonial dominion over vast First Nations territories in the form of a federal state, the government enacted legislation that created the juridical category of the Indian. Binding together identity with access to land, Indian status became a core aspect of the colonial regulation of the lives of First Nations people from the mid-nineteenth century until the present. The creation of both the Indian as a juridical category and the Indian reserve marks a specific historical conjuncture, one in which identity and property relations were explicitly bound to each other, constituting a core dimension of an apparatus of colonial knowledge and governance.[3] In this chapter, I seek to explore this conjuncture—what I refer to as the identity-property nexus—which continues as a very particular form of dispossession for many First Nations women and their children and grandchildren.

The relationship between status, broadly conceived, and property relations takes on a specific double valence with the evolution of the modern common law of property. Status signifies a position that one occupies, determined by the law (often a result of a legislative mechanism); it affords the bearer of that status privileges, property, and properties that are both tangible and intangible. As mentioned above, status can be conceived of as an apparatus itself, in that it signifies a conjunction between juridical, economic, and social forces that works to regulate and produce subjects and, crucially, relations between subjects. Status is not immutable but is transmissible in the sense that it can be inherited by one's descendants. Status as a concept does not reflect an essential quality about the bearer herself; it is more akin to a legal persona.

The double valence emerges, however, when legal status, and the privileges and the value afforded the bearer of such status, become affixed to the bodies of those occupying a specific juridical category (immigrant or refugee or Indian). In the settler colony, status expresses the coarticulation of racial and gendered properties of the subject and access to land; identity becomes affixed to specific property relations. With respect to the status created by the colonial government for First Nations people in Canada, the significance of this legal designation shows no sign of diminishing, as economies of reserve land, which scaffold and justify the continued existence of Indian status, remain under federal jurisdiction. Status, historically a legal fiction that designated a position that a person occupied rather than the person herself, has come in the modern era to reflect the articulation of abstract racial and gender characteristics with specific property relations (entitlement and access to land). Status has become a racialized designation that is determined by an individual's gender and marital status and upon which access to one's land depends; it expresses the identity-property nexus that was forged by a juridical apparatus that structured and justified the appropriation of indigenous land and the creation of reserves. Indian status, as I discuss below, is constituted in relation to the ideal, proper citizen-subject, the self-possessive individual.

Many authors have critiqued the imposition of Indian status on First Nations, and the particularly pernicious effects on the lives of First Nations women and children. For instance, writing about the recognition of Indian tribal status and membership in the American context, Joanne Barker argues that the focus on "cultural authenticity" in the legislative mechanisms of federal recognition is a primary means of asserting control over Indian tribes. She examines how tribes have deployed law in intratribal struggles over land, membership, and self-government. With regard to the specific disputes between the Cherokee and the Delaware tribes for example, she queries why the legitimacy of federal control over the definition of Indian tribal status is not challenged in this particular struggle for recognition. This reflects one of the primary power effects of state control over governing status and membership, which is, Barker argues, "really about the coercion of Native peoples to *recognize themselves* to be under federal power within federal terms."[4] Notwithstanding the historical differences in the American and Canadian approaches to the regulation of Indian tribal status and Indian status respectively, Barker's astute observations about the effects of the colonial regulation of First Nations' identity is certainly relevant to the Canadian context. The relation of dominance between the colonial sovereign state and First Nations (or Indian tribes in the U.S.) evident in laws governing Indian status works to shore up the power and status of the white (male) possessive individual: "Within the narrative practices of nation formation, laws that regulate Native status and rights are central in defining conditions of power for those classified as 'white.' These laws have worked so concertedly over time to normalize the legal, social and economic positions of privilege for 'whites' over Native lands, resources, and bodies that those classified as white have come not only to feel entitled to their privileges and benefits—but also to enjoy the right to exclude them from non-whites."[5]

Explicitly drawing on the work of Cheryl Harris, Barker examines "the production of tribal membership as a property right" that functions as a means of exclusion and inclusion, according to ideologies of gender, race, and sexuality.[6] I too argue that status in the Canadian context comes to function as a property right in and of itself; and my focus here extends beyond the ways in which legislative definitions of Indian status were tied to specific property relations and seeks to emphasize the long relationship between status and property itself. That is, status with respect to First Nations is part of the conceptual inheritance of the modern common law of property, wherein status has functioned both as a designation of legal standing and as a form of property in itself; its value is determined by social, economic, and racial hierarchies, particularly with the advent of the spatial and temporal configurations of colonial modernity. This conceptual inheritance of modern property law is traced through the figure of the self-possessive individual. This chapter aims to excavate the racial and gendered ontology of the self-possessive subject as the ideal status against which the juridical category of the Indian was created. Building on scholarship that has firmly established how the property relations imposed on reserves and reservations were defined in relation to the ideal white, proprietorial subject and forms of tenure that were defined by the English common law of property, the objective here is to further explore how the philosophical grounding of the self-possessive subject itself was defined in contradistinction to the racial, gendered subject of colonial domination, and how the very concepts of appropriation and ownership were shaped, in the colonial context, by a thoroughly racial and gendered logic.

Aileen Moreton-Robinson has identified the figure of the "white possessive" individual as central to the colonization of Australia. She outlines the meaning of possession both in an exterior, legal sense and on an ontological level, as a structure of modern subject formation. "To be able to assert 'this is mine' requires a subject to internalize the idea that one has proprietary rights that are part of normative behaviour, rules of interaction, and social engagement."[7] She argues that possession, functioning in a sociodiscursive manner, reinforces this "ontological structure of white subjectivity."[8] Here, my aim is to explore how the juridical concept of Indian status articulates the intimate bind between the racial, ontological structure of possessive individualism and the modern economy of private property relations in the settler colony.

In the remainder of this section, I explore concepts of status and status property as they have been conceived of in different legal paradigms. The contradictory and complex nature of how status has operated historically (and presently) in both British and colonial contexts places any general arguments about modern law and status beyond the reach of this chapter. In the work of William Blackstone, for instance, status and the entitlements it gives rise to find a place in his taxonomy of recognizable property interests. While the benefits attach to the position of the bearer, not the bearer himself, aristocratic titles certainly passed through lines of inheritance based on kinship. Casting our view further back in time, toward Roman law, status determined legal relations and was transmissible between generations, but was certainly not immutable. My aim in this chapter is not to make an overarching argument about status and property relations but specifically to examine the conjuncture of modern conceptualizations of identity and property in the figure of the self-possessive individual as elaborated by C. B. MacPherson. I argue that this conjuncture of identity, in the form of legal status, and property relations is firmly rooted in a racial and gendered ontology. Indian status figures as a legal persona oppositional to the self-possessive, appropriative subject, bound to the bodies of First Nations women in specific ways. My focus in the bulk of this chapter is largely historical; the aim is to excavate the different economies of identity and land that were constructed in the mid-nineteenth century by the colonial government, which express the fundamental centrality of race and gender thinking to the identity-property nexus. By way of conclusion, however, I turn to contemporary challenges to the Indian Act provisions that perpetuate the ongoing dispossession of First Nations women and emphasize that decolonization requires breaking with the logic of the identity-property nexus.

Status, as a legal concept, has long been a mechanism used to determine the political, economic, and legal conditions that an individual is subject to within both the public and private spheres. As Davina Bhandar has observed, "[o]fficial legal status has been used to define and legislate the very nature of personhood in society. Status determines membership, belonging and may also define the rights and entitlements a political subject or actor demands of the state."[9] Status derives from the Latin term *stare*, or legal standing, and in Roman law was used to define the rights of individuals vis-à-vis others, and to govern both populations and territory. For the Romans, at least according to one nineteenth-century English interpreter of Roman law, the status (or *conditio*) of the parties involved in a dispute was essential in determining the contours of the legal action.[10] The fourteenth-century Roman jurist Bartolus was acutely concerned with the status of individuals involved in a legal dispute, even more so than the actual facts of a particular crime.[11] Relatedly, Alain Pottage, in his discussion of the work of Roman law scholar Yan Thomas, elucidates how the objectivity of a thing, in the context of a legal action, was determined by the legal name or definition bestowed upon it, not some essential characteristic or property that defined its essence.[12]

Status was of central significance for two reasons, one being that it could shift, thereby changing quite completely the rules applicable to the disputants. Another reason that status was of prime import to Roman law concerned the exigencies of empire. With territorial acquisition and the assertion of sovereignty came the need to determine the substance and meaning of jurisdiction. The conceptualization of jurisdiction that took hold during a long period of territorial acquisition, as Elden has argued, was influenced by previous distinctions between the spiritual and temporal jurisdiction of canon law and civil law.[13] But as territory became the object of rule, the status of individuals within a given territory determined their legal rights, obligations, and incapacities.[14] Status became a means of governing populations who were incorporated into the jurisdiction of Roman rule through conquest.

One's legal status was not immutable, as is generally the case with the notion of legal capacity that we have inherited from the early modern common law. The legal status of women could change with marriage in the Roman world; for instance, if a freedwoman married, with the consent of her patron she would be released from the obligation of work.[15] A manumitted slave could gain full citizenship, including the right to vote and to occupy government offices.[16] As Orlando Patterson notes, in Rome a "group of slaves and freedmen exercised extraordinary power in both the executive and administrative branches of the imperial government."[17] Of course, Patterson also argues that Roman lawyers "invented the legal fiction of dominium or absolute ownership" in order to more categorically distinguish between categories of owner and thing, as a reaction to more relativistic conceptions of ownership and the mutability of one's status as a slave or free person. He asserts that the three constituent elements set out in the new legal paradigm that emerged in the first century BC—*persona*, *res*, and *dominium*—corresponded to master, slave, and enslavement.[18] That is to say, even with the mutability of legal persona or status, the treatment of slaves as objects of property was not less violent and brutal than in other systems of slavery.

While the manumitted classes would long be distinguished from those who were freeborn, the latter could also be subjected to extreme forms of disenfranchisement—the punitive nature of the exile or banishment of inhabitants of the Roman territories was marked by the loss of status. While we can glean the origins of status as a means of defining the legal rights of individuals and as a mode of governing populations as a part of consolidating jurisdiction over foreign territories, status was not, it seems, written on the body in the same way that it comes to be in the modern era.

In the modern era, status comes to function as a form of property in itself. William Blackstone categorized one's status (specifically referring to one's position or office in society) as a form of property in itself that carried with it economic value. These kinds of property interests were categorized as "incorporeal hereditaments," in distinction to corporeal hereditaments (or real property). Incorporeal hereditaments included the right to rents, annuities, tithes (taxes), commons, and several other property interests that were not tangible (although they generally gave rise to tangible benefits).[19] One's status as an officer of the court, to take one example, afforded that person economic and legal benefits that were attached to the office, not the person inhabiting it. Public offices, such as those of magistrates, functioned as a "right to exercise a public . . . employment and to take fees and emoluments thereunto belonging," which were defined as incorporeal hereditaments.[20] A man had an estate in such property, "either to him and his heirs, or for life or for a term of years."[21] An incorporeal hereditament was a species of property derived from a "thing corporate," collateral to the person who enjoyed its benefits.

Blackstone identifies the benefits accrued by patronage as a type of property that appears to incorporate a somewhat more metaphysical dimension. Patronage, "only conveyed by operation of law, *viz.*, by writing under seal," is evidence of "an invisible mental transfer" whereby it lies dormant until an event triggers it, "calls it forth," and then a "visible corporeal fruit" materializes.[22] While in the time that Blackstone was writing such formal patronage meant bestowing upon the beneficiary of such privileges possession of lands or perhaps the tenements of a church, we can see how patronage, in ways not formalized by writing under seal, operates in very much the same way in today's world. Informal networks of patronage, often (but not always) based on social position and shared identity characteristics such as gender, sexuality, and race, lead to material benefits with regard to employment and promotion.

Another species of what could be described as status property appears to carry with it the remnants of a more thoroughly feudal era, where the entitlements and privileges that attach to a particular status or arrangement capture the subject in a more totalizing embrace. For instance, Schmitt distinguishes the "status contract" from the "free contract" of the liberal bourgeois social order that rests on the will of each subject who is party to the contract. The status contract, by contrast, involves the whole person, "and founds an enduring life relationship that takes into account the person in his *existence* and incorporates the person into a total order."[23] Examples of such status contracts include engagement and marriage contracts (and Schmitt also points to the oath as a "characteristic sign of the existential engagement with the entire person").[24] Status, in this enlarged sense, gave rise to recognizable property interests in the modern common law, and intangible entitlements that bear social and material benefit. Status as a concept that denotes legal standing, and a particular social position in society vis-à-vis others, can thus function as a form of property in itself.

The lineages of social relations established through feudal hierarchies also point to a form of status property that encompasses individual subjects in a totalizing way, by which promises and entitlements are affixed not to an abstract legal persona but to the individual. Hereditary titles of nobility, for instance, based on the grounds of biological kinship and the doctrine of primogeniture that assured firstborn males of the powers associated with ownership, were forms of status that ensured the reproduction of sociocultural norms and economic structures that prevailed in the United Kingdom throughout the colonial era. In considering how status has functioned to determine rights and entitlements of individuals and entire classes of people in colonial contexts, a more complex set of relations emerges. The transmissibility of status through biological inheritance was articulated through the racial and gendered schemas germane to the colonial appropriation of indigenous lands and, of course, the institution of slavery in the United States. With regard to the latter case, the transmissibility of slave status was deemed to be matrilineal, ensuring the reproduction of a slave labor force and, to some extent, indemnifying white slave owners against the crimes of rape and sexual violence (or, in other circumstances, evidence of relationships with black slave women), given that the children borne of these situations remained the property of the white owner.

In considering how status, as a juridical concept, comes to signify differential value along axes of race and gender, I argue that Indian status was defined in relation to the legal subjectivity of the possessive individual, who bears the status of the ideal citizen-subject. As I explore in the following section, the creation of Indian status was concomitant with legislation that established federal jurisdiction over reserve lands and stipulated in great detail the rules governing life on the reserve. This took place within the same space and temporal framework as the appropriation of First Nations lands and the privatization of the land base, particularly in provinces such as British Columbia, as explored in chapter 1. The ideal legal and political subject of the burgeoning settler state was the possessive individual, and the "Indian" of the Indian Act was defined in contradistinction to this figure.

ECONOMIES OF LAND AND IDENTITY

The identity-property nexus, in the settler colony of Canada, was forged in relation to two distinct economies of land. One was the Indian reserve, the other a market for individual private property ownership that rested upon the fiction of underlying Crown sovereignty. Landlaw was evidently informed by Lockean justifications for ownership. In British Columbia, for instance, land that was not visibly populated by agricultural settlements in the English vein was often deemed to be wasteland, open for appropriation by settlers, as discussed in chapter 1.[25] Concerns for creating and expanding commercial markets reflected the influence of Smithian political economy on the mentality of Canada's first legislators.[26] The self-possessive and appropriative subject was the ideal archetype of the settler. The legal designation "Indian" was in many ways its inverse, defined in order to establish who had the right to reside on reserves, which, as I explore below, were spaces intended to be kept outside and insulated from the market economy of mainstream society. Reserves were intended to be anachronistic spaces bounded by time and place, with the paternalistic aims of protecting First Nations from white settlers making incursions onto their lands and encouraging First Nations to assimilate by placing them in the extreme margins of the young settler nation-state.

The first federal piece of legislation pertaining to Indian status and Indian lands was An Act Providing for the Organisation of the Department of the Secretary of State of Canada, and for the Management of Indian and Ordinance Lands, S.C. 1868, c.42 (31 Vict.). This act was passed shortly after the British North America Act 30 & 31, Vict. Ch 3, (also known as the Constitution Act), the imperial legislation that united the Canadian provinces into a unified dominion. This act provided the constitutional architecture for the division of powers over a range of matters between federal and provincial governments. Indian lands were to fall under federal jurisdiction and initially were the responsibility of the Department of the Secretary of State of Canada. As John Milloy has written, the early legislation regulating the lands and lives of Indians reflected the colonial policy objectives of assimilation.[27] The earlier imperial policy of civilizing the natives was displaced by the objective of assimilating First Nations into the larger white settler population. Indeed, as Milloy notes, the passage in 1869 of the "Act for the Gradual Enfranchisement of Indians, the Better Management of Indian Affairs, and to Extend the Provisions of the Act 31st Victoria" rendered bare the colonial "dedication to assimilation."[28]

The 1868 act defined who an "Indian" was "for the purposes of determining what persons are entitled to hold, use or enjoy the lands and other immoveable property" (section 15). The "Indians" were defined as those who had "Indian" blood, and those "reputed to belong to the particular tribe, band or body of Indians interested in such lands or immoveable property" (section 15). The first comprehensive statute that amalgamated the various pieces of legislation that applied to Indians was An Act to Amend and Consolidate the Laws Respecting Indians, S.C. 1876, c.18. Finally, the Indian Act, R.S.C. 1886, c.43, provided the following definition of "Indian" that would remain intact until well into the twentieth century:

> *First.* Any male person of Indian blood reputed to belong to a particular band;
> *Secondly.* Any child of such person;
> *Thirdly.* Any woman who is or was lawfully married to such person.

Milloy argues that the concept of status in the Indian Act derived from "Victorian cultural assumptions: that property ownership was the foundation of civilized society," which, firmly patriarchal in nature, linked descent and ownership (of status and land) to males.[29] And certainly, in the definition of "Indian" we see the erasure of First Nations women as subjects independent from the juridical category of Indian; they are categorized either as the child or the wife of a man.

Early legislation governing Indians is revealing of the intensely gendered nature of racial difference. The attempt to civilize the native, reflecting a bourgeois, Victorian sensibility, required Indian women to be treated as property of their husbands.[30] Thus, in 1857, the Dominion Government of Canada passed a piece of legislation titled An Act to Encourage the Gradual Civilization of the Indian Tribes in the Province, and to Amend the Laws Respecting Indians, S. Prov. C. 1857, 20 Vict., as c.26. As Justice Ross recounts in her judgment in *McIvor v. Registrar, Indian and Northern Affairs Canada*, this was perhaps the first act to inflict upon First Nations women and children the involuntary loss of status. If the husband of an Indian woman were enfranchised and thus assimilated (at least partially) into the mainstream economy of property ownership, she too would have had her status removed.[31]

If a First Nations woman married a person who was not registered as an Indian, she (and her children) lost her status. If she married a man who belonged to another band, then her name was automatically transferred to his band.[32] It is difficult to underestimate the radical effect of the imposition of this patriarchal system governing identity and access to land on First Nations women and communities. Scores of indigenous feminists have written about the violence of this system and its continuing legacies.[33] European explorers and settlers who "described Aboriginal women of the plains as slaves and drudges" bequeathed their racist-sexist imagery to colonial administrators and modern-day anthropologists, who in their turn saw reserve life as a way of providing aboriginal women with the potential for respectable domesticity.[34]

The racial and gendered configuration of Indian status led to the dispossession and disenfranchisement of generations of First Nations women. Indian status was the necessary precondition for access to one's community, one's reservation, one's kinship and social networks, and the benefits and entitlements that attached to both the place of the reservation and the ascription of Indian status. Indian status, however, for First Nations women is not simply the means through which one accesses reserve land and has the right of residency on the reserve; status has over time come to signify and encapsulate identity itself for many women. The forms of psychic, existential, and material exile suffered by First Nations women who were stripped of their status by marrying nonaboriginal men remain an ongoing legacy for women and their children who still have not obtained a just remedy for the dispossession of their rights to reside on their land. This is not to argue that Indian status is wholly determinative of First Nations women's identities or, indeed, their relationships to their communities, their reserves, and ancestral land. Certainly the heterogeneity of First Nations and their internal modes of governance and ways of dealing with the Indian Act bureaucracy have meant that First Nations have engaged a plethora of ways of resisting and negotiating these draconian laws; however, it is also clear that for a vast number of First Nations women, the status provisions amounted to a radical form of dispossession.

The requirement that an aboriginal man who belongs to a band must have Indian blood reflects a biological conception of race that prevailed during the nineteenth century. As Bonita Lawrence has noted, "with the exception of the 1869 legislation . . . the *Indian Act* has regulated Indianness without reference to *actual* blood quantum."[35] However, the difference between blood quantum and Indian status has been obscured by both the state and bands themselves, who have come to equate full Indian status with "full bloodedness."[36] The notion of Indian blood functions persistently, it seems, in a way strangely parallel to the American context in which racial boundaries were policed through explicit legal rules regarding blood quantum. As there is no way to actually measure blood, as Hartman notes, "the tangled lines of genealogy and association . . . determine racial identity."[37]

A First Nations woman who was not married to an Indian man but belonged to a particular band was not recognized as an Indian. However, non-aboriginal women who married Indian men found themselves recognized as Indian. The racial categorization that subtended the transmissibility of status was thoroughly patrilineal and patriarchal. Relatedly, the prevailing gender ideology was thoroughly racialized—with First Nations women falling outside the bounds of propriety in relation to the gendered criteria of citizenship (and constituted property) on the one hand and, on the other, cast as immoral, hypersexual, or depraved in relation to white women.[38]

Bonita Lawrence has argued that the gendered nature of the Indian Act legislation reflects the attempts of the colonial state to break indigenous relationships to their land. "Removing women," writes Lawrence, "was the key to privatizing the land base."[39] The imposition of patriarchal governance structures on reservations, combined with other means of weakening First Nations' self-governance, severely impeded the ability of First Nations women (particularly in female-led clans) to protect the land base and provide for future generations.[40]

The privatization of the land base was intimately connected to colonial identity formation. In the province of British Columbia, an economy of private property ownership was created through the assertion of blanket sovereignty over the territory, followed by the surveying and appropriation of land by settlers. Through cultivating the land according to the conditions set by the colonial government, white, and for the most part male, settlers were afforded the opportunity to become recognized as bona fide property owners and citizens of the burgeoning nation-state.[41] Contemporaneous with the recognition of the proper settler was the creation of the juridical category "Indian," whose interest in land was confined to lands reserved initially by the provincial government and later held in trust for them by the dominion government. The expulsion of First Nations communities from vast areas of their territories and the creation of reserves, access to which depended on the acquisition of Indian status, happened in conjunction with the state's attempt to annihilate First Nations ways of life and being.

If one desired to be granted the franchise, and thus, at least in theory, participate in the growing state as a full citizen, one had to give up one's Indian status. Indian men and unmarried Indian women who were twenty-one years of age could apply to be enfranchised. After satisfying certain requirements, he or she would be granted a "location ticket as a probationary Indian for the land occupied by him or her" or such proportion as the superintendent general deemed fair and proper.[42] At the end of three years, letters patent would be issued, granting the Indian the land in fee simple. This right to the land in fee simple, however, did not carry with it the power to sell, lease, or otherwise alienate the land without the sanction of the governor in council. Along with the letters patent would come the recognition of his or her enfranchisement. Laws applying to Indians would no longer apply to the enfranchised man (along with his wife and any minor unmarried children, who would also become enfranchised) or enfranchised woman, except for rights concerning annuities and interest moneys, and rents and councils of the band to which they belonged.[43] This rather Manichean juridical structure was resisted in all manner of ways but most particularly through refusing to participate in it. It is important to note that very few First Nations individuals pursued enfranchisement, as the cost—giving up one's Indian status—was so high. As Robert Nichols notes, in the first twenty years after the Gradual Civilization Act 1857 was passed, only one man, Elias Hill, availed himself of the opportunity to become a full subject of the British Crown.[44] Nichols analyzes the involuntary or compulsory enfranchisement of the Michel Nation in northwestern Alberta in 1958 as a prime instance of how enfranchisement operates as "a political technology of assimilation in settler colonialism."[45] Nichols argues that the near twenty-year period between 1857 and the first Indian Act of 1876 was marked by a "major conceptual reordering" whereby individual, voluntary enfranchisement shifted to compulsory enfranchisement provisions aimed at the wholesale assimilation of First Nations into a "settler colonial body politic."[46] What is clear is that the intention of colonial authorities was characterized by the desire to eliminate indigenous sovereignty, radically diminish First Nations' land base, and control nearly every aspect of aboriginal lives on reserve lands.

The ideal British subject, as Nichols notes, was male, propertied, and "of good moral character."[47] This proprietorial or self-possessive subject was in many ways the standard by which indigenous men and women were evaluated, which in turn became the basis for policies aimed at their civilization and assimilation. The concept of Indian status is, in some ways, a by-product of Locke's understanding of the proprietorial subject. As I explore below, drawing on the work of Étienne Balibar, modern legal personality rooted in Lockean notions of self-possession is constituted through acts of appropriation that take place in both the interior realm of knowledge and the exterior realm of the world. This philosophical structure of the self-possessed subject was defined in relation to the figure of the savage Indian or child, who lacked the capacity for self-possession. In reality, the status Indian was also denied the ability to appropriate land in a manner that would satisfy the conceptual criteria of the proper subject of law; as aboriginal people were to be assimilated into the nonaboriginal population, the Indian was confined to the economy of the reserve, and the colonial government attempted to control and regulate every aspect of Indian life.

THE APPROPRIATIVE SUBJECT:
LOCKE AND THE INDIAN QUESTION

Without memory, without an account of how one has come to know a proposition, we are nothing more than children, for whom the mind is heedless of perceptions, and thus incapable of forming ideas, the latter of which are, for Locke, the aggregated, metabolized data of repeated sense impressions.

—Jordana Rosenberg, *Critical Enthusiasm*

The economy of the reserve bespeaks a regime of governance over land, labor, mobility, and cultural practices. The imbrication of identity with property relations here reflects the dominant episteme of a long era that remains very much with us. C. B. Macpherson most famously captured the relationship between market forces and the constitution of modern political subjectivity in his theory of possessive individualism. Analyzing theories of ownership as postulated by Locke, Macpherson explores how the emergence in the seventeenth century of a market society inaugurated a concept of the subject who was defined primarily through his self-possession, his capacity to alienate his labor in the marketplace, and his ostensible freedom from reliance on others.[48] Those who could not alienate their labor in this way of course fell outside the bounds of the self-possessed, proper subject.

Macpherson's thesis has been challenged on numerous bases. James Tully, for instance, critiques Macpherson's reading of Locke on the basis that it fails to deal squarely with the questions of political sovereignty and universal rights and duties, and further that Macpherson puts forth an argument about the nature of individual sovereignty that is reductively economistic in nature.[49] In the same volume, Tully argues that Locke's "concepts of political society and property are inappropriate to and misrepresent . . . the problems of aboriginal self-government and ecology."[50] Tully places the colonial at the forefront of his reading of Locke, making vital connections between Locke's own colonial interests and his interpretation of the natural law foundation for appropriation of land in the Americas.

Neal Wood has also challenged Macpherson on the basis of his assumption that seventeenth-century England was a purely market society, and points to what he views as a troubling ahistoricism in Macpherson's work. Arguing that the influence of Baconian philosophy and natural history on Locke's thinking cannot be underestimated, Wood exposes the complex interrelation between the scientific drive for agricultural improvement, the increasing appetite for mercantile imperialism, and the theories of governance that would secure the "peace, toleration and security" necessary for economic development at a particular historical juncture, all of which influenced Lockean theories of ownership. Wood finds Macpherson's reading of Locke lacking in his failure to account for a number of historical contingencies that influenced his political philosophy of government.[51]

While these criticisms of C. B. Macpherson's work highlight several significant omissions in his reading of Locke and, in turn, the weaknesses in his concept of the self-possessive individual, neither of them turns their attention to the place of race in the scientific, political, and economic dimensions of Locke's thought on property. Both Wood and Tully illuminate (in different ways) the relationship between the ontology of Locke's subject and the social formations that were becoming concretized during the seventeenth and eighteenth centuries. Drawing from the critiques of these scholars and others, I would like to shift direction here and explore the racial dimensions, assumptions, and consequences of Locke's theorization of individual subjectivity and identity. How might we consider the ontological formation of the self-possessive subject in its relationship to property and commerce as thoroughly racial in its constitution?

If the logic of property relations in settler colonies largely derives from the political-philosophical justifications for ownership engineered by Locke, how do we account for the identity-property nexus upon which these property logics depend?[52] I want to follow a different line of thought on Locke that in my view potentially holds explanatory value for understanding the identity-property nexus that continues to inform modern forms of ownership and dispossession. Balibar's *Identity and Difference: John Locke and the Invention of Consciousness* begins to bridge the long-standing gap between Locke's theory of consciousness in the *Essay Concerning Human Understanding* and his theory of property elaborated in *Two Treatises of Government*. Here, I aim to reflect on the place of race and patriarchy in the identity-property nexus, or the contact point between propriety and property.

Balibar's analysis of the relationship between the *Essay Concerning Human Understanding* and the *Two Treatises* has opened up a path for reconsidering Locke's notion of the self-owning subject. In drawing out and emphasizing the temporal dimension of Locke's concept of self-consciousness, the concept of the self in the *Essay* not only moves closer to the political philosophy of property in the *Two Treatises* but bears traits or qualities that mirror Lockean concepts of property and ownership. There are two in particular that I focus on here. First, identity and property for Locke are formed through appropriation, which is a temporal concept, and takes place through memory, over time. Second, the connection between identity and property ownership is relational, encompassing both an interiority of the self and the exteriority of the world (and social relations) outside of it. This relational aspect of the self in Locke's thought mirrors the relational nature of property itself.[53] In the settler colonial context, the attributes of this identity-property nexus are harnessed to push forward the civilizational imperative of the colonial authorities.

Temporality and duration, two hallmarks of the property form, characterize the nature of appropriation that defines Lockean self-consciousness.[54] Appropriation takes place through a process of identification, wherein the individual "practically *identifies himself* with that property which forms his essence, . . . he recognizes his identity in the actual process of appropriation and acquisition" of reflection, or thought.[55] It is the recognition that one has a memory of past thoughts, and thus one's ability to observe one's thoughts and reflections over time, that constitutes the self.[56] While this in itself is not a novel insight, Balibar's interpretation usefully emphasizes that the reflection on memory takes place as, or in the form of, appropriation. This concept of appropriation reveals two things. One is that for self-consciousness, or identity, appropriation is the mode through which the self constitutes (or recognizes) itself and is thus a continual process rather than a static one. I want to suggest that the ongoing nature of this process of appropriation finds a conceptual counterpart in the temporality of property ownership found in *Two Treatises*, where Locke provides us with an origin story of private property. In the movement he makes from a divine to secular justification for the accumulation of property, Locke rationalizes the removal of common property for the use of individuals. At various stages of this transition, temporality and duration inform his concept of appropriation and ownership itself. Labor (an extension of one's life into the external world) is the initial measure of how much one can legitimately appropriate.[57] This is quickly bound, however, by the amount that one can consume, in relation to the time it takes for goods to spoil.

> [I]f gathering the Acorns, or other Fruits of the Earth, *&c.* makes a right to them, then any one may *ingross* as much as he will. To which I Answer, Not so. The same Law of Nature, that does by this means give us Property, does also *bound* that *Property* too. *God has given us all things richly*, 1 Tim. vi 17. is the Voice of Reason confirmed by Inspiration. But how far has he given it us? *To enjoy.* As much as any one can make use of to any advantage of life before it spoils; so much he may by his labour fix a Property in.[58]

Locke specifically writes that the "measure of Property, Nature has well set off, by the Extent of Mens *Labour, and the Conveniency of Life.*"[59] Finally, we move into the abstract, limitless and infinite accumulation of property facilitated by the introduction of currency.[60] Even improvement, the motor force of scientific, political, and legal innovation in the eighteenth and nineteenth centuries, is conceptualized as being teleological and progressive, growing in and with time.

Second, Balibar's explanation of appropriation presents a fundamental challenge to an unnecessarily narrow interpretation of Locke's famous dictum, that "every Man has a *Property* in his own *Person*."[61] Property here signifies many things that are, or constitute, Man: lives, liberties, and estates.[62] Balibar argues that the list represents "the development of the progress of legitimate appropriation." The *power of appropriation* is the point of origin for the Lockean subject. The "transcendental power of appropriation" is exercised by and on the subject himself, which is called "labor and its work."[63] The subject's acts of appropriation in the external world, where labor is the origin of property ownership, are analogous with, and indeed a reflection of, the metaphysical nature of constituent property.

Thus it is not, Balibar asserts, merely that "property ownership is the precondition for man's liberty, what he calls property." This reading focuses, too narrowly in his view, on the "juridical criterion for acquiring political rights or citizenship in a given *polity*."[64] As discussed above and in chapter 2, in the settler colony the juridical criteria for property ownership were thoroughly racial and gendered. In his more expansive reading of Locke, Balibar outlines a theory of constituent property: "an originary property that is not 'measured' by pre-existing institutions because it is 'individuality itself.' "[65] With constituent property, "property as such is the exercise of liberty" in the sense that "every free man must always be considered *somehow a proprietor, or an 'owner' of something*," which is individuality itself. Individuality, as noted above, is constituted through the self-recognition of one's memory of past and present thoughts. The idea that every man has property in himself brings propriety back into contact with property; or, to put it another way, Balibar presents a theory of a relation between constituted property and constituent property, contra Radin (for example), who argues that there need be no relation between these two phenomena. The proper subject is not only he who actually owns property or is able to freely alienate his labor but is, fundamentally, he who has the capacity to engage in the conscious reflection that marks out or defines the internal stage, "an indefinitely open field in which [self-consciousness] is both actor and spectator."[66]

The modern subject captures a "paradoxical unity of opposites"; that is, he is composed of qualities that are both alienable (I alienate my labor in the external world and, through this act of alienation, come to own things) and inalienable (the labor of continually constituting myself through reflection and exercising my power of appropriation over my own processes of reflection). Here property meets propriety; interiority and exteriority are conjoined through my power of appropriation, which has a double valence: one that exposes and spends an aspect of my self that is alienable within capitalist relations of production, and the other movement which is conserving and protective of my very capacity for self-constitution. Without these capacities, I am less than a fully individuated human being.

The move from a metaphysics of interiority to colonial governance is not simple or straightforward. We are attempting to excavate the philosophical structure of dispossession and how it surfaces in the specific space of the settler colony in the nineteenth century and continues on into the present. Locke's primary concern was with fashioning a theory of self-consciousness that justified and fit, organically, with a nonabsolutist form of government. Colonial governance and juridical representations of colonial subjects frame the constitution of categories of Indian and settler and indeed the Indian Act regime. Let's return for a moment to Balibar's insight that actual property ownership is not necessarily a precondition for the recognition of one's identity as a fully individuated person, but rather, one whose interior life is marked by the movement of a self-appropriation that resists the type of alienation that social-economic formations (wage labor, for instance) demand of modern subjects. How are assumptions about racial superiority smuggled into the formation of constituent property?

The primary place of interiority in the conceptualization of the Lockean subject—one version of Spivak's "transparent 'I'"—sets the scene for an analytic of raciality that emerges in the nineteenth century.[67] By locating the sovereign source of the self in reason, Ferreira da Silva finds "the negation, the declaration of the onto-epistemological inexistence of, exterior things, that is, the affirmation that, as objects of knowledge, phenomena, they constitute but effects of the interior tools of 'pure reason.'"[68] Racial subjects, the black slave, the native, the savage, are located in an exterior realm of nature by scientific and philosophical discourses that give primacy to the subject of interiority. Ferreira da Silva intervenes in our understanding of how the relationship between interiority and exteriority—as a defining characteristic of the modern subject—is mapped onto the globe and world history, so as to render most inhabitants of the non-European world as mere effects of the powers of reason, which lie in the sole custody of their European superiors.

Locke's theory of consciousness and identity, as elaborated in the *Essay Concerning Human Understanding*, focuses on the ability of man to appropriate (to himself) recollections of his own thoughts and sensations. As

Balibar emphasizes, appropriation is central to his constitution, and property metaphors are far from rare throughout the text. In the introduction, Locke sets the scene of the *Essay* by analogizing the quest for knowledge and understanding with the treacherous journey through a terra incognita and the unbounded dark space of the unknown:

> I suspected we began at the wrong end, and in vain sought for satisfaction in a quiet and sure possession of truths that most concerned us, whilst we let loose our thoughts into the vast ocean of Being; as if all that *boundless extent* were the natural and undoubted possession of our understandings, wherein there was nothing except from its decisions, or that escaped its comprehension. Thus men, extending their inquiries beyond their capacities, and letting their thoughts wander into those *depths where they can find no sure footing*, it is no wonder that they raise questions and multiple disputes. . . . Whereas, were the capacities of our understandings well considered, the extent of our knowledge once discovered, and the horizon found which sets *the bounds between the enlightened and dark parts of things*; between what is and what is not comprehensible by us, men would perhaps with less scruple acquiesce in the avowed ignorance of the one.[69]

It is arguable that just as with the attempt to secularize the foundations of property and natural law in the *Two Treatises*, there is in the *Essay* a history of the "first beginnings of human knowledge" that incorporates a racial anthropology of the human,[70] just as in the *Two Treatises* and the chapter "Of Property," there is the prehistory of modern law in which Indians nourish themselves in the absence of enclosure.[71] Locke's favorite quadrumvirate in the early part of the *Essay*, composed of illiterate people, savages, idiots, and children, prove that there are no universal principles of knowledge.[72] General propositions of knowledge are, to the contrary, "the language and business of schools and academies of learned nations."[73] While the chapter "Identity and Diversity" distinguishes between brute animals and men in considering capacities for reflection, rather than between civilized men and the aforementioned quadrumvirate, it is arguable that the barbarians of a seventeenth-century political imaginary, defined by their godlessness and lack of agricultural science, were also lacking in the capacity for interior reflection and recollection.

The figure of the savage in Locke's *Essay* and *Two Treatises* finds its reflection in the juridical category of the Indian. The Indian is a subject without a past.[74] The settler who has the capacity to preempt land fits into the Enlightenment historicism that equated cultivation with a narrative of civilizational progress. The property logic of Indian identity is entirely different from that of the self-possessed, proprietorial subject—its temporality is static, rather than dynamic and of a cognizable duration. Indian status flattens time and congeals space into an economy that prohibits appropriation. The concept of memory, of recollection, for Locke is not the same as memory of a historical past. However, both memory and recollection are "indispensable *to the use of any of our intellectual faculties* precisely because," as Balibar notes, our intellectual faculties involve the "selective 'retention' and reactivation of 'dormant' thoughts."[75] Balibar argues that ultimately, Locke bestows a "quasi-transcendental function on memory" as central to consciousness itself. The recognition of personal identity is limited or demarcated by the memory of consciousness's past acts and thoughts. It is the "memory trace that binds the present to the past and to which identity remains attached."[76] This theory of consciousness, when cast in the domain of settler colonial relations, can be used to understand both regimes of governance over identity and resistance to them. Of course, First Nations have resisted the imposition of a racial regime of ownership that binds together identity (and a particular theory of consciousness) with access to and ownership of land, precisely through remaining attached to recollection of ways of being and thinking that import their own histories and temporalities. On the other hand, it is also clear that the apparatus of the Indian Act and the residential school system were premised on the denial of First Nations' capacity and ability to keep hold of the memory trace that binds identity to the form of consciousness associated with full and proper legal subjects. In particular, the punishment of First Nations children for speaking their native languages in the residential school system was central to the colonial attempt to radically diminish the connection between memory and the consciousness of one's identity as an indigenous person. And thus, while the concept of recollection for Locke is not the same as memory of a historical past, it is quite clear that the Indian Act, along with the imposition of private property relations, were premised on the denial of First Nations' living memory of their relationships to land and place. As Mahmoud Darwish reminds us, writing of another settler colonial context, the refusal to credit the colonized with a memory of place before settlement, before civilization, is intimately connected to the theft of rights, to the theft of land.[77]

The Indian Act 1886 was apparently designed to create a separate juridical space, with the state attempting to regulate nearly all aspects of labor, the use of natural resources, and exchange on the reserve. Here, I discuss the legislative provisions of the Indian Act that reflect the juridical construction of the Indian as the inverse of the self-possessive liberal subject. Indians were not only prohibited from appropriating land in contrast to the ideal, white male citizen subject but were barred from engaging in collective cultural practices that were integral to their own self-constitution as First Nations, and these two aspects of subject constitution are closely entwined. The appropriation of land as property is contingent upon particular ontological qualities, and vice versa. Thus, in thinking through the nature of the dispossession of First Nations women's entitlement to reside on their land and to be part of their communities, this is not solely about the gendered and racialized nature of the registration provisions; this is about the very structure of settler subjectivities and prevailing conceptualizations of property ownership.

It is imperative to emphasize that my interest is in the legislative provisions governing the reserve economy, the discursive and textual constructions of Indian status and the economy of the reserve, not the actual development of indigenous economies that included waged labor off the reserve, limited agricultural development on reserve lands, and other income-generating work, all of which varied remarkably across the country. In regard to labor on the reserve, section 33 of the Indian Act 1886 provided for the forced (or compulsory) labor of Indians on "public roads laid out or used in or through or abutting upon" their reserves. The Indians who were liable were those who were residing upon any reserve and engaging in agriculture as their principal means of support. The labor was to be performed "under the sole control of the Superintendent General or officer or person aforesaid." The section provides that this authority "shall have the power to enforce the performance of such labour by imprisonment or otherwise, as may be done by any power or authority under any law, rule or regulation in force in the Province or Territory in which such reserve is situate, for the non-performance of statute labour." Furthermore, for any labor not performed by any band of Indians on roads, bridges, ditches, and fences within its reserve in accordance with instructions by the superintendent general, the work would be performed at the cost of the band (or relevant individual); funds would come out of the annual allowances of the band or otherwise.[78]

The regulation of the land and natural resources found on reserves was an integral part of the Indian Act. The act attempted to prohibit the development of any kind of independent reserve economy by penalizing the sale, barter, exchange, or gift of certain crops or natural resources from reserve land. If Indians were to harvest natural resources from their reserve land for commercial sale, they would have to be licensed by the superintendent general or one of his agents. For instance, section 27 of the act provided penalties for "every Indian who, without the license in writing of the Superintendent General" or one of his agents, cut down any trees or timber or removed any hay, soil, stone, minerals, metals, or other valuables from reserve land. This provision applied to Indians who did not have a license for the removal of such resources for sale; if it was for the immediate use of the family, it was not penalized.[79]

Any money or securities "of any kind" that were for the support or benefit of Indians or any band of Indians, including all money from the sale of Indian lands or timber on Indian lands, were subject to the provisions of the Indian Act 1886, section 69. The money from the sale of land and resources that was "for the benefit" of Indian bands was controlled and managed by the governor in council.[80] A Victorian morality permeated the control of money, as the superintendent general could stop the payment of the annuity and interest of any woman who had no children and who "deserted her husband and lived immorally with another man."[81]

The Indian Act made provision for the colonial control of exchange; as noted above, the act ensured that legally, the capacities of Indian subjects to exchange and own as status Indians on the reserve were limited or nonexistent. (As we will see below, waged labor off the reserve was encouraged as a means of assimilating Indians into the nonaboriginal population.) On the reserve, no property purchased with Indian annuities or presents given to Indians were to be sold, bartered, exchanged, or given by any band of Indians or individual Indian to any person or Indian other than an Indian of such band.[82] Without consent of the superintendent general or his agent for such exchanges, a person was liable to a fine or imprisonment.[83] This was yet another provision that had the objective of containing and isolating Indians within the confines of the reserve through the contemporaneous containment of their capacity to create and sustain a viable economic independence within the reserve territory alone. More significant for our purposes here, the prohibition of the transmission of gifts and currency reflects the control that the state exerts over the transmissibility of Indian status.

Finally, the Indian Act 1886 established a regime of governance over land and identity that wreaked havoc on preexisting social relations and governance structures in native communities.[84] The act's creation of the Indian band established the primary mechanism through which colonial rule of native communities was facilitated. The superintendent general or his agent had the power to determine membership in the band.[85] The Indian Advancement Act, R.S.C. 1886, ch.44, provided specifically for the creation of the band council. On such reserves as the governor in council deemed fit to be governed by the act, the Indian men who were at least twenty-one years of age, termed electors, would meet in order to elect the members of the council of the reserve, who would in turn elect the chief councilor.[86] Preexisting structures of governance were replaced with patriarchal band councils that were given control over several important aspects of social life on the reserve. First Nations women who have challenged the sexist provisions of the Indian Act and sought reinstatement in their reserve communities, as I explore in the final section, have keenly felt the legacy of this system of colonial control established through male-dominated band governance.

The colonial authorities attempted to create an absolute division between the nature of the reserve economy and that of the settler economy. However, the reality of First Nations economic life, in British Columbia for instance, was not, at least in the earlier phases of settlement, overdetermined by the image that arises from the legislation regulating the reserve, a stunted, underdeveloped Bantustan-like sphere controlled by the colonial authority. The demands of the fur trade, and subsequently the development of the settler economy, depended on aboriginal labor.[87] Aboriginal workers populated the burgeoning lumber industry, worked as seasonal farm laborers, were "integral to the successes of the [salmon] canning industries," and participated in gold mining as "part of their modified seasonal cycle" of waged labor.[88] As Lutz notes, by 1885 Indian agents estimated "that of the 28,000 aboriginal people in British Columbia in 1885, over 85 per cent belonged to bands that earned substantial incomes through paid labour."[89] After the turn of the twentieth century, the effects of colonial settlement on the aboriginal population (including increased disease and death) and an increase in migrant labor (Chinese, Indian, and European) led to the decline in aboriginal waged labor. But it is clear that the colonial objective of assimilation meant that First Nations men and women were encouraged to become industrious, and waged labor off the reserve was one means of drawing aboriginal peoples into the dominant economy.[90]

Preexisting economies such as that of the potlatch—which could be understood not only as a cultural practice but also as a practice that was integral to a particular economy of social relations and resources—were outlawed and criminalized by the colonial settler state. Section 114 (infamously) outlawed the potlatch, along with the dance known as the Tamanawas. What is of significance here, however, is that aboriginal laborers would save their wages in order to contribute to potlatches. Lutz argues that the potlatch ban was driven by the colonial view that the activity "kept aboriginal people poor and mitigated against the accumulation of individual dwellings, land holdings, and private property."[91] Elizabeth Furniss notes that in the 1880s in the interior of British Columbia, the Secwepemc bands were prohibited from holding potlatches by the Indian agent William Meason on the basis that they were a "distraction from 'work,' leaving the host poorer through generous provisions for the guests."[92]

The intention to assimilate aboriginal peoples into the space of the white settler nation-state required the regulation of life on the reserve so as to stunt independent, aboriginal ways of holding land and self-governance. Despite the place of the reserve in the colonial apparatus of governance, the effects of being cast out of the reserve were also, as explored above, severe and debilitating for many First Nations women. Since the 1970s, First Nations women have brought successive legal challenges to the discriminatory provisions of the Indian Act.[93] In the conclusion of this chapter, I consider the cases brought by First Nations women to challenge the continuing legacy of their disenfranchisement. It is clear that imposition and control of indigenous women's status continues to operate as a means of weakening the indigenous presence on their land, with the ultimate aim of assimilation.

After the Supreme Court of Canada rejected Jeanette Lavalle and Yvonne Bédard's jointly heard claim that section 12(1)(b) of the Indian Act was invalid on the basis that it violated the constitutional provision prohibiting discrimination on the basis of sex, Sandra Lovelace brought a petition before the Human Rights Committee established by the International Covenant on Civil and Political Rights, claiming the same section to be in violation of several articles of the covenant.[94] The committee found Canada to be in violation of article 27, which provides for the rights of minorities, "in community with the other members of their group, to enjoy their own culture, to profess and practice their own religion, or to use their own language."[95] It would take another four years, however, after *Lovelace*, before the Canadian government would remedy the sexist provisions of the Indian Act. However, the amendments passed in Bill C-31 have reproduced paternalistic and racist categories of identification: the children of women who are reinstated gain reinstatement pursuant to section 6(2) of the Indian Act, R.S.C. 1985, c.32, which stipulates that the reinstated child must marry a status Indian in order to maintain his or her status. If reinstated children marry out, their children will lose Indian status permanently. Pursuant to section 6(1) of the act, children who are reinstated where both parents can be reinstated as status Indian are not subject to this condition. There is an implicit and built-in mechanism to phase out Indian status for those who marry non–First Nations people, regardless of how and where they reside and live. Status continues to signify an ethnoracial concept of indigeneity and affects the children of women who were disenfranchised disproportionately to others. As Palmater has discussed at length, status is analogous "to imposing a blood quantum requirement on applicants that measure[s] their degree of descent from a section 6(1) status Indian (i.e. full blood)."[96]

These provisions were legally challenged by Sharon McIvor on the basis that they violate the constitutional guarantee of freedom from discrimination based on sex.[97] Despite a resounding victory at trial level, the British Columbia Court of Appeal (BCCA) narrowed the findings of the trial judge quite dramatically, as noted above. The BCCA found that while section 6(1) of the Indian Act violates the charter, the trial judge erred in finding the charter violation extended to section 6(2).[98] On December 15, 2010, the Gender Equity in Indian Registration Act came into effect. Following the BCCA judgment, the grandchildren of women who had been disenfranchised upon marrying out prior to 1985 were able to register for status. However, their children, if they married non-Indians, would be registered under section 6(2). Thus, the legislative remedy extended enfranchisement to one more generation but kept the structure intact.[99] The discriminatory provisions relating to the transmission of status that inhere in the legislative attempts to fix the twin problems of disenfranchisement and dispossession thus remain to a great degree unaddressed.

The reinstatement of one's status as Indian has come with its own set of difficulties. Women who have had their status removed due to sexist provisions of the Indian Act continue to confront many obstacles, as even after reinstatement they must obtain membership within their band. The objectives of Bill C-31 included remedying the sexist provisions regarding loss of status and, also, increasing band control over membership.[100] Giving control over membership to bands was one means of increasing the autonomy of bands, but it has given rise to a host of other difficulties as racial and gender-based bias continues to inform membership criteria.[101] Thus, women who have gained reinstatement of their Indian status under Bill C-31 have faced further obstacles because their bands have not necessarily been willing to grant them membership, which involves sharing and redistributing limited resources.[102] As Glen Coulthard has argued, "[t]he essentialist defense of certain First Nations' gender exclusionary practices also cannot be understood outside the context of the eliminatory logic of state's [sic] historical approach to the dealing with its so-called Indian Problem."[103] Interventions by Bonita Lawrence and Audra Simpson complicate a framework that has largely pitted individual First Nations women's rights against the collective sovereign rights of First Nations.[104]

Evidently, the problems that inhere in the Bill C-31 amendments illuminate how the regulation and control of First Nations peoples' identity that began during the colonial era lingers on with little sign of abatement. The Indian Act continues to define First Nations peoples as Indian and non-Indian according to an anachronistic and patrilineal notion of racial difference, signified by the transmissibility of status.[105] The state maintains the power to grant recognition of Indian status and to register this interest in an administrative archive controlled by an officer of the Crown. The recognition by courts that Indian status is purely the creation of a colonial order points to the troubled history not only of Bill C-31 but, significantly, the entire apparatus of the Indian Act.[106] While long-standing efforts to rectify the most egregious and sexist aspects of Bill C-31 remain necessary in order to halt the specific form of dispossession that the regime of status inaugurated in the nineteenth century, this particular mode of colonial governance points to a deeper structure of dispossession: the fusing together of identity and property ownership, encapsulated in the notion of Indian status.

By way of conclusion, I want to draw on the work of Cheryl Harris and to consider the ways in which status can be understood as a form of property itself. In "Whiteness as Property," Harris traces the transmutation of whiteness from status property to a sense of entitlement to the social goods once reserved for white people. Prior to desegregation, the status of whiteness as having economic and social value (in terms of reputational capital) is recognized explicitly in judgments such as *Plessy v. Ferguson* 163 U.S. 537 (1896), the judgment that upheld the separate but equal doctrine. With the celebrated judgment of *Brown v. Board of Education* 347 U.S. 483 (1954), and the subsequent failures to ameliorate the vast inequalities in educational resources between black students and their white peers, Harris argues that whiteness becomes a more abstract, intangible form of property that affords its owners economic benefits as well as social and cultural forms of capital. Identities such as whiteness are formed through relations of ownership and eventually operate within a racial-economic system that, even in the post-slavery era, continues to be based on the twin pillars of a heavily racialized and gendered labor market on the one hand and a political structure based on a legal form rooted in private property on the other.[107]

As such, whiteness continues to operate as a form of currency across generations. No longer based in nineteenth-century racial scientific discourses that posit race as a biological concept, whiteness becomes a sign that represents social, economic, and even moral value.[108] Can Indian status also be understood as a form of currency? We have seen how status encapsulates both tangible and intangible properties, in the sense of qualities and characteristics that are interdependent with access to land. Indian status binds together identity with access to land and all of the social, material, and cultural benefits appended to the place of the reserve. Status is a form of property that takes a legal form, as well as the abstract, intangible properties that attach to physical and actual access to land afforded by Indian status recognition. In this sense, it functions as a sign, much in the same way as money once did.

I say as it once did because before money became a pure signifier, its value regulated by uniform types of currency and standardized by universal rates of exchange, debates raged over the origins and status of its value. Did it lie in the value of the precious or semiprecious metals that constituted the coin itself? Or, rather, was its value derived from its use as a sign in relations of exchange?[109] Thinking of seventeenth-century debates over currency, in which Locke was an important protagonist, I want to draw a parallel with the concept of Indian status, whose value derives from its abstract function as a sign of an identification and identity as a recognized, bona fide subject entitled to reside upon and hold reserve land, and at the same time remains tethered to biological concepts of racial difference. In this way, Indian status both signifies (a particular state-controlled category of identity) and reifies racial difference as an actual, embodied substance. Like currency, status retains a degree of flexibility and mobility as something that is passed on and transmitted, a sign that has economic, cultural, and social value, but at the same time is regulated and controlled by the state. Status carries with it the double valence of being both a tangible and intangible form of property.

How does one think identity outside of its relationship to property? Or to put it another way, is it possible to conceive of identity outside of the relations of ownership in which it remains embedded? Indian status remains a relic of a nineteenth-century property logic, which still determines access to band membership and reserve lands. The various remedies sought by individuals and associations, through both domestic and international legal forums, have focused on the discriminatory aspects of the Indian Act but do not necessarily address the deeper structure of dispossession outlined in this chapter.[110] Many scholars have written about the value and necessity of engaging in strategic forms of litigation to ameliorate various forms of discrimination, while at the same time acknowledging the profound limits of this approach.[111] To consider this question, of decolonizing and depropertizing status, it is necessary to consider political strategies that might break the bind between relations of ownership and identity. It requires us to turn to completely different conceptualizations of subjectivity that are not based in acts or processes of appropriation—as an internal mechanism of self-constitution or externally as regards resources and wealth creation. This is not solely a question of indigenous sovereignty over land and membership in their communities; if the figure of the self-possessive individual is the ideal standard against which racialized and gendered minority populations are measured, the notion of de-propertization must take it, or rather "him," as its target too.

While theories of relationality are rife within contemporary social theory, exposing the phantasmatic nature of the bounded, proprietorial subject, it is clear from the discussion above that both private property relations in the settler colony and the figure of the possessive individual are also, indeed, relational by nature. Considering the idea of relationality as a potential political resource for a politics of decolonization and de-propertization brings into focus the larger political dynamics wherein settler states both continue in their attempts to eliminate indigenous control and presence on the land, and embark on new forms of primitive accumulation that are exacerbating income disparity and radical forms of inequality. As the settler colonial state continues to shore up its power through the regulation of indigenous women's status in particular, this aspect of the colonial apparatus of control must also be understood within the larger context of neoliberal governance and new modes of primitive accumulation. The figure of the self-possessive individual, and the juridical counterpart found in Indian status, can only be undone in tandem.

Conclusion

Life beyond the Boundary

We need to know where we live in order to imagine living elsewhere.
We need to imagine living elsewhere before we can live there.
—Avery Gordon, *Ghostly Matters*

This book's exploration of racial regimes of ownership reflects an attempt to better "know where we live"; to shed light, for instance, on how specific ideas of what constitutes use and improvement, which remain influential (if not determinative) of access to and ownership of land in colonial contexts, encapsulate an articulation of modern rationales for ownership and modern conceptualizations of racial value. The notion that land requires improvement because its inhabitants are also in need of civilizational uplift, and vice versa, is no accident of history. As explored in chapter 1, an ideology of improvement was present in the work of William Petty, who rendered the value of human life and labor in the guise of general equivalences with the value of land, and constructed this equation through forms of measurement and quantification designed to further the objectives of agrarian capitalism in colonial Ireland and beyond. Determining the value of land was necessary to settle debts accrued during the violent colonial suppression of the Irish in the seventeenth century. This objective coalesced with evaluations of Irish colonial subjects as inferior to the English because of their ways of life, how they cultivated their lands and to what end, the architecture of their homes, their cultural practices, and their language. Evaluations of the land and its people were born through methods that gave rise to the beginnings of statistical knowledge and were transmuted into a measure of national wealth based on newly emergent ideas of population. Further, we observed how this ideology of improvement that bound together the valuation of land with its people reappeared in other settler colonial contexts, notably British Columbia in the nineteenth century. In chapter 3, we saw how this ideology took an explicitly political-theological turn, as cultivation and agricultural labor became for early Zionists the means of redeeming the fate of the Jewish peoples in Palestine. Reinstantiating the figure of the nomad, the ideology of improvement has long rendered indigenous people (and others) as lacking in the required degree of fixity and immobility to be legally legible as owners of their land.

As explored in chapter 2, a commodity logic of abstraction that culminated in the nineteenth century in the wide-scale development of a system of title by registration in the colonies was articulated in conjunction with racial abstractions that relegated indigenous people to a position low on the hierarchy of racial difference, reflected in a burgeoning racial science. At the same time, as we observed in the case of Palestine, the commodity logic that underlies contemporary relations of ownership in many settler-colonial jurisdictions is at times displaced by the colonial animus to possess, which requires physical occupation and control. The contestation over land between Palestinians and settlers remains tethered to forms of dispossession marked by eviction, displacement, and exile; it is wrought through legal mechanisms that span the fields of land use and urban planning laws, the historical abuse of state custodianship of the property of absentee owners, military laws, and the cynical deployment of Ottoman-era concepts of use and cultivation that have led to the misappropriation of vast swathes of Palestinian land.

The articulation of racial subjectivity and modern property laws finds its clearest expression in the identity-property nexus explored in chapter 4. Here, identity, in the form of Indian status, is defined through access to reserve land. The capacity to appropriate takes on a dual valence in Lockean rationales for ownership and Lockean ontology, whereby the true subject of Reason is defined through his capacity for appropriation, both in the external world and in the realm of interiority and self-consciousness. The philosophical structure of the self-possessed subject was defined in relation to the figure of the Savage, Indian, woman, or child, who lacked the capacity for self-possession—an idea that found its mirror image materialized in the legislative denial of the right for status Indians to appropriate land in a manner that would satisfy the conceptual criteria of the proper subject of law.

How does one reimagine a legal form so central to colonial capitalist modernities? How do we imagine forms of property and place that are unbound from the racial and commodity logics of abstraction that continue to take root through land laws aimed at maintaining settler possession over indigenous territory? How might we privilege the social uses of property and resist the real estate developers and mortgage lenders that prey on vulnerable communities in their drive to accumulate as much capital as the law encourages and permits them to do? How do we think about intervening in globalized circuits of financial speculation where ownership of what Marx termed "fictitious capital" is obscured by financial instruments whose baroque opacity is less the product of esoteric knowledge than an index of grossly cynical and instrumental forms of incompetence?[1] Avery F. Gordon also invokes a sense of place and presence in her insistence on thinking the past and present differently, her invitation to cast our gaze toward a future that could be otherwise.[2] How do we reconceive place, territory, land, or property when it appears settled, firmly ensconced in real estate and financial markets organized according to capitalist rationalities that bear the mark of historically embedded processes of abstraction? Is the task thus best described as one of decolonizing property law? Or is such a disaffiliation best understood as only one site, albeit a crucial one, in a broader struggle against modes of governance developed during the era of colonial expansion and seemingly perfected by neoliberal rationalities?

The racial regimes of ownership explored throughout this work are neither absolute nor transhistorical, and I have stressed the need to account for the contradictions that arise in particular articulations of race and modern laws of property. To recall Stuart Hall, the fact that nothing guarantees that this articulation will manifest in the same way across different jurisdictions and at different political and historical conjunctures reminds us that along with dominant forms of modern property ownership, there has always been a space for property to be contested, upended, and subverted, radically altered by those bearing the brunt of the deprivation and exclusion created by private relations of ownership. Indeed, there is a rich and vibrant history of the marginalized creating counterlegalities and subverting modern laws of private property as a form of resistance to colonial capitalist modes of governance.[3]

I would like to first consider here the capacity of property law to transform the established social order, a question that arises at moments of profound political change. While alternative property practices (such as cooperatives, to take one example) have long provided spaces of relief from the burdens of individual private ownership, increasing autonomy, and perhaps creating conditions that make life for specific communities more livable, they can also be understood as examples of how hegemonic property relations operate to incorporate what can amount to a form of minority difference in a globalized system of accumulation reliant upon a plethora of different forms of ownership. Indeed, contemporary notions that taking ownership and asserting mastery over a space from which one is normally excluded (summed up in the rhetoric of a contemporary female empowerment slogan: "Own it!") constitute an act of subversion reflect a misapprehension of the nature of this hegemony and its reliance upon and exploitation of the presence of difference in institutions such as the university, across many sectors of the labour market, and, most poignantly perhaps, in urban spaces of gentrification.[4]

The fabrication of the modern law of property requires, as Nicholas Blomley notes, "sustained enactment," and crucially, as he continues, so "does its denial."[5] Legal techniques of fabrication exist in tension with "counterstories and mappings [that] complicate the certainties of the settler-city in intriguing and unsettling ways."[6] The contestation of settler representations of urban space by indigenous and impoverished, propertyless residents of Vancouver's downtown Eastside, to take one example, is a necessary precondition for any potentially radical transformation of the spatial dynamics of both ownership and dispossession. These counterrepresentations are vital to the struggle to halt real estate development premised upon the removal and displacement of the poor and racialized.

Countermovements of representation and use of First Nations land exist (as they always have) in relation to and tension with a spatial order of property law that remains fundamentally bound and shaped by capitalist, liberal, and/or neoliberal political-economic structures—a genealogy of which includes at its foundations the racial regimes of ownership excavated throughout this book. The foremost question I want to pose in these concluding reflections is thus whether actual transformative changes to property law can go any distance in dismantling racial regimes of ownership. South Africa, a paradigmatic instance of a settler political order founded on a racial regime of ownership, witnessed radical changes to the law of property in the constitutional transition to democracy in the aftermath of apartheid. Did these legal changes rupture the juridical formation that bound forced evictions and displacement to the radical devaluing of black life? André van der Walt has critically evaluated reforms to property law in relation to eviction, which played a massive role in the oppression of black South Africans during apartheid.

Van der Walt's project is to distinguish between the reform of property law that reinforces the status quo and "the larger, system-threatening changes and qualifications that are sometimes required in a transformational setting."[7] He concludes that genuine political transformation requires perspectives from the margins—those of the evicted, propertyless, impoverished—to either complement or indeed replace the lexicon of traditional rights that is the focal point of much property doctrine. Van der Walt's understanding of what constitutes a view from the margins is not just about the experience and perspective of the disenfranchised; it is also about positioning oneself as a legal theorist on the margins of settled law, "a place where one is precariously placed in such a way as to be constantly looking into the abyss of problems that cannot be solved by 'normal' legal science."[8]

Did changes to property laws governing eviction, and their interpretation by South African courts, "challenge the hegemony of the rights paradigm, or ... [were they] simply accommodated within the rights paradigm as 'normal' regulatory restrictions on the exercise of rights?"[9] This is a crucial question, and not just in the South African context, as many of the much-touted limitations on the perceived absolute right of owners in nontransformative settings, where political stability is assumed (such as North America), often amount to nothing more than regulatory restrictions, which, while not unimportant, are part of the law of property that ensures the smooth functioning of the status quo.[10] Van der Walt focuses on the potential for legislative changes to land law to alter the logic and orientation of the common law of eviction, which, with its strong emphasis on the rights of the owner, was ripe for abuse under apartheid's racial regime of ownership.

In the remainder of this chapter, I want to explore van der Walt's engagement with the transformative potential of postapartheid laws relating to eviction, setting the scene with a brief discussion of forced removals during the apartheid era and the impact of mass evictions on black South Africans. The legislative changes relating to the rights of unlawful occupiers (defined below) vis-à-vis privately or state-owned land "represent a major shift, not only in approach but also in [the] terminology, language, metaphor and logic" of eviction law.[11] However, while the high courts in South Africa have rendered judgments that reflect a transformative change in accounting for the social, economic, and personal needs of the unlawful occupier, van der Walt notes that this does not mean that "unlawful occupiers are now favoured above landowners and that landownership is undervalued or denied protection because of the history of apartheid."[12]

To imagine how and where we might live otherwise, I then turn, by way of conclusion, to some recent work by radical scholars who variously identify the essential role of subjugated knowledges in the task of reimagining the political orders that we inhabit and in refashioning the self and our relations to others in their engagements with colonial oppression, the legacies of slavery, and contemporary forms of racial capitalism. The essentially political nature of property law and the fact that property as a field of practices is open to radical contestation raise fundamental questions about the potentialities and the limits of law or, more specifically, the capacity for the legal form of property to be fundamentally reconceived. While property law may have the capacity, in theory, to support social transformation, as the example of eviction law from South Africa demonstrates, the political imaginary and will to fundamentally reorder racial regimes of ownership will inevitably, as history has demonstrated thus far, emerge from the radical political traditions of the oppressed.

FORCED REMOVALS AND EVICTION

Eviction law in the postapartheid era can be assessed only if we take stock, however, briefly, of the harm and injustices it attempts to remedy. The history of forced removals and evictions in South Africa is long and complex, incorporating varying modes of colonial and apartheid governance from the late nineteenth century onward. Contrary to what some may think, the removal and eviction of black South Africans from their land and homes began long before the rise of the Nationalist Party to power in 1948 and the explicit apartheid policies of racial segregation. Decades prior to the formation of the Union of South Africa, both the Dutch and British colonial powers introduced legislation to spatially segregate the population based on race and indigeneity.[13] While the motivations behind the creation of the multitude of laws aimed at transforming the landscape of ownership and labor relations along racial and gendered lines differed according to the (sometimes conflicting) labor requirements of the agricultural and industrial sectors, they also had much in common: the destruction of black ownership and tenure of agricultural land; the removal of black populations from urban areas; the prohibition of black ownership except on reserve lands (which, like reserves in Canada, amounted to a very small fraction of native territory); and, consequently, the criminalization of vast numbers of the indigenous population as illegal trespassers throughout much of the territory of which they had been dispossessed.[14] Millions of black Africans were forcibly displaced in South Africa during the twentieth century, and the cost and legacies of this colonial and apartheid social engineering cannot easily be reckoned with.[15]

Some of the techniques used in both the Dutch and British colonies to dispossess black South Africans are common to other settler colonial jurisdictions. For instance, in the late nineteenth century Dutch colonies of the Transvaal and the Orange Free State, Africans were not allowed to purchase land freely, and very few held titles to their land. In the Transvaal, the black population "could only acquire individual title to land under a complicated and restricting system of trusteeship—the land had to be held in trust for them, by the Commission for Native Affairs."[16] In the South African colonies as elsewhere, land title was used as a means to dispossess the indigenous population of their ownership (see chapter 2). Another example can be drawn from the Glen Grey Act of 1894, which augmented the reserve policy begun earlier by Sir Grey in the Cape.[17] This act, developed by none other than Cecil Rhodes, imposed a limited form of self-government on the reserves in the Glen Grey district and introduced individual land tenure in the form of small garden plots.[18] Rural black communities objected to the act on the basis that communal tenure was understood as their primary means of access to the use and ownership of land. With echoes of the Indian Act of 1876 (discussed in chapter 4), the act marked the beginnings of the imposition of a colonial native governance structure within the reserve and the prohibition of indigenous forms of land use. Furthermore, the act's importance also lay in the fact that it provided the groundwork for the apartheid policies of segregation that would follow in the mid-twentieth century, which reflected the continued objective of creating cheap migrant labor forces for industry while maintaining exclusively white possession of urban spaces.

Three very significant pieces of legislation were passed after the Union of South Africa came into being in 1910: the Native Land Act of 1913, the Native Administration Act of 1927, and the Development Trust and Land Act of 1936. These acts had a profound and long-lasting effect on the formation and sedimentation of the racial regimes of ownership in South Africa. The Native Land Act of 1913 made reserves the only lawful place where black Africans could legally acquire land. Those black sharecroppers and tenant farmers who had been renting land from white owners were to "be slowly phased out over time."[19] The total amount of land allocated to reserves at that point in time was approximately 7 percent, and its occupants could not use the land to farm commercially but could only grow food for subsistence purposes. Unsurveyed land and land held in freehold by black owners were both omitted from the official schedules that identified reserve land; the latter, termed "black spots," would be dealt with through subsequent pieces of legislation that aimed to isolate the already small pockets of black land ownership to the point of unsustainability.

The Native Administration Act of 1927 (later renamed the Black Administration Act 38 of 1927), provided for the forced removal of "any tribe or portion thereof or any Native from any place to any other place within the Union" in the general public interest.[20] Where tribes objected to their removal, the order would require a resolution approving the removal by both houses of Parliament. This particular section was repeatedly amended until the removal order did not even require prior notice to be given to those who were to be evicted.[21] The Development Trust and Land Act of 1936 included an attempt to augment the total amount of reserve land to 13 percent of all the territory of South Africa, but even this paltry gesture would not be realized for many decades to come.[22] Significantly, this act made the state "the registered owner of almost all of the reserves—title was not to be vested in the people who lived there, except in a few exceptional cases."[23] The dispossession of black communities who had long settled state land but whose rights were not recognized, and whose lands were not incorporated into existing reserves, led to the classification of black communities living on state land as illegal squatters.[24]

The laws described above built the foundation for the racial segregation, disenfranchisement, and dispossession of black South Africans that were the hallmarks of apartheid. The 1950s saw the continuation of mass forced removals under the auspices of the Group Areas Act of 1950, with the continued objective of depriving black communities of ownership and occupation rights. The Prevention of Illegal Squatting Act of 1951 was a primary means of controlling squatters in urban areas and determining where and how they would live.[25] What is evident from the complex legal framework constructed over centuries of colonial and then apartheid rule is that while the architecture of the regime of forced removals and eviction was thoroughly legal in nature, backed by the force of police power and militarized violence, its effects on the political and economic structures, as well as the psychic and social fabric of South Africa, were wide ranging and profound, arguably transcending the domain of the law and its effects. In other words, while law was a central mode of structuring and effecting the radical engineering of racial regimes of ownership and dispossession in South Africa, the legal imaginary, in this case as in others, remains too constrained in its conceptualization of justice and political-social transformation to go beyond a meaningful if basic balancing of interests.

EVICTION AND POSTAPARTHEID LEGAL TRANSFORMATION

Eviction, as opposed to removal, takes us squarely into the juridical realm of ownership and property relations. Eviction is incidental to the ownership right, the logical corollary of the right to exclude others from your property, and the right to possess your property exclusively. As such, the right to evict is engaged "whenever someone else occupies the property against the owner's will or without her permission."[26] With an ownership model constructed according to a hierarchy of rights, with private ownership occupying its apex, the right to evict, as van der Walt observes, remains relatively undisturbed by "even quite dramatic restrictions imposed by legislative regulation of the landlord-tenant relationship." He also argues that "the landowner's right to evict is seldom curtailed purely with reference to the general socio-economic context or the personal or economic circumstances of the tenant. It can therefore be said that eviction is still largely based on the hierarchical power of the landowner's superior right to possession, even when that right has been restricted quite severely for public policy considerations related to the regulation of the rental housing market."[27]

The position of lawful occupier describes those tenants who had a legal right to reside in a property, but whose tenure has come to an end for one reason or another (end of lease, cancellation of tenancy, breach of contractual term, etc.). An unlawful occupier, which I focus on below, is that person (or community) who never had a legally recognized right to reside on or occupy property owned privately by an individual or by the state. I focus on the position of the unlawful occupier because in South Africa, as in many other settler colonial sites, rendering indigenous and racialized populations as illegal or unlawful, often on the basis of their ways of living or relating to land, has been used as a primary means of dispossession, as explored throughout chapters 1, 2, and 3. Unlawful occupiers are defined by van der Walt as "persons who occupy land without any legally recognised right, permission or licence"; a definition that, as the forced removals of black communities under apartheid amply demonstrated, "is very much a matter of political choice."[28]

In response to the wide-scale forced removals and evictions under apartheid, legislation was passed for the express purpose of protecting the rights of unlawful occupiers.[29] Specifically, the Prevention of Illegal Eviction from and Unlawful Occupation of Land Act 19 of 1998 (PIE) was enacted to give effect to the constitutionally enshrined right to not be evicted from one's home or to be subject to house demolition without a court order.[30] The PIE act was enacted to prohibit unlawful evictions and to repeal a key piece of apartheid legislation, the Prevention of Illegal Squatting Act, act 52 of 1951 (PISA), and several other related legislative amendments and acts. In the judgment of *Port Elizabeth Municipality v. Various Occupiers* [2005] 1 (SA) 217 (CC), Justice Sachs gives a compelling and forward-looking interpretation of PIE.

Justice Sachs also sums up succinctly the effects of PISA on black communities:

> PISA was an integral part of a cluster of statutes that gave a legal/administrative imprimatur to the usurpation and forced removal of black people from land and compelled them to live in racially designated locations. For all black people, and for Africans in particular, dispossession was nine-tenths of the law. Residential segregation was the cornerstone of the apartheid policy. This policy was aimed at creating separate "countries" for Africans within South Africa. Africans were precluded from owning and occupying land outside the areas reserved for them by these statutes. The Native Urban Areas Consolidation Act, 25 of 1945, was premised on the notion of Africans living in rural reserves and coming to the towns only as migrant workers on temporary sojourn. Through a combination of spatial apartheid, permit systems and the creation of criminal offences the Act strictly controlled the limited rights that Africans had to reside in urban areas. People living outside of what were defined as native locations were regarded as squatters and, under PISA, were expelled from the land on which they lived.[31]

Briefly, the facts of the case involved nine families (about sixty-eight people, including twenty-three children) who faced eviction at the hands of the Municipality of Port Elizabeth, located in the Eastern Cape province. The occupiers had settled on undeveloped, privately owned land after they had been evicted from a different place. They made it clear that they were willing to leave the land if given reasonable notice and provided with a suitable alternative upon which to construct their dwellings.[32] They had rejected the offer of being moved to a township by the name of Walmer on the basis that it was "crime-ridden and unsavoury" and that, moreover, they would not enjoy any sort of security of tenure there, rendering them vulnerable to further eviction.[33]

The municipality alleged that the occupiers would be "queue-jumping" if they were granted alternative accommodation after illegally occupying private land, as they would be disrupting the municipality's housing program and "forcing the Municipality to grant them preferential treatment."[34] Ultimately, the Constitutional Court found in favor of the occupiers; they held that neither the municipality nor the owners of the land needed to evict the occupiers and that it would not be "just and equitable" in all of the circumstances to evict this group of occupiers.[35]

The court reached this decision by considering PIE and section 25, the constitutional property guarantee, as part of a "constitutional matrix" that does not simply seek to restore common-law property rights in the absence of explicitly racist statutes but seeks actively to remedy or restore "secure property rights for those denied access to or deprived of them in the past."[36] The court proceeded to interpret section 25 in light of societal considerations and also, significantly, the economic, social, and personal conditions of those facing eviction. Combined with the constitutional protection for the right to adequate housing (found in section 26 of the Constitution), the public and social nature of property rights was given new meaning. As Sachs noted, "the Constitution imposes new obligations on the courts concerning rights relating to property not previously recognized by the common law. It counterposes to the normal ownership rights of possession, use and occupation, a new and equally relevant right not arbitrarily to be deprived of a home."[37]

The court made a significant incursion on the common-law paradigm of ownership in which an owner's right to evict is typically paramount where a person is in unlawful occupation of the owner's property. Bringing to bear "substantive justice and equality considerations" on the adjudication of a contest between property and housing rights, van der Walt argues that the significance of this judgment (and others that followed) is the explicit acknowledgment of the political nature of property relations.[38] The interpretation of PIE and sections 25 and 26 of the Constitution in light of the legacies of apartheid significantly altered the ownership paradigm: "through land reform, eviction law has become sensitive to social, economic and political marginality, weakness and vulnerability." However, as van der Walt goes on to note, "the rights paradigm still exercises a stabilising effect that can inhibit reforms of the property regime."[39]

While dramatic constitutional reforms in postapartheid South Africa certainly provide recognition of the importance of shelter and housing, and protection for some of the most vulnerable communities, they remain situated within a legal framework that seeks to find a balance between the rights of private property owners and illegal occupiers. In other words, even these highly progressive legal reforms did not, and perhaps could not, create conditions in which the right to housing, the right to shelter, is paramount when in conflict with the rights of a property owner. Can the recognition of the right to not be arbitrarily deprived of one's home subvert or radically transform the racial regimes of ownership that took hold from the late nineteenth century onward? Does this legal recognition and the potential protection it affords disrupt the economic and political legacies of two different colonial powers, who constructed a legal regime based on private property ownership and white possessive nationalism? Clearly, the logic of possessive individualism retained its force in the transition from apartheid to a liberal democracy, carrying with it the traces of a racial regime that were foundational to its development in South Africa.

ALTERNATE POLITICAL IMAGINARIES OF PROPERTY

I want to suggest by way of conclusion that the undoing or dismantling of racial regimes of ownership requires nothing less than a radically different political imaginary of property. This means at least three different yet related things. The first is to understand, study, and revive the ontologies of property relations that have been suppressed by colonial techniques of dispossession and appropriation.[40] The second is to imagine what radically alternate ways of holding and relating to land might look like. The third is to consider the kinds of transformation of the self and our relations with one another that are a precondition for wider social and political transformations. Considering how to dispense with characteristics of the self-possessive or indeed the entrepreneurial subject of contemporary capitalist rationalities is arguably at the core of any consideration of dismantling the forms of subjectivity presupposed and shored up by racial regimes of ownership.

There is an urgent need to grasp other ways of relating to land, those obscured and repressed through the imposition of the cadastral survey and imperial modes of mapping, through systems of title registration, through the rendering of entire communities as illegal squatters based on their ways of living; ways of relating to land that are not premised on the exploitation of its resources and the often-unbridled destruction of the environment for corporate profit. Indigenous scholars and activists have explained how indigenous ontologies incorporate an embodied and conceptual relationship to the land, animals, and plants that reflect ways of being quite alien to capitalist, commoditized visions of land.[41]

Leanne Simpson, for instance, has written cogently about the relationship between the need for a radical political imaginary that would recenter and revive the forms of knowledge and everyday practices of the Nishnaabeg First Nation, of which she is a member. She begins her article "Land as Pedagogy: Nishnaabeg Intelligence and Rebellious Transformation" with a Michi Saagiig Nishnaabeg origin story of making maple syrup. After recounting the story of how the Nishnaabeg learned to make maple syrup, with a young girl as one of the main protagonists, she imagines herself, she says, "at seven [years of age] running through a stand of maples with the first warmth of spring marking my cheeks with warmth. I imagine everything good in the world. My heart, my mind and my spirit are open and engaged and I feel as if I could accomplish anything. I imagine myself grasping at feelings I haven't felt before—that maybe life is so good that it is too short; that there really isn't enough time to love everything."[42] Simpson continues that this imagining is just that—a made-up memory, because her reality growing up as a child in a colonial society was so radically different. "My experience of education, from kindergarten to graduate school was one of coping with someone else's agenda, curriculum, and pedagogy, someone neither interested in my well being as a *kwezens* [a girl], nor interested in my connection to my homeland, my language or history, nor my Nishnaabeg intelligence."[43]

This imagining forms part of a radical politics that seeks to transform the world. Simpson's anticolonial politics requires nothing less than a deep rupture with settler colonial ways of seeing and thinking. Embracing Michi Saagiig Nishnaabeg epistemology means that knowledge is cultivated through love and trust in family and community, rather than coercion and authority. I quote from Simpson again: "Coming to know is the pursuit of whole body intelligence practiced in the context of freedom, and when realised collectively it generates generations of loving, creative, innovative, self-determining, inter-dependent and self-regulating community minded individuals."[44] Simpson presents her readers with a concept of knowledge formation that has as its precondition a different conception of freedom, one rooted in embodied, community-supported practices that operate in multiple registers of understanding. Freedom is the context in which such knowledge formation takes place. It is not an ideal to be striven for, a goal to be reached through individualistic, disciplinary modes of abstract thought. These epistemological practices have, since colonization took root in Canada, often required indigenous people and others to act in defiance of the laws, that is, in defiance of the racial regimes of ownership premised on their assimilation or erasure.

John Borrows, an Anishinaabe legal scholar, has not pursued a line of refusal or rejection of the settler legal order *tout court*, but has sought to theorize the transformation of the legal architecture of the Canadian state to recognize the full import of treaties made during colonial settlement with First Nations, and constitutional promises held out in the aftermath of reform in 1982 regarding the recognition of aboriginal title and rights. Borrows's work, however, is neither reformist nor accommodationist in outlook. In his most recent book, *Nookomis' Constitution: Revitalizing Law in Canada*, he struggles with the contradictory nature of a radical form of mutual recognition that would require Anishinaabe laws, values, and philosophy to be deployed in the legal adjudication of indigenous rights claims (and presumably more widely too). Borrows grapples with the question of why First Nations should require any form of recognition from a colonial state apparatus whose claim to underlying title lacks legal, political, and ethical legitimacy. At the same time, as a legal scholar invested in a form of reconciliation that is not simply another manifestation of colonial violence, Borrows's vision of justice requires adjudication of political-legal claims to be rooted in Anishinaabe forms of legal knowledge and subjectivity.[45] Perhaps, not unlike the work of Patricia J. Williams, who argues for a radical de-reification of rights to privacy and property, expanding them with a legal consciousness informed by a historically inflected awareness of the value of civil rights for racially oppressed peoples, Borrows's vision bears the hallmark of a radical legal project that is an immanent form of critique, drawing on legal precedent and common-law forms of reasoning in order to subvert some of its more pernicious effects (particularly in relation to the recognition of indigenous legal knowledge and First Nations' sovereignty).[46] While both Borrows and Williams engage with common-law forms of legal reasoning and argumentation, their reconceptualizations of the bounds and boundaries of law, the maps they have charted for its undoing and transformation, demonstrate the centrality of epistemologies and intellectual resources rooted in the experiences of racially marginalized and colonized subjects and communities.

Indigenous practices of anticolonial resistance and refusal are ones to be grasped and learned by nonindigenous scholars, activists, and anyone else interested in decolonization. Identity-based politics and the real threat of the (mis)appropriation of these practices by nonindigenous communities need to be surpassed or overcome through active solidarity movements and forms of relationality and self-transformation that actively counter the ontological and epistemic traits of the self-possessive individual.[47] Eva Mackey notes that "reinventing, altering and renegotiating" settler-indigenous relations "have a multitude of possible dangers if not carried out in mindful and self-critical ways, because disengaged (or possessive) curiosity *about* the 'other' can easily become both fetishizing and objectifying." She goes on to remark that "[s]ettler states and citizens have rarely found it difficult to enjoy and appropriate colourful aspects of Indigenous cultures and traditions, and have made a habit of mobilizing Indigenous imagery and ritual to legitimate settler nations and events, rituals and paternalistic programs."[48]

History shows us that there are plenty of precedents for affiliations that are not plagued by the difficulties Mackey warns against. Several scholars have in recent years looked to histories of marronage in the Americas to uncover and revive their attendant radical political imaginaries, sorely needed in the present. These histories tell of cross-racial solidarities formed for survival.[49] These histories unfolded in a time when escaping from slavery was a radical act of self-reclamation in defiance of the law and often required the solidarity of others who were differently but no less enmeshed in colonial settlement enterprises. As Cedric J. Robinson notes, "American marronage was not just a Black phenomenon. Indeed, American maroon communities frequently acquired the multicultural and multiracial character that liberal historians of the early twentieth century had expected of the whole nation."[50] These histories tell of the reclamation of land by communities of ex-slaves, for physical survival and for the constitution of a social fabric that would bind newly formed community. The demand for and reclamation of land by ex-slaves whose lives and labor generated immense wealth for their owners continued into the twentieth century. As Robin D. G. Kelley has noted, reparations movements in the United States included land re-distribution as a key demand. In the 1970s, Nelson Peery, author of *The Negro National Colonial Question*, argued for a concept of black national-ism that had a territorial dimension. His concept of nationalism was not, however, about color. Southern whites were also to be included in the Negro nation, composed of the black-belt counties of the southern United States or, as Kelley notes, the thirteen states of the old Confederacy.[51] Na-tional identity was to be defined by the unique cultural practices and his-tories of African Americans but was to include everyone who shared the same territory. Kelley concludes that including whites in this concept of nationalism was "ingenious" because it essentially destabilized racial cat-egories.[52] Being a citizen of the Negro nation was premised not on one's racial identity but on shared practices, language, and customs. While I am not advocating nationalism as a desirable political formation toward which efforts to unmask and take apart racial regimes of ownership could be di-rected (particularly given the relationship of colonial state formation and the ideology of the possessive individual), the sovereignty of indigenous and subjugated peoples could take forms rooted in epistemological tradi-tions that counter what I referred to earlier as possessive nationalism.

Decolonization and freedom require a reconfiguration of the relation be-tween racial identities and the epistemological traditions of First Nations and other, radical political traditions that have emerged from struggle. Transformative political solidarities require us to consider what conditions might permit them to emerge, including a rejection and remaking of the identity-property nexus of the self-possessive individual.

In *The Hawthorn Archives: Letters from the Utopian Margins*, Gordon priv-ileges the idea of use over possession in her theorization of "in-difference: the capacity to let go of the ties that bind you to an identification with that which is killing you, to assume a freedom or an autonomy that you can own because you are one of its most important sources, and to share it with others so that it is 'usable,' not simply a private possession."[53] Drawing on the work of Toni Cade Bambara and Herbert Marcuse in her theorization of in-difference and preparation, two concepts central to her ideas about free-dom, Gordon elaborates a notion of freedom as a practice, one that can only happen in relation with others. "Freedom," writes Gordon, "is the process by which you develop a practice for being *unavailable for servitude*. Freedom is an uneven process, not very linear, always looping around, catching folks at different moments—facing up, healing, becoming in-different, already in-different."[54] Freedom "requires a certain practice or preparation in property relations with which we are often less familiar."[55] The itinerant contributors to the Hawthorn Archive, of which Avery Gordon is the keeper/curator and sometimes author, echo Frederick Douglass and say in unison, *"own nothing, own nothing, own nothing. . . . We were now prepared for anything."*[56]

In Douglass's autobiography, he recounts the moment when he and his fellow slaves are caught during their attempt to escape slavery. He beseeches Henry, one of his companions, to destroy the evidence of their attempted escape, the pass indicating they were free to travel, which Douglass had himself forged.[57] He urges him to "eat [the pass] with his own biscuit, and *own nothing*." They "passed the word around," and through repeating this phrase, Douglass recounts, "we were resolved to succeed or fail together, after the calamity had befallen us as much as before." For Douglass, in that moment, separation from his fellow slaves, from his fellow freedom seekers, would be a worse fate than death itself. The eventual breakup of the group as they were repossessed by their former masters caused Douglass "more pain than anything else in the whole transaction."[58] The struggle for freedom, and the psychic, physical, and emotional cost it would exact could only be pursued collectively.

The appearance of property, ownership, and sovereign subjectivity as concerns in Gordon's book, which takes marronage and abolitionist politics among other histories and contemporary instances of radical practices of freedom as its focus, is not surprising. Ownership conceived as an exclusive right to control and possess land and bodies in the contexts of colonialism and slavery found its counterpart in racial thinking that continues to license forms of racial subjugation. But what does this thinking of freedom mean, vis-à-vis property relations? In contemporary times, what might it mean to "own nothing" as a practice of (preparing for) freedom? Perhaps this requires a recognition of how we are unwittingly caught by the figure of the self-possessive individual in the ways we work, live, and relate to one another, not simply as an abstraction. Gordon's text, for example, attests to an attempt to break with a form of authorship and authorial voice that is singular, sovereign. By including correspondence with other members of the

Hawthorn Archives in the book, and explicitly engaging in conversations with others where the nature or form of the interaction is as important as the content, she has composed a series of reflections on freedom that defy the notion that she is sole proprietor of the text. She has in fact shared, with an autonomous collective that comes to exist through her work as the archivist in pulling all and sundry together, thoughts on freedom that are at the same time her creation but also usable by others. One gets the sense that the Hawthorn Archive was created by a self who is disaffiliated from the typical ownership model of authorship. The relations embedded in the text, I surmise, speak to deeply felt forms of friendship as solidarity, ones that are quite explicitly acknowledged and made on the basis of a common and shared political worldview.

The ways in which we understand, practice, and perform modes of subjectivity that are rooted in possession and domination are intimately bound to the juridical apparatus of private property relations. One cannot be undone without dismantling the other. If ever there were a moment when collective attempts to disaffiliate ourselves from what Richard Wright called the "fever of possession," it is now, as we witness the rise of pernicious forms of authoritarianism and possessive nationalism on a global scale. What are the contact points, if any, between property as a legal form and radical political imaginaries that seek to break free of, to break with, the political order sustained by racial capitalism?

As I've argued above, even radical reforms of property and constitutional law in South Africa, the paradigmatic settler nation built on a racial regime of ownership and labor exploitation, could not adequately displace or diminish the power of private ownership. Could privileging the social uses of property over the rights of owners effectively redistribute the security and social power usually attached to ownership? If the right to housing and shelter were rendered paramount, rather than placed in opposition to the rights of the private owner, how would this alter the value of private property ownership and the ideology of possessive individualism? Could using things in a way that is disaffiliated from the typical hallmarks of individual possession (exclusivity, the right to sell, rent, etc.) alienate property ownership from its current form so much as to be unrecognizable as a property right? Is this estrangement of the legal form of property from itself one way of conceiving of a metamorphosis of ownership as we know it into something else altogether? Piercing the "protective hues of rationalism"[59] and thinking anew about the meaning of justice and freedom require of us nothing less than radical acts of imagining how we might relate to and use things that we usually expect to own, and how to collectively create the conditions for turning away from property as we know it.

Notes

INTRODUCTION

1 Edward Said, *Culture and Imperialism* (New York: Vintage, 1993), 71.

2 Sara L. Maurer, *The Dispossessed State: Narratives of Ownership in 19th-Century Britain and Ireland* (Baltimore, MD: Johns Hopkins University Press, 2012), 20.

3 Even if we take a broader view of colonial endeavors, the role of property in colonization beyond land was also central to the formation of capital markets and revenue extraction. See Ritu Birla, *Stages of Capital: Law, Culture, and Market Governance in Late Colonial India* (Durham, NC: Duke University Press, 2009), particularly the discussion of trusts law in chapters 2 and 3.

4 Nasser Hussain, *The Jurisprudence of Emergency: Colonialism and the Rule of Law* (Ann Arbor: University of Michigan Press, 2003), 3; and see also, in the context of colonial India, Piyel Haldar, *Law, Orientalism and Postcolonialism: The Jurisdiction of the Lotus Eaters* (London: Routledge, 2007).

5 Kalyan Sanyal, *Rethinking Capitalist Development: Primitive Accumulation, Governmentality and Post-Colonial Capitalism* (New Delhi: Routledge, 2013); Birla, *Stages of Capital*.

6 Peter Fitzpatrick, *The Mythology of Modern Law* (London: Routledge, 1992), 83.

7 See Laura Brace, *The Politics of Property: Labour, Freedom and Belonging* (Edinburgh: Edinburgh University Press, 2004).

8 See, for example, Margaret Jane Radin, *Reinterpreting Property* (Chicago: University of Chicago Press, 1993); Carol Rose, *Property and Persuasion: Essays on the History, Theory, and Rhetoric of Ownership* (Boulder, CO: Westview, 1994);

Margaret Davies, *Property: Meanings, Histories, Theories* (Abingdon: Routledge-Cavendish, 2007).

9 Frantz Fanon, *The Wretched of the Earth* (London: Penguin, 2001), 28.

10 For example, see Eric Williams, *Capitalism and Slavery* (Chapel Hill: University of North Carolina Press, 1944); Sterling Stuckey, *Slave Culture: Nationalist Theory and the Foundations of Black America* (Oxford: Oxford University Press, 1987); Colin Dayan, *The Law Is a White Dog: How Legal Rituals Make and Unmake Persons* (Princeton, NJ: Princeton University Press, 2011).

11 See Lisa Lowe, *The Intimacy of Four Continents* (Durham, NC: Duke University Press, 2015).

12 Cedric J. Robinson, *Forgeries of Memory and Meaning: Blacks and the Regimes of Race in American Theater and Film before World War II* (Chapel Hill: University of North Carolina Press, 2007), 4–5.

13 Cornel West, "Race and Social Theory: Towards a Genealogical Materialist Analysis," in *The Year Left: Toward a Rainbow Socialism*, vol. 2, ed. Mike Davis, Manning Marable, Fred Pfeil, and Michael Sprinkler (London: Verso, 1987), 83.

14 Robinson, *Forgeries of Memory and Meaning*, 29. Robinson distinguishes, for instance, the "racial passions infecting English consciousness" during the Elizabethan era that were primarily confined to a nationalist stage, to the white racism that would follow in subsequent centuries, which "aggregate[d] the global to the domestic" (29).

15 Robin D. G. Kelley, "What Did Cedric Robinson Mean by Racial Capitalism?," *Boston Review*, January 12, 2017, 7.

16 Cheryl Harris, "Whiteness as Property," *Harvard Law Review* 106, no. 8 (June 1993): 1716.

17 Harris, "Whiteness as Property," 1716.

18 Ruth Wilson Gilmore, "Fatal Couplings of Power and Difference: Notes on Racism and Geography," *Professional Geographer* 54, no. 1 (2002): 16.

19 Harris, "Whiteness as Property," 1722.

20 My use of the term "recombinant" bears little relation to the content or context of the piece that inspired its use: David Stark, "Recombinant Property in East European Capitalism," in *Laws of the Market*, ed. Michel Callon (Oxford: Blackwell, 1998), 117–46. Stark defines recombinant property as a type of hedging used in emerging capital markets in postcommunist Hungary in order to "hold resources that can be justified or assessed by more than one standard of measure" (119).

21 Paul Gilroy, *After Empire: Melancholia or Convivial Culture?* (London: Routledge, 2004).

22 Avery F. Gordon, " 'I'm Already in a Sort of Tomb': A Reply to Philip Scheffner's *The Halfmoon Files*," *South Atlantic Quarterly* 110, no. 1 (winter 2011): 133.

23 Stuart Hall, "Gramsci's Relevance for the Study of Race and Ethnicity," *Journal of Communication Inquiry* 10, no. 5 (1986): 23–24.

24 Stuart Hall, "Signification, Representation, Ideology: Althusser and Post-structuralist Debates," *Critical Studies in Mass Communication* 2, no. 2 (June 1985): 91.

25 Although underexplored by Hall, the gendered nature of particular forms of labor, as the feminist literature on the centrality of reproductive labor to capital-ist social formations recalls, draws our attention to how patriarchal constructions of gender similarly determine the value attributed to work traditionally done by women. In considering the geopolitical specificity of some of the worst forms of labor exploitation, labor relations and class formations cannot be adequately understood without considering the gendered and racialized nature of labor practices. See, for example, Silvia Federici, *Revolution at Point Zero: Housework, Reproduction, and Feminist Struggle* (Oakland, CA: PM Press / Common Notions, 2012).

26 Hall, "Signification, Representation, Ideology," 93.

27 Étienne Balibar, "Plus-value et classes sociales: Contribution à la critique de l'economie politique," in *Cinq études de matérialisme historique* (Paris: Francois Maspéro, 1974), 165–67.

28 Louis Althusser, "Contradiction and Overdetermination: Notes for an Investiga-tion," in *For Marx* (London: Verso, 2005), 112.

29 Hall, "Signification, Representation, Ideology," n2, 113–14.

30 Stuart Hall, "Race, Articulation and Societies Structured in Dominance," in *Sociological Theories: Race and Colonialism*, ed. UNESCO (Paris: UNESCO, 1980), 312.

31 Witness, for instance, how ownership has become a prime strategy for racial-ized groups to achieve long-denied economic and social security, and to assert their equal value and respectability as individual persons. The powerful fallacy that ownership is sufficient to render groups of people long denied recognition as having the same value and worth as middle-class white proprietors certainly exacerbated the effects of the exploitative reverse redlining practices present during the subprime crisis. Indeed, grasping the complexity and contradictions of the racial character of contemporary real estate markets in North America, among other places, requires an account of the histories of racial dispossession that inform current ideologies of ownership. See Brenna Bhandar and Alberto Toscano, "Race, Real Estate and Real Abstraction," *Radical Philosophy* 194 (November/December 2015): 8–17.

32 Robinson, *Forgeries of Memory and Meaning*, xii.

33 Robinson, *Forgeries of Memory and Meaning*, xi.

34 For instance, Robinson argues that English abolitionists, mainly white middle-class professionals who were driven in part by a sense of moral superiority and a belief in their Christian duty to assist in the uplift of black slaves, induced (the implication here is unintentionally) the creation of literature and visual repre-sentations of black people that subverted notions of black inferiority. Robinson, *Forgeries of Memory and Meaning*, 41.

35 Robinson, *Forgeries of Memory and Meaning*, xiv.

36 Robinson, *Forgeries of Memory and Meaning*, xii.

37 Robinson, *Forgeries of Memory and Meaning*, 184.

38 Robinson, *Forgeries of Memory and Meaning*, 185.

39 "Race presents all the appearance of stability. History, however, compromises this fixity. Race is mercurial—deadly and slick. And since race is presumably natural, the intrusion of convention shatters race's relationship to the natural world." Robinson, *Forgeries of Memory and Meaning*, 4.

40 Ranajit Guha, *A Rule of Property for Bengal: An Essay on the Idea of Permanent Settlement* (Durham, NC: Duke University Press, 1996), 8–9. The illusory divide between the public and the private that is an organizing rationale for liberal, capitalist democratic forms of governance travels to the postcolonial space of transition, where, as André van der Walt has shown in the context of postapartheid South African property jurisprudence, the public/private divide so central to juridical forms is porous indeed. A. J. van der Walt, "Un-doing Things with Words: The Colonization of the Public Sphere by Private Property Discourse," *Acta Juridica* (1998): 235–81.

41 While her book covers much more ground than this, see on the competition of interests Laura Underkuffler, *The Idea of Property* (Oxford: Oxford University Press, 2003). See, in the American context of historical development, Gregory Alexander, *Commodity and Propriety: Competing Visions of Property in American Legal Thought, 1776–1970* (Chicago: University of Chicago Press, 1997); Jennifer Nedelsky, *Private Property and the Limits of American Constitutionalism* (Chicago: University of Chicago Press, 1990). On social norms, see Joseph W. Singer, *Entitlement: The Paradoxes of Property* (New Haven, CT: Yale University Press, 2000). On distribution, see Radin, *Reinterpreting Property*; Rose, *Property and Persuasion*.

42 Singer, *Entitlement*, 6, 31–32.

43 Jennifer Nedelsky has challenged the idea of the autonomous, bounded self in the context of constitutional provisions governing property law, and argues instead for a relational theory of the self. See Jennifer Nedelsky, "Should Property Be Constitutionalized? A Relational and Comparative Approach," in *Property on the Threshold of the 21st Century*, ed. G. E. van Maanen and A. J. van der Walt (Antwerp: Maklu, Blackstone, Nomos, Jurdik and Samhaelle, Schulthess, 1996), 417; Jennifer Nedelsky, "Law, Boundaries, and the Bounded Self," *Representations*, no. 30 (spring 1990): 162.

44 Nicholas Blomley, "The Boundaries of Property: Complexity, Relationality, and Spatiality," *Law and Society Review* 50, no. 1 (2016): 224–55.

45 Gregory Alexander notes that the metaphor of the bundle of rights "was intended to signify three key insights. First, it indicates that ownership is a complex legal relationship. Second, the metaphor illuminates the fact that the constitutive elements of that relationship are legal rights. Third, and most important, it underscores the social character of that relationship." Alexander, *Commodity and Propriety*, 319.

46 Underkuffler, *The Idea of Property*, 25–26.

47 Singer, *Entitlement*, 29–31.

48 Singer, *Entitlement*, 37.

49 See, for instance, Lee Godden, "Grounding Law as Cultural Memory: A 'Proper' Account of Property and Native Title in Australian Law and Land," *Australian Feminist Law Journal* 19, no. 1 (2003): 61–80; Patrick Macklem, *Indigenous Difference and the Constitution of Canada* (Toronto: University of Toronto Press, 2001); and Kent McNeil, *Common Law Aboriginal Title* (Oxford: Clarendon, 1989), among others.

50 For instance, Patricia J. Williams's classic study *The Alchemy of Race and Rights* (Cambridge, MA: Harvard University Press, 1991); Harris, "Whiteness as Property."

51 Patrick Wolfe, *Traces of History: Elementary Structures of Race* (London: Verso, 2016), 18.

52 André van der Walt, *Property in the Margins* (Oxford: Hart, 2009), 15.

53 Van der Walt, *Property in the Margins*, 14.

54 Hall, "Gramsci's Relevance for the Study of Race and Ethnicity," 23–24; see Achille Mbembe, *On the Postcolony* (Los Angeles: University of California Press, 2001).

55 David Lloyd, *Irish Times: Temporalities of Modernity* (Dublin: Field Day, 2008), 3.

56 Audra Simpson, *Mohawk Interruptus: Political Life across the Borders of Settler States* (Durham, NC: Duke University Press, 2014); Joanne Barker, *Native Acts: Law, Recognition, and Cultural Authenticity* (Durham, NC: Duke University Press, 2011); Bonita Lawrence, *"Real" Indians and Others: Mixed-Blood Urban Native Peoples and Indigenous Nationhood* (Lincoln: University of Nebraska Press, 2004); Glen Coulthard, *Red Skin, White Masks: Rejecting the Colonial Politics of Recognition* (Minneapolis: University of Minnesota Press, 2014); Noenoe K. Silva, *Aloha Betrayed: Native Hawaiian Resistance to American Colonialism* (Durham, NC: Duke University Press, 2004); in relation to Australia, Aileen Moreton-Robinson, *The White Possessive: Property, Power, and Indigenous Sovereignty* (Minneapolis: University of Minnesota Press, 2015); Jodi Byrd, *The Transit of Empire: Indigenous Critiques of Colonialism* (Minneapolis: University of Minnesota Press, 2011).

57 Brenna Bhandar, "Resisting the Reproduction of the Proper Subject of Rights: Recognition, Property Relations and the Movement towards Post-colonialism in Canada," PhD diss., University of London, 2007.

58 On legacies of territorial reorganization, see Mahmood Mamdani, *Citizen and Subject: Contemporary Africa and the Legacy of Late Colonialism* (Princeton, NJ: Princeton University Press, 1996); Mahmood Mamdani, *Saviours and Survivors: Darfur, Politics, and the War on Terror* (New York: Pantheon, 2009).

59 Patrick Wolfe, "Settler Colonialism and the Elimination of the Native," *Journal of Genocide Research* 8, no. 4 (2006): 387.

60 Byrd, *The Transit of Empire*, xxiii.

61 Byrd, *The Transit of Empire*, 39.

62 For a critical discussion of this tendency, see Brenna Bhandar and Rafeef Ziadah, "Acts and Omissions: Framing Settler Colonialism in Palestine Studies," *Jadaliyya*, January 14, 2016, http://www.jadaliyya.com/pages/index/23569/acts-and-omissions_framing-settler-colonialism-in-.

63 David Lloyd and Patrick Wolfe, "Settler Colonial Logics and the Neoliberal Regime," *Settler Colonial Studies* 6, no. 2 (2016): 112.

64 In the Australian context, in relation to the Northern Territory Emergency Legislation, see Irene Watson, "Aboriginal Women's Laws and Lives: How Might We Keep Growing the Law?," *Australian Feminist Law Journal* 26, no. 1 (2007): 95–109; and in the Canadian context, in relation to the First Nations Property Ownership Act, see Shiri Pasternak, "How Capitalism Will Save Colonialism: The Privatization of Reserve Lands in Canada," *Antipode* 47, no. 1 (January 2015): 179–96.

65 Lloyd and Wolfe, "Settler Colonial Logics and the Neoliberal Regime," 113.

66 Lloyd and Wolfe, "Settler Colonial Logics and the Neoliberal Regime," 109, 111. On Israel's settlement practices, see Adam Hanieh, *Lineages of Revolt: Issues of Contemporary Capitalism in the Middle East* (London: Haymarket, 2013); R. Khalidi and S. Samour, "Neoliberalism as Liberation: The Statehood Programme and the Remaking of the Palestinian National Movement," *Journal of Palestine Studies* 40, no. 2 (2011): 6–25.

67 Avtar Brah, *Cartographies of Diaspora: Contesting Identities* (London: Routledge, 1996), 154.

68 Brah, *Cartographies of Diaspora*, 155–56. For a discussion of some of these feminist traditions of thought, see Delia Aguilar, "From Triple Jeopardy to Intersectionality: The Feminist Perplex," *Comparative Studies of South Asia, Africa and the Middle East* 32, no. 2 (2012): 415–48; Brenna Bhandar and Davina Bhandar, "Cultures of Dispossession: Rights, Status and Identities," *Darkmatter* 14 (2016), http://www.darkmatter101.org/site/2016/05/16/cultures-of-dispossession/; Silma Birge and Patricia Hill Collins, *Intersectionality* (London: Polity, 2016).

1. USE

1 A genuinely absentee owner, versus owners who are absent due to being displaced at the hands of an occupying power. The abuse of the Absentees' Property Law 1950 by the state of Israel is summed up by Adalah: "Property belonging to absentees was placed under the control of the State of Israel with the Custodian for Absentees' Property. The Absentees' Property Law was the main legal instrument used by Israel to take possession of the land belonging to the internal and external Palestinian refugees, and Muslim Waqf properties across the state." See "Absentees' Property Law," Adalah, accessed August 14, 2017, https://www.adalah.org/en/law/view/538.

2 One goal of PAH's political campaign is to reassert the right to housing that is enshrined in article 47 of the Spanish Constitution, which provides that "all Spaniards have the right to enjoy decent and adequate housing." The article places a positive duty on the government to make this right effective and to "prevent speculation." Article 33, which stipulates that private property must be limited by the social function of property, is also relevant. Despite these constitutional guarantees, mortgage laws, the deregulation of credit and lending, and the unrestrained bolstering of real estate development at any cost hollowed out the substance of article 47. See Adrià Alemany and Ada Colau, *Mortgaged Lives* (Los Angeles: Journal of Aesthetics and Protest Press, 2014), 38–44.

3 See Giorgio Agamben, *The Highest Poverty: Monastic Rules and Forms of Life* (Stanford, CA: Stanford University Press, 2013).

4 Thomas Frank, "Exploring the Boundaries of Law in the Middle Ages: Franciscan Debates on Poverty, and Inheritance," *Law and Literature* 20, no. 2 (summer 2008): 244–46.

5 Frank, "Exploring the Boundaries of Law in the Middle Ages," 257.

6 The concept of use underlying "the use" or its modern form, the trust, reflected the social and economic conditions of a time when warfare in far-flung places (including, infamously, the Crusades), religious prohibitions on ownership, and laws relating to primogeniture made the splitting of ownership an attractive proposition.

7 The modern trust has come to operate, as noted by Roger Cotterrell, in ways that obscure the social power that beneficial ownership endows upon a beneficiary, and is used to great effect today to avoid tax liability. See Roger Cotterrell, "Power, Property and the Law of Trusts: A Partial Agenda for Critical Legal Scholarship," *Journal of Law and Society* 14, no. 1 (1987): 85.

8 See Nicholas Blomley, *Unsettling the City: Urban Land and the Politics of Property* (London: Routledge, 2003).

9 Eva Mackey describes improvement as a concept foundational to Western epistemologies, whereby "the highest value in human relationships with land and the natural world is based on particular kinds of labour perceived as 'improvement'; specific kinds of improvement can make a human being into the owner and master of land and nature; and that other kinds of relationships with land preclude that ownership." Eva Mackey, *Unsettled Expectations: Uncertainty, Land and Settler Decolonization* (Halifax: Fernwood, 2016), 126.

10 Peter Fitzpatrick, *The Mythology of Modern Law* (London: Routledge, 1992).

11 Robin Fisher, *Contact and Conflict: Indian-European Relations in British Columbia, 1774–1890*, 2nd ed. (Vancouver: University of British Columbia Press, 1992), 66; and see John McLaren, Andrew R. Buck, and Nancy E. Wright, eds., *Despotic Dominion: Property Rights in British Settler Societies* (Vancouver: University of British Columbia Press, 2005).

12 Michel Foucault, *The Punitive Society* (Basingstoke: Palgrave Macmillan, 2015), 46.

13 Edmond Fitzmaurice, *The Life of Sir William Petty, 1623–1687* (London: Murray, 1895), 20.

14 Fitzmaurice, *The Life of Sir William Petty*, 34.

15 Mary Poovey, *A History of the Modern Fact: Problems of Knowledge in the Sciences of Wealth and Society* (Chicago: University of Chicago Press, 1998), 143.

16 Fitzmaurice, *The Life of Sir William Petty*, 40–41.

17 Peter Linebaugh and Marcus Rediker, *The Many-Headed Hydra: The Hidden History of the Revolutionary Atlantic* (London: Verso, 2002), 122.

18 T. C. Barnard, "Sir William Petty as Kerry Ironmaster," *Proceedings of the Royal Irish Academy Section C: Archeology, Celtic Studies, History, Linguistics, Literature* 82C (1982): 4.

19 Barnard, "Sir William Petty as Kerry Ironmaster," 2, 30.

20 Barnard, "Sir William Petty as Kerry Ironmaster," 28.

21 William Petty, *Political Anatomy of Ireland with the establishment for that kingdom when the late Duke of Ormond was Lord Lieutenant: to which is added Verbum sapienti; or, An account of the wealth and expences of England, and the method of raising taxes in the most equal manner* (London: D. Brown and W. Rogers, 1691), 38–39.

22 Petty, *Economic Writings*, 34.

23 Petty, *Economic Writings*, 39.

24 Petty, *Economic Writings*, 43.

25 Petty, *Economic Writings*, 44.

26 Petty, *Economic Writings*, 45.

27 Petty, *Political Anatomy*, 170.

28 The volume of trade in Ireland was inhibited, in Petty's view, by a population who "led a largely self-sufficient life." Adam Fox, "Sir William Petty, Ireland, and the Making of a Political Economist, 1653–87," *Economic History Review*, New Series, 62, no. 2 (May 2009): 398; Petty, *Political Anatomy*, 190.

29 Petty, *Economic Writings*, 45.

30 Petty, *Political Anatomy*, 108.

31 Paul Slack, "Material Progress and the Challenge of Affluence in Seventeenth-Century England," *Economic History Review*, New Series, 62, no. 3 (August 2009): 596.

32 In referring to Irish laborers, Petty writes, "Their Lazing seems to me to proceed rather from want of Imployment and Encouragement to Work, than from the natural abundance of Flegm in their Bowels or Blood" (Petty, *Political Anatomy*, 201).

33 Adam Fox explains Petty's plan in greater detail. It involved "a five-year plan for repatriating 100,000 Irish Catholic families who spoke little or no English, and distributing them evenly around England such that there would be one for every 11 indigenous families. They were to be accompanied by 40,000 unmarried women between 15 and 30 years old and 10,000 youths aged between 15 and 20 years. . . . In return, 100,000 of the families which the English hearth tax

returns revealed to be insolvent were to be shipped in the other direction, or alternatively 40,000 single women, 'to marry with Irish men.'" Fox, "Sir William Petty," 397. See Petty, *Political Anatomy*, 158.

34 Fox, "Sir William Petty," 398.

35 Petty, *Economic Writings*, 84.

36 Stanley G. Mendyk, *Speculum Britanniae: Regional Study, Antiquarianism, and Science in Britain to 1700* (Toronto: University of Toronto Press, 1989), 146.

37 Francis Bacon, *Novum Organum: Or, a True Guide to the Interpretation of Nature* (London: Bell and Daldy, 1859), 16.

38 Bacon, *Novum Organum*, 15. See Londa Schiebinger and Claudia Swan, eds., *Colonial Botany: Science, Commerce, and Politics in the Early Modern World* (Philadelphia: University of Pennsylvania Press, 2007).

39 Petty, *Economic Writings*, 302.

40 As quoted in R. Hooykaas, "The Rise of Modern Science: When and Why?," in *The Scientific Revolution*, ed. Marcus Hellyer (Oxford: Blackwell, 2003), 39.

41 Slack, "Material Progress and the Challenge of Affluence," 578.

42 Siep Stuurman, "François Bernier and the Invention of Racial Classification," *History Workshop*, no. 50 (autumn 2000): 4.

43 François Bernier, "The Division of the Earth According to the Different Types of Races of Men Who Inhabit It," *History Workshop*, no. 51 (spring 2001): 248.

44 Neal Wood, *John Locke and Agrarian Capitalism* (Berkeley: University of California Press, 1984), 65.

45 A full discussion of the labor theory of self-proprietorship appears in chapter 3.

46 John Locke, "Of Property," in *The Two Treatises of Government* (Cambridge: Cambridge University Press, 1960), 40.

47 Locke, *Two Treatises of Government*, 336.

48 William Blackstone, *Commentaries on the Laws of England* (London: Routledge, 2001), 4.

49 Locke, *Two Treatises of Government*, 213–14.

50 Locke, *Two Treatises of Government*, 209.

51 Pat Moloney, "'Strangers in Their Own Land': Capitalism, Dispossession and the Law," in *Land and Freedom: Law, Property Rights and the British Diaspora*, ed. A. R. Buck, John McLaren, and Nancy E. Wright (Aldershot: Ashgate, 2001), 23–26; and see Mackey, *Unsettled Expectations*, 49–55.

52 Locke, *Two Treatises of Government*, 213.

53 Locke, *Two Treatises of Government*, 209.

54 Locke, *Two Treatises of Government*, 209.

55 Blackstone, *Commentaries on the Laws of England*, 6–7.

56 Blackstone, *Commentaries on the Laws of England*, 6–7.

57 Eva Mackey has elucidated how settler communities who are actively opposed to aboriginal land rights in Canada and the United States come to have expectations of security and certainty in their property rights. She argues that "such certainty in property, enacted through philosophy, law and land claims policies, has

been, and continues to be, pivotal in establishing and maintaining the 'fantasy of entitlement' and the 'settled expectations' of settler society." Mackey, *Unsettled Expectations*, 67.

58 See Vaughn Palmer, " 'The Finest Savage I Have Met with Yet'—but Judge Begbie Sent Him to Hang Anyway," *Vancouver Sun*, October 25, 2014, http://www.vancouversun.com/news/Vaughn+Palmer+finest+savage+have+with+Judge+Begbie+sent+hang+anyway/10323091/story.html.

59 Matthew Begbie to Governor Frederick Seymour, September 30, 1864, *Papers Connected with the Indian Land Question*, BC Provincial Archives (Victoria: Government Printing Office, 1875).

60 Begbie to Governor Frederick Seymour, September 30, 1864.

61 Fisher, *Contact and Conflict*, 35.

62 Fisher, *Contact and Conflict*, 35.

63 Blomley, *Unsettling the City*, 7–8.

64 Cole Harris, *Making Native Space: Resistance, Colonialism and Reserves in British Columbia* (Vancouver: UBC Press, 2002), 32.

65 Harris, *Making Native Space*, 45.

66 Harris, *Making Native Space*, 32.

67 Harris, *Making Native Space*, 19.

68 Harris, *Making Native Space*, 30.

69 Harris, *Making Native Space*, 34.

70 As I discuss below, preemption was one of the two principle ways in which aboriginal lands were appropriated by colonial settlers. In order to preempt land that was unsurveyed, unoccupied, or unreserved for other settlers or Indians, a settler merely needed to stake out the land that he desired with posts or even natural markers such as a tree trunk. After staking out the land physically, one needed to complete various types of registration in order to solidify one's ownership interest in law and equity. An Act to Amend and Consolidate the Laws Affecting Crown Lands in British Columbia, Statutes of the Province of British Columbia, 4th Session of First Parliament of BC, 1875, section 5.

71 Harris elaborates on why it was so difficult for aboriginal peoples to acquire land through preemption: the initial fee and the requirements of crop production were arduous to begin with; and also, taking out preemptions cast natives into a "bureaucratic environment that assumed English language literacy, paperwork and the rudiments of Cartesian geometry." Harris, *Making Native Space*, 36, 68.

72 Dispatches between the Right Honourable Sir Edward Bulwer-Lytton and Governor James Douglas, *Papers Connected with the Indian Land Question*, 15–16.

73 *Papers Connected with the Indian Land Question*, 15.

74 *Papers Connected with the Indian Land Question*, 16.

75 *Papers Connected with the Indian Land Question*, 15, 16.

76 *Papers Connected with the Indian Land Question*, 36, 37, 45.

77 *Papers Connected with the Indian Land Question*, 46.

78 As Patrick Wolfe has pointed out, settler colonialism is a process, a structure, not a singular event. The diminishing of reserve boundaries was intended to impoverish and eliminate indigenous populations seen as waste. More recently, the notion of the border as a technique of control has emerged as a way of understanding the shifting territorial terrain marked by unstable boundaries. In Israel/Palestine, Eyal Weizman argues that in the post-Oslo period, the rapidly shifting boundaries policed by flying checkpoints has become a primary technique of destabilizing and controlling the Palestinian population in the West Bank. Eyal Weizman and Fazal Sheikh, *The Conflict Shoreline: Colonization as Climate Change in the Negev Desert* (Brooklyn: Steidl, 2015).

79 In addition to significant property holdings, Trutch "successfully bridged the Fraser [River] a short distance [above the town of] Yale" in 1863 and held this under a toll charter right until 1870. Gilbert Malcolm Sproat, "Sir Joseph William Trutch, K.C.M.G.," in the Provincial Archives of British Columbia, 3. In fact, as Lynch notes, he was granted by charter tolls on the roads that he had built as a private contractor during the years 1859–1864. Hollis R. Lynch, "Sir Joseph William Trutch, a British-American Pioneer on the Pacific Coast," *Pacific Historical Review* 30, no. 3 (August 1961): 249.

80 Joseph Trutch's father was employed as a clerk of the peace in St. Thomas, Jamaica, and Joseph Trutch "spent his boyhood on the family estates on the British island." Lynch, "Sir Joseph William Trutch," 243. Trutch's sister, Emily Pinder, married and spent several years in India. Trutch Archives, Box 1, File 5, University of British Columbia Library, Vancouver, BC.

81 Joseph Trutch to John Trutch, September 13, 1858, Trutch Archives.

82 Robin Fisher, "Joseph Trutch and Indian Land Policy," *BC Studies*, no. 12 (winter 1971–72): 12–16.

83 Fisher, "Joseph Trutch and Indian Land Policy," 7.

84 Joseph Trutch to John Trutch, March 6, 1857, 1; Joseph Trutch to John Trutch, March 6, 1857, 3; Joseph Trutch to John Trutch, July 31, 1857, 1–2; Joseph Trutch to John Trutch, September 13, 1858, 1; Joseph Trutch to John Trutch, November 15, 1858, 3–4, Trutch Archives.

85 Joseph Trutch to John Trutch, July 27, 1858, 3, Trutch Archives.

86 Joseph Trutch to John Trutch, July 27, 1858, 3, Trutch Archives.

87 Joseph Trutch to John Trutch, July 27, 1858, 1, Trutch Archives.

88 Joseph Trutch to John Trutch, July 27, 1858, 3, Trutch Archives.

89 Joseph Trutch to John Trutch, July 27, 1858, 4, Trutch Archives.

90 Joseph Trutch to John Trutch, July 27, 1858, 5, Trutch Archives.

91 Joseph Trutch to Charlotte Trutch, June 23, 1850, 4, Trutch Archives.

92 Joseph Trutch, "Lower Fraser River Indian Reserves," August 28, 1867, 1, Trutch Archives; and see Fisher, "Joseph Trutch and Indian Land Policy," 16.

93 Trutch, "Lower Fraser River Indian Reserves," 4.

94 Trutch, "Lower Fraser River Indian Reserves," 6–7.

95 Trutch, "Lower Fraser River Indian Reserves," 8.

96 Joseph Trutch to Colonial Secretary, September 20, 1865, *Papers Connected with the Indian Land Question*, 30.

97 Joseph Trutch to Secretary of State for the Provinces, September 26, 1871, *Papers Connected with the Indian Land Question*, 101.

98 Frantz Fanon, *The Wretched of the Earth* (London: Penguin, 2001), 34.

99 *Papers Connected with the Indian Land Question*, 46.

100 *Papers Connected with the Indian Land Question*, 46.

101 *Papers Connected with the Indian Land Question*, 77.

102 An Act to Consolidate and Amend the Acts Respecting the Public Lands of the Dominion ("The Dominion Lands Act"), 1908, ch.20, 7–8, section 2.

103 An Act Respecting the Land of the Crown, RSBC, 1911, vol. 2, ch.128, section 7.

104 I have thus far emphasized that the preemption of land and homesteading were racialized processes in their near-categorical exclusion of aboriginal peoples from the ability to preempt land. However, it was not only aboriginal peoples who could not preempt land but also immigrants from China and, later, those who arrived from India to work as laborers in British Columbia's resource industries. The ability to own property privately through preemption of the land was a racialized phenomenon, generally speaking. For instance, section 160 of An Act Respecting the Land of the Crown stipulates that "it is unlawful for the Commissioner or other person to issue a pre-emption record of any Crown land or sell any portion thereof to any Chinese." During the late nineteenth and early twentieth centuries, Asian immigrants, who constituted a large labor force in British Columbia's natural resource industries, were also excluded from the burgeoning economy of private property relations. For an analysis of the relationship between race, immigration, labor, and nation building, see B. Singh Bolaria and Peter S. Li, *Racial Oppression in Canada* (Toronto: Garamond, 1988). For reference to discriminatory laws that were passed against Chinese and Japanese immigrants during the nineteenth and early twentieth centuries, see Joel Bakan et al., eds., *Canadian Constitutional Law*, 3rd ed. (Toronto: Emond Montgomery, 2003), 644–56.

105 Paul Tennant, *Aboriginal Peoples and Politics: The Indian Land Question in British Columbia, 1849–1989* (Vancouver: University of British Columbia Press, 1990), 34–35.

106 Tennant, *Aboriginal Peoples and Politics*, 34–35.

107 Peter Hogg, *Constitutional Law of Canada* (Toronto: Thompson Reuters, 2000), 53.

108 Hogg, *Constitutional Law of Canada*, 56.

109 Section 52(1), Constitution Act, 1982; Hogg, *Constitutional Law of Canada*, 53.

110 See Brenna Bhandar, "The First Nations of Canada Are Still Waiting for the Colonial Era to End," *Guardian*, October 21, 2013, http://www.theguardian.com/commentisfree/2013/oct/21/canada-colonial-mentality-first-nations.

111 Shin Imai, *Aboriginal Law Handbook* (Toronto: Carswell, 1999), 10.

112 John Borrows, *Nookomis' Constitution: Revitalizing Law in Canada* (Toronto: University of Toronto Press, forthcoming), chapter 3, manuscript on file with author.

113 *Delgamuukw v. British Columbia* [1997] 3 S.C.R. 1010, para. 7.

114 *Delgamuukw v. British Columbia*, para. 1.

115 John Borrows, *Recovering Canada: The Resurgence of Indigenous Law* (Toronto: University of Toronto Press, 2007), 84, 85.

116 *Delgamuukw v. British Columbia*, para. 108.

117 Borrows, *Recovering Canada*, 85.

118 *Delgamuukw v. British Columbia*, para. 143.

119 Peter R. Grant, interview with author, June 25, 2015, Vancouver, BC.

120 *Delgamuukw v. British Columbia*, para. 134.

121 *Delgamuukw v. British Columbia*, para. 114.

122 *Delgamuukw v. British Columbia*, para. 114.

123 *Delgamuukw v. British Columbia*, para. 115.

124 *Delgamuukw v. British Columbia*, para. 117.

125 *Delgamuukw v. British Columbia*, para. 125.

126 *Delgamuukw v. British Columbia*, para. 125.

127 *Delgamuukw v. British Columbia*, para. 128.

128 *Delgamuukw v. British Columbia*, para. 131.

129 *Delgamuukw v. British Columbia*, para. 148.

130 *Delgamuukw v. British Columbia*, para. 149.

131 *Delgamuukw v. British Columbia*, para. 156.

132 *Delgamuukw v. British Columbia*, para. 158.

133 *R. v. Gladstone* [1996] 2 S.C.R. 723, para. 39.

134 *R. v. Gladstone*, para. 54.

135 *Delgamuukw v. British Columbia*, para. 161.

136 *Delgamuukw v. British Columbia*, para. 161.

137 *Delgamuukw v. British Columbia*, per Chief Justice Lamer, para. 165.

138 Sherene Razack, *Dying from Improvement: Inquests and Inquiries into Indigenous Deaths in Custody* (Toronto: University of Toronto Press, 2015).

139 Razack, *Dying from Improvement*, 95.

140 *Tsilhqot'in Nation v. British Columbia* [2014] 2 S.C.R. 256, para. 72.

141 *Tsilhqot'in Nation v. British Columbia*, para. 72.

142 *Tsilhqot'in Nation v. British Columbia*, para 74. With regard to the issue of economic development on indigenous land, the court also reiterates the duty to consult with aboriginal title holders owed by the government and others that was established in *Haida Nation v. British Columbia (Minister of Forests)* [2004] 3 S.C.R. 511.

143 For the webcast of the appeal at the Supreme Court of Canada, see Web-cast 34986, July 11, 2013, http://www.scc-csc.ca/case-dossier/info/webcast -webdiffusion-eng.aspx?cas=34986.

144 Appellant factum, para. 176, on file with author.
145 Appellant factum, para. 177.
146 Appellant factum, para. 180.
147 Appellant factum, para. 38.
148 Appellant factum, para. 41.
149 Appellant factum, para. 42.
150 Appellant factum, para. 30.
151 Martin Lukacs, "The Indigenous Land Rights Ruling That Could Transform Canada," *Guardian*, October 21, 2014, http://www.theguardian.com/environment/true-north/2014/oct/21/the-indigenous-land-rights-ruling-that-could-transform-canada.
152 Blomley, *Unsettling the City*, xx.
153 *Delgamuukw v. British Columbia*, para. 82, quoting from para. 49 of *R. v. Van der Peet* [1996] 2 S.C.R. 507.
154 Borrows, *Nookomis' Constitution*, 73.

2. PROPERTIED ABSTRACTIONS

1 Hernando de Soto, *The Mystery of Capital* (Reading: Bantam Press, 2000), 6.
2 Rashmi Dyal-Chand queries the sufficiency of de Soto's explanation for the subprime mortgage crisis, which amounted to a criticism of the lack of transparency involved in the securitization of subprime mortgages. For de Soto, it was the failure to maintain the system of recording typical of property registration that was largely to blame, as it was impossible to identify and attribute risk to the chain of actors involved. The MERS system has received critical commentary by both scholars and the judiciary: see Joseph Singer, "Foreclosure and the Failures of Formality, or Subprime Mortgage Conundrums and How to Fix Them," *Connecticut Law Review* 46, no. 2 (December 2013): 497–557; *Jackson et al v. MERS Inc* 770 N.W.2d 487 (Minn. 2009). Rashmi Dyal-Chand, "Leaving the Body of Property Law? Meltdowns, Land Rushes, and Failed Economic Development," in *Hernando de Soto and Property in a Market Economy*, ed. D. Benjamin Barros (Surrey: Ashgate, 2010), 83–96.
3 Timothy Mitchell, "The Work of Economics: How a Discipline Makes Its World," *European Journal of Sociology* 46, no. 2 (2005): 297–320.
4 Dyal-Chand, "Leaving the Body of Property Law?," 92.
5 De Soto, *The Mystery of Capital*, 110.
6 Dipesh Chakrabarty, *Provincialising Europe* (Princeton, NJ: Princeton University Press, 2007); Gayatri Spivak, *A Critique of Postcolonial Reason: Toward a History of the Vanishing Present* (Cambridge, MA: Harvard University Press, 1999).
7 See, for instance, Ezra Rosser, "Anticipating de Soto: Allotment of Indian Reservations and the Dangers of Land-Titling," in *Hernando de Soto and Property in a Market Economy*, ed. D. Benjamin Barros (Surrey: Ashgate, 2010), 61–81.

8 J. Kēhaulani Kauanui, *Hawaiian Blood: Colonialism and the Politics of Sovereignty and Indigeneity* (Durham, NC: Duke University Press, 2008), 76.

9 Kēhaulani Kauanui, *Hawaiian Blood*, 76; and in relation to the use of allotment and homesteading as a means of "propelling Indians from the collective inertia of tribal membership into the progressive individualism of the American dream" in the late nineteenth-century United States, see Patrick Wolfe, *Traces of History: Elementary Structures of Race* (London: Verso, 2016), 182–83.

10 Kēhaulani Kauanui, *Hawaiian Blood*, 77.

11 Kēhaulani Kauanui, *Hawaiian Blood*, 77.

12 Kēhaulani Kauanui, *Hawaiian Blood*, 77.

13 See J. C. Altman, C. Linkhorn, and J. Clarke, "Land Rights and Development Reform in Remote Australia," discussion paper no. 276/2005 (Canberra: Centre for Aboriginal Economic Policy Research, 2005).

14 Aileen Moreton-Robinson, *The White Possessive: Property, Power, and Indigenous Sovereignty* (Minneapolis: University of Minnesota Press, 2015), 69.

15 See Ranajit Guha, *A Rule of Property for Bengal: An Essay on the Idea of Permanent Settlement* (Durham, NC: Duke University Press, 1996).

16 Geremy Forman, "Settlement of the Title in the Galilee: Dowson's Colonial Guiding Principles," *Israel Studies* 7, no. 3 (2002): 63.

17 Bill Maurer and Gabriele Schwab, *Accelerating Possession: Global Futures of Property and Personhood* (New York: Columbia University Press, 2006), 2.

18 Maurer and Schwab, *Accelerating Possession*, 1–4.

19 E. P. Thompson, *Customs in Common* (London: New Press, 1992); Ellen Meiksins Wood, *Liberty and Property: A Social History of Western Political Thought from the Renaissance to Enlightenment* (London: Verso, 2011).

20 Alain Pottage, "The Originality of Registration," *Oxford Journal of Legal Studies* 15, no. 3 (1995): 377.

21 The term "affective" is used here to denote the sentiments, emotions, and sensibilities that come to explicitly ground justifications for ownership in the work of Bentham, Blackstone, and others; namely, desires, expectations, and fear of loss and insecurity. For an excellent discussion of how affect operates in contemporary Canadian settler colonial property relations, to engender a sense of entitlement to and expectation of property ownership among settler communities, see Eva Mackey, "(Un)Settling Expectations: (Un)Certainty, Settler States of Feeling, Law and Decolonization," *Canadian Journal of Law and Society* 29, no. 2 (2014): 235–52.

22 For analysis of the imposition of a system of title by registration in colonial Bengal, see Guha, *A Rule of Property for Bengal*; for Mandate Palestine, see Zeina B. Ghandour, *A Discourse on Domination in Mandate Palestine: Imperialism, Property and Insurgency* (London: Routledge, 2009).

23 However, land registries now run the risk of being privatized, as proposed in the Neighbourhood Planning and Infrastructure Bill. It is briefly outlined in the Queen's Speech of May 2016. See https://www.gov.uk/government/uploads

/system/uploads/attachment_data/file/524040/Queen_s_Speech_2016
_background_notes_.pdf. Relatedly, the privatization of the Mortgage Electronic Registration System in the United States has been identified as a major
detriment to the interests of homeowners in their struggles against foreclosure;
see Singer, "Foreclosure and the Failures of Formality."

24 Lee Godden, "Grounding Law as Cultural Memory: A 'Proper' Account of
Property and Native Title in Australian Law and Land," *Australian Feminist Law
Journal* 19, no. 1 (2003): 61–80.

25 See David J. Hayton, *Registered Land* (London: Sweet and Maxwell, 1981),
10–12; Alfred William Brian Simpson, *An Introduction to the History of Land
Law* (Oxford: Oxford University Press, 1961), 254.

26 The Registration Act 1617 provided for a system of registration of land in
Scotland.

27 Avner Offer, *Property and Politics, 1870–1914: Land Ownership, Law, Ideology
and Urban Development in England* (Cambridge: Cambridge University Press,
1981), 69.

28 Richard Robert Torrens, *Notes on a System of Conveyancing by Registration of
Title (with instructions for the guidance of parties dealing, illustrated by copies of
the books and forms in use in the land titles office)* (Adelaide: Register and Observer General Printing Office, 1859), 6–7.

29 Offer, *Property and Politics*, 69.

30 As noted below, the Torrens system was introduced in the colony of British
Columbia in 1870, and a system of land registration was introduced into Ghana
(or the Gold Coast as it was known at the time) in 1883. See Patrick McAuslan,
Bringing the Law Back In: Essays in Land, Law and Development (Abingdon:
Ashgate, 2003), 74.

31 David Sugarman and Ronnie Warrington, "Land Law, Citizenship, and the
Invention of Englishness: The Strange World of the Equity of Redemption," in
Early Modern Conceptions of Property, ed. John Brewer and Susan Staves (Lon-
don: Routledge, 1996), 111.

32 Sugarman and Warrington, "Land Law, Citizenship, and the Invention of
Englishness," 112. See also Philip Girard, "Land Law, Liberalism, and the
Agrarian Ideal: British North America, 1750–1920," in *Despotic Dominion:
Property Rights in British Settler Societies*, ed. John MacLaren, Andrew R.
Buck, and Nancy E. Wright (Vancouver: University of British Columbia
Press, 2005), 131.

33 And presumably, in some instances, trust between individuals who were attached
to others through social and kinship relations.

34 Robert T. J. Stein and Margaret A. Stone, *Torrens Title* (London: Butterworths,
1991), 4.

35 Alain Pottage, "The Measure of Land," *Modern Law Review* 57, no. 3 (May 1994):
363.

36 Pottage, "The Measure of Land," 365.

37 Pottage, "The Measure of Land," 366. See Tithe Commission and Ordnance Survey, *First Report of the Registration and Conveyancing Commission* PP (London: House of Commons, 1850), 32.

38 Pottage, "The Measure of Land," 366.

39 *Copy of the Second Report made to His Majesty by the Commissioners appointed to inquire into the Law of England respecting Real Property*, dated 29 June 1830 (575) Sess. vol. XI, p. 1.

40 Greg Taylor, *The Law of the Land: The Advent of the Torrens System in Canada* (Toronto: University of Toronto Press, 2008), 24.

41 Torrens wrote, "If the comparative indivisibility in land constitutes a difficulty, it exists in a yet greater degree in a ship. Here also we find the characteristic of individuality. We must identify the particular ship to be transferred by a long description in the register. Here again the contingency of adverse possession requires to be guarded against. Finally the attribute of immobility renders transfer by registration more suitable for that description of property than for shipping which may be removed beyond the ken and jurisdiction of the registering officer; yet the transfer and encumbrance of shipping property through the instrumentality of registration has given universal satisfaction, ensuring certainty, simplicity and economy." Torrens, *Notes on a System of Conveyancing by Registration of Title*, 10–11.

42 Torrens, *Notes on a System of Conveyancing*, 10–11.

43 Torrens, *Notes on a System of Conveyancing*.

44 Torrens, *Notes on a System of Conveyancing*, 43.

45 Torrens, *Notes on a System of Conveyancing*, 10–11.

46 William Searle Holdsworth, *The History of English Law*, vol. 2 (London: Sweet and Maxwell, 1936), 224.

47 See, for instance, Nicholas Jickling (Customs Officer), *A Digest of the Laws of the Customs Comprising a Summary of the Statutes in Force in Great Britain and Its Foreign Dependencies Relating to Shipping, Navigation, Revenue and other matters within the cognizance of the officers of the Customs, from the earliest Period to the 53 Geo. III inclusive, Part II* (London: No. 41, Pall Mall, 1815). For a discussion of the importance of customs records to revenue collection, as customs duties provided a more reliable source of income than excise taxes or Parliament, see Mary Poovey, *A History of the Modern Fact: Problems of Knowledge in the Sciences of Wealth and Society* (Chicago: University of Chicago Press, 1998), 126.

48 Henry Thring, *A Memorandum of the Merchant Shipping Law Consolidation Bill; Pointing Out and Explaining the Points in Which the Existing Acts Are Altered* (London: George E. Eyre and William Spottoswoode, HM Stationery Office, 1854), 4–5.

49 Thring, *A Memorandum of the Merchant Shipping Law Consolidation Bill*, 4, 5.

50 Thring, *A Memorandum of the Merchant Shipping Law Consolidation Bill*, 9.

51 William Pietz, "Material Considerations: On the Historical Forensics of Contract," *Theory, Culture and Society* 19, no. 5/6 (2002): 42. On bookkeeping, see Poovey, *A History of the Modern Fact*.

52 Pottage, "The Measure of Land," 383.

53 Jonathan Levy, *Freaks of Fortune: The Emerging World of Capitalism and Risk in America* (Cambridge, MA: Harvard University Press, 2012), 99.

54 Pottage, "The Originality of Registration," 377.

55 Pottage, "The Originality of Registration," 381–82.

56 South Australia Parliamentary Debates, June 4, 1857, 202, British Library archives, London.

57 Another perceived defect with the system of conveyancing was the cost involved. The perusal of title deeds and related investigations into the land, the lucrative preserve of lawyers, was indeed expensive, and this proved particularly onerous in the colonies, where the initial outlay of expenses to obtain land were high. In the colonies of New South Wales and South Australia, immigrants would first purchase land orders that they could sell on the private market. Speculation became rife, and with an especially transient settler population in the early days of settlement, problems relating to the insecurity of title were exacerbated.

58 James Scott, *Seeing Like a State: How Certain Schemes to Improve the Human Condition Have Failed* (New Haven, CT: Yale University Press, 1998), 4.

59 Scott, *Seeing Like a State*, 35.

60 Nicholas Blomley, *Unsettling the City: Urban Land and the Politics of Property* (London: Routledge, 2003).

61 Blomley, *Unsettling the City*, 55; and see Lee Godden, "The Invention of Tradition: Property Law as a Knowledge Space for the Appropriation of the South," *Griffith Law Review* 16, no. 2 (2007): 375–410.

62 Pottage, "The Measure of Land," 363; and see Alain Pottage and Brad Sherman, *Figures of Invention: A History of Modern Patent Law* (New York: Oxford University Press, 2010), for a novel discussion of how abstraction (and Marx's labor theory of value) were central to modes of propertization in the development of patent law doctrine, particularly chapter 2.

63 Writing about the colonization and commercialization of the Mississippi Valley, Walter Johnson notes how the surveying, mapping, and sale of land was concomitant with its "racial pacification." Walter Johnson, *River of Dark Dreams: Slavery and Empire in the Cotton Kingdom* (Cambridge, MA: Harvard University Press, 2013), 34.

64 See Cole Harris, *Making Native Space: Resistance, Colonialism and Reserves in British Columbia* (Vancouver: UBC Press, 2002), and discussion of Trutch in Harris's chapter 3; Blomley, *Unsettling the City*.

65 Torrens, *Notes on a System of Conveyancing*, 13.

66 Torrens, *Notes on a System of Conveyancing*, 19.

67 *Fourth Annual Report of the Colonization Commissioners for South Australia (1839)* (London: House of Commons, 1836–40), 3.

68 *Fourth Annual Report of the Colonization Commissioners*, 4.

69 *Fourth Annual Report of the Colonization Commissioners*, 4.

70 *Fourth Annual Report of the Colonization Commissioners*, 4.

71 *Fourth Annual Report of the Colonization Commissioners*, 4.

72 Henri Lefebvre's insight that "capitalism and neo-capitalism [produce] an abstract space that is a reflection of the world of business on both a national and international level, as well as the power of money and the *politique* of the state" seems quite apt here. Henri Lefebvre, *State, Space, World: Selected Essays*, ed. N. Brenner and S. Elden, trans. G. Moore, N. Brenner, and S. Elden (Minneapolis: University of Minnesota Press, 2009), 187.

73 Torrens, *Notes on a System of Conveyancing*, 7.

74 Elizabeth Povinelli, "The Governance of the Prior," *interventions* 13, no. 1 (2011): 20.

75 See, for instance, Godden, "Grounding Law as Cultural Memory"; Blomley, *Unsettling the City*.

76 Of course, the reality of how land was used, exchanged, mortgaged, and so on was to some extent conditioned, as explored above, by a general suspicion among landowners of the fictive nature of these propertied abstractions, and resulted in a mixture of real estate practices that reflected multiple property logics.

77 Derek Sayer, *The Violence of Abstraction: The Analytical Foundations of Historical Materialism* (London: Basil Blackwell, 1987), 86.

78 Sayer, *The Violence of Abstraction*, 88.

79 Karl Marx, *Poverty of Philosophy* (1847), 154, quoted in Sayer, *The Violence of Abstraction*, chapter 2.

80 Alberto Toscano, "The Open Secret of Real Abstraction," *Rethinking Marxism: A Journal of Economics, Culture and Society* 20, no. 2 (2008): 275. See also Jordana Rosenberg, *Critical Enthusiasm: Capital Accumulation and the Transformation of Religious Passion* (Oxford: Oxford University Press, 2011), 22–25; and Alberto Toscano's thorough exploration of the way in which abstraction functions in the work of Whitehead, Stengers, and Marx in "The Culture of Abstraction," *Theory, Culture and Society* 25 (2008): 57.

81 See China Miéville, *Between Equal Rights: A Marxist Theory of International Law* (London: Pluto, 2005), 77–84; Evgeny Pashukanis, *Law and Marxism: A General Theory* (London: Pluto, 1989), 51.

82 Pashukanis, *Law and Marxism*, 51.

83 Pashukanis, *Law and Marxism*, 112.

84 For an insightful analysis of the feminist critiques of this Marxist theory of law, which obscures forms of labor that fall outside commodification, such as reproductive labor in the home, see Ruth Fletcher, "Legal Form, Commodities and Reproduction: Reading Pashukanis," in *Feminist Encounters with Legal Philosophy*, ed. Maria Drakopoulou (London: Routledge, 2013). Fletcher presents a cogent and critical reappropriation of Pashukanis's theory of law in the context of valuing women's labor in the realm of reproductive biotechnology. See Pashukanis, *Law and Marxism*, 110.

85 Pashukanis, *Law and Marxism*, 122.

86 Pashukanis, *Law and Marxism*, 110–11; see also Karl Marx, "On the Jewish Question," in *Early Writings*, trans. D. McLellan (London: Penguin, 1972), and discussion of C. B. MacPherson above.

87 Pashukanis, *Law and Marxism*, 110, 114, 119.

88 Paul Hirst, *On Law and Ideology* (London: Macmillan, 1979), 98–100.

89 Hirst, *On Law and Ideology*, 138.

90 Hirst, *On Law and Ideology*, 101.

91 Possession and occupation precede this shift, this transformation that marks the commodification of land, and eventually do not provide a justification for ownership. However, possession remains central to the lifeworld of property; notions of privilege and entitlement shape the contours of one's consciousness, based on the possession of particular qualities and characteristics that once constituted the prerequisites of one's ability to own. See Cheryl Harris, "Whiteness as Property," *Harvard Law Review* 106, no. 8 (June 1993): 1707–91.

92 Jeremy Bentham, *Theory of Legislation* (London: Kegan Paul, Trench, Trübner, 1896), 120.

93 Bentham, *Theory of Legislation*, 118–19.

94 Bentham, *Theory of Legislation*, 118.

95 Bentham, *Theory of Legislation*, 117, 116, 89.

96 Bentham, *Theory of Legislation*, 113.

97 See Laura Brace, "Colonisation, Civilisation and Cultivation: Early Victorians' Theories of Property Rights and Sovereignty," in *Land and Freedom: Law, Property Rights and the British Diaspora*, ed. A. R. Buck, John McLaren, and Nancy E. Wright (Aldershot: Ashgate, 2001), 23–38; Peter Fitzpatrick, "'No Higher Duty': *Mabo* and the Failure of Legal Foundation," *Law and Critique* 13, no. 3 (2002); Irene Watson, "Aboriginal Laws and the Sovereignty of Terra Nullius," *borderlands* 1, no. 2 (2002).

98 See Michael O'Malley, *Face Value: The Entwined Histories of Money and Race in America* (Chicago: University of Chicago Press, 2012).

99 On this issue, see Wolfe, *Traces of History*, 38–40.

100 Nancy Stepan, *The Idea of Race in Science: Great Britain, 1800–1960* (London: Macmillan, 1982), xx.

101 See A. S. Curran, *The Anatomy of Blackness: Science and Slavery in an Age of Enlightenment* (Baltimore, MD: Johns Hopkins University Press, 2011).

102 Ivan Hannaford, *Race: The History of an Idea in the West* (Baltimore, MD: Johns Hopkins University Press, 1996), 156.

103 Hannaford, *Race*, 156.

104 Mary Louise Pratt, *Imperial Eyes: Travel Writing and Transculturation* (London: Routledge, 1992). See A. W. Crosby, *The Measure of Reality: Quantification and Western Society, 1250–1600* (Cambridge: Cambridge University Press, 2007), for a history of the long development of quantification in science, mathematics, and aesthetic forms.

105 Stephen J. Gould, *The Mismeasure of Man* (New York: Norton, 1996), 56.

106 Stepan, *The Idea of Race in Science*, xvii–xviii.

107 See Colin Perrin and Kay Anderson, "Reframing Craniometry: Human Exceptionalism and the Production of Racial Knowledge," *Social Identities: Journal of Race, Nation and Culture* 19, no. 1 (2013): 90–103; Patrick Wolfe, *Settler Colonialism and the Transformation of Anthropology: The Politics and Poetics of an Ethnographic Event* (London: Cassell, 1999), 48–49; Gould, *The Mismeasure of Man*, 105–40. See Curran, *The Anatomy of Blackness*, 2, where he discusses the identification of "black bile and blood" by eighteenth-century French anatomists in their attempt to understand the "anatomical and conceptual status of blackness." For a fascinating account of how racial identity based on the notion of biological difference required, in the context of racial identity trials in the United States, the performance of whiteness or blackness, and other modes of fashioning of racial selves, see Ariela J. Gross, *What Blood Won't Tell: A History of Race on Trial in America* (Cambridge, MA: Harvard University Press, 2008); and see generally Wolfe, *Traces of History*.

108 Michel Foucault, *The Order of Things: An Archaeology of the Human Sciences* (New York: Vintage, 1994), chapter 2.

109 William H. Tucker, *The Science and Politics of Racial Research* (Chicago: University of Illinois Press, 1994), 9; Stephen Jay Gould, "The Geometer of Race," *Discover*, November 1, 1994.

110 Gould, *The Mismeasure of Man*, 66.

111 Gould, *The Mismeasure of Man*, 66.

112 Cuvier, *Recherches sur les ossemens fossils*, vol. 1 (Paris: Deterville, 1812), 105, cited in Gould, *The Mismeasure of Man*, 66.

113 Pratt, *Imperial Eyes*, 30.

114 Pratt's work provides something between a supplement and corrective to Foucault's analysis of eighteenth-century natural history, which, as she notes, "[does] not always underscore the transformative, appropriative dimensions of its conception." Pratt, *Imperial Eyes*, 31.

115 Gould, *The Mismeasure of Man*, 106.

116 Gould, *The Mismeasure of Man*, 106.

117 Hannaford, *Race*, 148.

118 Warwick Anderson, *The Cultivation of Whiteness: Science, Health and Racial Destiny in Australia* (Melbourne: Melbourne University Press, 2002), 186.

119 Anderson, *The Cultivation of Whiteness*, 195.

120 Anderson, *The Cultivation of Whiteness*, 190.

121 Wolfe, *Settler Colonialism and the Transformation of Anthropology*.

122 South Australia Parliamentary Debates, January 27, 1858, 792.

123 Shitong Quio, "Planting Houses in Shenzhen: A Real Estate Market without Legal Titles," *Canadian Journal of Law and Society*, no. 29 (2013): 253–72.

124 Forman, "Settlement of the Title in the Galilee," 63.

125 Ghandour, *A Discourse on Domination in Mandate Palestine*.

126 Ghandour, *A Discourse on Domination in Mandate Palestine*, 53.

127 Forman, "Settlement of the Title in the Galilee."

128 Martin Bunton, "'Home,' 'Colony,' 'Vilayet': Frames of Reference for the Study of Land in Mandate Palestine," paper presented at workshop, Brown University, March 2014.

129 Martha Mundy and Richard Saumarez Smith, *Governing Property, Making the Modern State: Law, Administration and Production in Ottoman Syria* (London: I. B. Tauris, 2007), 7.

130 Mundy and Saumarez Smith, *Governing Property*.

131 Bunton, "'Home,' 'Colony,' 'Vilayet.'"

132 See "Land Registration and Settlement of Rights Department," Land Regulation and Registry, Israel, accessed July 14, 2014, http://index.justice.gov.il/En/UNITS/LANDREGISTRATION/Pages/default.aspx.

133 The difference between unsettled land described here, and unregistered land in jurisdictions such as the United Kingdom, is that in the latter context, the land is automatically registered upon sale, or alternately can be initiated as a "first registration" in the land registry pursuant to its guidelines.

134 Daniel Seidemann, interview with author, Jerusalem, July 2011.

135 Seidemann, interview.

136 Seidemann, interview.

137 Elias Dauoud Khoury, interview with author, Jerusalem, July 2011.

138 Jac Isac and Fida' Abdul-Latif, *Jerusalem and the Geopolitics of De-Palestinianisation* (Jerusalem: Arab League Educational, Cultural and Scientific Organisation, 2007), 53.

139 Khoury, interview.

140 Khoury, interview.

141 See Forman, "Settlement of the Title in the Galilee."

142 In Jerusalem, the construction of the light rail system led to the expropriation of occupied land in East Jerusalem, and literally "cements the presence of settlements in East Jerusalem, making their presence more permanent and perhaps irreversible." See Hanna Baumann, "The Heavy Presence of Jerusalem Light Rail: Why Palestinian Protestors Attacked the Tracks," Open Democracy, July 6, 2014, https://opendemocracy.net/north-africa-west-asia/hanna-baumann/heavy-presence-of-jerusalem-light-rail-why-palestinian-protesters-attac.

143 Dawood Hamoudeh, interview with author, July 12, 2011; and see Nadera Shalhoub Kevorkian, "Stolen Childhood: Palestinian Children and the Structure of Genocidal Dispossession," *Settler Colonial Studies* 6, no. 2 (2016): 142–52.

144 Edward Said, *After the Last Sky* (Somerset: Butler and Tanner, 1986), 82.

3. IMPROVEMENT

1 That day, I was traveling through the area with Fazal Sheikh, Alberto Toscano, Eyal Weizman, and Ines Weizman.

2 As Haneen Naamnih has pointed out (pers. comm.), the term "unrecognized village" is a creation of the Israeli government and works to discursively situate the displaced Bedouin as a problem to be solved.

3 Oren Yiftachel, *Ethnocracy: Land and Identity Politics in Israel/Palestine* (Philadelphia: University of Pennsylvania Press, 2006), 202.

4 The Prawer Plan, or, in its most recent legislative iteration, the Prawer-Begin Bill, "will result in the destruction of 35 unrecognised Bedouin villages and the forced displacement of up to 70 000 people." Adalah, "Demolition and Eviction of Bedouin Citizens of Israel in the Naqab (Negev)—the Prawer Plan," accessed January 27, 2017, https://www.adalah.org/en/content/view/7589#What-is-the -Prawer-Plan. The plan was officially suspended in 2013, but the destruction of Bedouin villages continues into the present.

5 Shirly Deidler, "Israel Begins Razing Bedouin Village of Al-Arakib—for 50th Time," *Haaretz*, June 12, 2014, http://www.haaretz.com/news/israel /.premium-1.598414; and see Eyal Weizman and Fazal Sheikh, *The Conflict Shoreline: Colonization as Climate Change in the Negev Desert* (New York: Steidl, 2015), 9.

6 Alison Deger, "Bedouin Village Razed 83 Times Must Pay $500,000 for Demolitions, Israel Says," *Mondoweiss*, May 9, 2015, http://mondoweiss.net/2015/05 /bedouin-village-demolitions.

7 Thabet Abu Ras, "Land, Power and Resistance in Israel," lecture, Leo Baeck Institute, London, December 3, 2015.

8 Hanna Nakkarah, unpublished manuscript, on file with author, 154. Nakkarah (1912–84) was one of the first legal advocates for Palestinian rights.

9 Atheel Athameen, interview with author, Khasham Zaneh, April 2014, translator Thabet Abu Rasa.

10 Josef Fraenkl, *Herzl: A Biography* (Jerusalem: Ararat, 1946), 111, 126.

11 Gabriel Piterberg, *Returns of Zionism: Myths, Politics and Scholarship in Israel* (New York: Verso, 2008).

12 Piterberg, *Returns of Zionism*, 65, 85.

13 Shlomo Avineri, *Arlosoroff* (London: Peter Halban, 1989), 46.

14 Alex Bein, ed., *Arthur Ruppin: Memoirs, Diaries, Letters*, trans. Karen Gershon (London: Weidenfeld and Nicolson, 1971), 22–24.

15 Bein, *Arthur Ruppin*, xiii.

16 Bein, *Arthur Ruppin*, 60–63.

17 Bein, *Arthur Ruppin*, 75–76.

18 Bein, *Arthur Ruppin*, 76.

19 Arthur Ruppin, *The Agricultural Colonisation of the Zionist Organisation in Palestine* (London: M. Hopkinson, 1926), 5.

20 Ruppin, *The Agricultural Colonisation*, 23.

21 Ruppin, *The Agricultural Colonisation*, 5–6.

22 Ruppin, *The Agricultural Colonisation*, 2, 66–68.

23 Ruppin, *The Agricultural Colonisation*, 2.

24 The focus on the specific exploitation of women recurs throughout Ruppin's writings, and the significance that Ruppin places on women's role in the colonization effort is discussed below.

25 Ruppin, *The Agricultural Colonisation*, 3.

26 Ruppin, *The Agricultural Colonisation*, 28–29.

27 Ruppin, *The Agricultural Colonisation*, 28–29.

28 Ruppin, *The Agricultural Colonisation*, 29. The notion of possessive nationalism can be understood as a corollary of possessive individualism. The psychoaffective dimensions of the possessive individual, including the desire to possess exclusively, to fulfill the need for security and to calm the fear of losing one's property, are transmuted to the stage of the nation-state; the possessive individual develops a close identification with national identity. Frank Cunningham describes possessive nationalism as a coalescence of the "worst aspects of national or ethnic chauvinism and aggressive capitalism" with the values of the self-possessive individual, including greed and selfishness. Frank Cunningham, "Could Canada Turn into Bosnia?," in *Cultural Identity and the Nation-State*, ed. Carol C. Gould and Pasquale Pasquino (Lanham, MD: Rowman and Littlefield, 2001), 36–37. Judith Butler observes, in relation to Palestine, "In the early years of Zionism, it was clear that Jews invoked Lockean principles to claim that because they worked the land and established irrigation networks, this labouring activity implied rights of ownership, even rights of national belonging grounded on territory. We can see how, in fact, the aims of both the nation and the colony depended upon an ideology of possessive individualism that was recast as possessive nationalism." Athena Athanasiou and Judith Butler, *Dispossession: The Performative in the Political* (London: Polity, 2013), chapter 1.

29 Ruppin, *The Agricultural Colonisation*, 33.

30 Amos Morris-Reich, "Arthur Ruppin's Concept of Race," *Israel Studies* 11, no. 3 (fall 2006): 1–30.

31 Arthur Ruppin, *Three Decades of Palestine: Speeches and Papers on the Upbuilding of the Jewish National Home* (Jerusalem: Schocken, 1936), 78–79.

32 Ruppin, *Three Decades of Palestine*, 78.

33 Morris-Reich, "Arthur Ruppin's Concept of Race," 11.

34 Reproduced in Morris-Reich, "Arthur Ruppin's Concept of Race," 20.

35 Ruppin, *The Agricultural Colonisation*, 51.

36 Ella Shohat, "The Narrative of the Nation and the Discourse of the Modernization: The Case of the Mizrahim," *Critique: Critical Middle Eastern Studies* 6, no. 10 (1997): 11.

37 Ruppin, *The Agricultural Colonisation*, 134–35.

38 Fraenkel, *Herzl*, 70.

39 Fraenkel, *Herzl*, 75–76.

40 Theodor Herzl, *The Jewish State* (1896), trans. Sylvie D'Avigdo, 15–16, MidEast-Web, http://www.mideastweb.org/jewishstate.pdf.

41 Herzl, *The Jewish State*, 16.

42 Walid Khalidi, "The Jewish-Ottoman Land Company: Herzl's Blueprint for the Colonisation of Palestine," *Journal of Palestine Studies* 22, no. 2 (winter 1993): 30.

43 Khalidi, "The Jewish-Ottoman Land Company," 31.

44 Articles 1 and 2, Khalidi, "The Jewish-Ottoman Land Company," 44.

45 Khalidi, "The Jewish-Ottoman Land Company," 33–34. See Stuart Banner, where he argues that the colonization of New Zealand occurred primarily through the use of contracts that enabled individuals to make truly massive land purchases on behalf of colonization companies. Stuart Banner, "Conquest by Contract: Wealth Transfer and Land Market Structure in Colonial New Zealand," *Law and Society Review* 34, no. 1 (2000): 47–96.

46 The Anglo-Palestine Bank went on to become Bank Leumi, one of the most important banks in Israel and a core part of what would become the capitalist class. Adam Hanieh, personal correspondence, December 10, 2015.

47 Fraenkel, *Herzl*, 71.

48 Ruppin, *Three Decades of Palestine*, 148.

49 The tension of using private-law mechanisms for the acquisition of land held collectively by an ethnonational entity produced certain legal complexities. For instance, until 1920, there was no legal recognition of cooperative activity in Palestine. As of 1920, the Kvutzah, the primary type of cooperative agricultural settlement in Palestine, gained the right to be registered as a cooperative society with a definite legal status. However, when the American professor Mead visited Palestine in 1923 on the invitation of Ruppin, he identified the lack of contracts between individual settlers and the colonization company as a dangerous omission; it was virtually impossible to account for the financial obligations owed by settlers to the companies that had supported their endeavors financially. Investing in Palestine could hardly be an attractive proposition for Jews in the diaspora under these conditions. Ruppin, *The Agricultural Colonisation*, 172.

50 Gershon Shafir, *Land, Labor and the Origins of the Israeli-Palestinian Conflict, 1882–1914* (Cambridge: Cambridge University Press, 1989), 41.

51 Shafir, *Land, Labor and the Origins*, 23.

52 Shafir, *Land, Labor and the Origins*, 33–34.

53 Shafir, *Land, Labor and the Origins*, 29.

54 Shafir, *Land, Labor and the Origins*, 41; and see Patrick Wolfe, "Purchase by Other Means: The Palestine *Nakba* and Zionism's Conquest of Economics," *Settler Colonial Studies* 2, no. 1 (2012): 155–59.

55 Wolfe, "Purchase by Other Means," 153.

56 Carlo Ginzburg, preface to Amnon Raz-Krakotzkin, *Exil et Souveraineté: Judaïsme, sionisme, et pensée binationale* (Paris: La Fabrique, 2007), 11.

57 Amnon Raz-Krakotzkin, "Exile, History and the Nationalisation of Jewish Memory: Some Reflections on the Zionist Notion of History and Return," *Journal of Levantine Studies* 3, no. 2 (winter 2013): 42.

58 Raz-Krakotzkin, "Exile, History and the Nationalisation of Jewish Memory," 42.

59 Piterberg, *Returns of Zionism*, 78.

60 Ruppin, *The Agricultural Colonisation*, 127.

61 Patrick Wolfe, in discussing the conquest of labor as a primary strategy of settlement in Palestine, argued that it was sustained ideologically through the figure of the "New Jew, whose distinctive iconography bore the marks of the extreme national-isms that were emerging in Europe." This observation is accompanied by a Jewish National Fund poster calling for Zionist colonization of the Galilee from 1938 titled "The New Jew" and depicts a strong, muscular man wielding an axe as he looks across at a plowed field and mountains. Wolfe, "Purchase by Other Means," 152.

62 *Israel's Agriculture*, a pamphlet produced by Orit Noked, Minister of Agriculture and Rural Development (Tel Aviv: The Israel Export and International Coopera-tion Institute), 8, http://www.a-id.org/pdf/israel-s-agriculture.pdf.

63 Michael Palgi, "Organization in Kibbutz Industry," in *Crisis in the Israeli Kib-butz: Meeting the Challenge of Changing Times*, ed. U. Leviatan, H. Oliver, and J. Quarter (New York: Praeger, 1998).

64 Ivan Vallier, "Social Change in the Kibbutz Economy," *Economic Development and Cultural Change* 10, no. 4 (July 1962): 341–42.

65 Vallier, "Social Change in the Kibbutz Economy," 343.

66 Palgi, "Organization in Kibbutz Industry."

67 Palgi, "Organization in Kibbutz Industry."

68 Tobias Buck, "The Rise of the Capitalist Kibbutz," *Financial Times*, January 26, 2010, http://www.ft.com/cms/s/0/d50b3c20-0a19-11df-8b23-00144feabdc0 .html#axzz3gXdG9hgy.

69 Yiftachel, *Ethnocracy*, 144.

70 Noked, *Israel's Agriculture*, 30.

71 See Hussein Abu Hussein and Fiona McKay, *Access Denied: Palestinian Land Rights in Israel* (London: Zed, 1993); Raja Shehadeh, *Occupier's Law: Israel and the West Bank* (Beirut: Institute for Palestine Studies, 1988); George Bisharat, "Land, Law and Legitimacy and the Occupied Territories," *American University Law Review* 43 (1994): 467–561; Salman Abu Sitta, *An Atlas of Palestine, 1917–1966* (London: Palestine Land Society, 2010).

72 Abu Sitta, *An Atlas of Palestine*, 1.

73 Abu Sitta, *An Atlas of Palestine*, 54.

74 Abu Sitta, *An Atlas of Palestine*, 54.

75 Abu Sitta, *An Atlas of Palestine*, 56.

76 Abu Sitta, *An Atlas of Palestine*, 141.

77 Abu Sitta, *An Atlas of Palestine*, 142.

78 However, Oren Yiftachel, Alexandre (Sandy) Kedar, and Ahmad Amara argue that the 1858 reforms merely codified already existing practices in land owner-ship. Oren Yiftachel, Alexandre (Sandy) Kedar, and Ahmad Amara, "Question-ing the 'Dead (*Mewat*) Negev Doctrine': Property Rights in Arab Bedouin Space," paper prepared for "Socio-Legal Perspectives on the Passage to Moder-nity in the Middle East," Ben Gurion University, Be'er Sheba, June 2012, 13, on file with author.

79 Bisharat, "Land, Law and Legitimacy," 493–94.

80 Nakkarah, unpublished manuscript, 141.

81 Bisharat, "Land, Law and Legitimacy," 494.

82 Bisharat, "Land, Law and Legitimacy"; Alexandre (Sandy) Kedar, "The Legal Transformation of Ethnic Geography: Israeli Law and the Palestinian Landholder 1948–1967," *NYU Journal of International Law and Politics* 33, no. 4 (2001): 933.

83 Kedar, "The Legal Transformation of Ethnic Geography," 933.

84 Sami Hadawi, *Land Ownership in Palestine* (New York: Palestine Arab Refugee Office, 1957), 12–14. Sami Hadawi worked at the Mandatory Land Registration Office and the Land Settlement Department until he was forced into exile in 1948.

85 Nakkarah, unpublished manuscript, 144.

86 Oren Yiftachel, "'Ethnocracy' and Its Discontents: Minorities, Protests and the Israeli Polity," *Critical Inquiry* 26, no. 4 (summer 2000): 725–56.

87 Zeina B. Ghandour, *A Discourse on Domination in Mandate Palestine: Imperialism, Property and Insurgency* (London: Routledge, 2009), see discussion in chapter 2.

88 Martin Bunton, *Land Legislation in Palestine* (Cambridge: Cambridge University Press, 2009).

89 Nakkarah, unpublished manuscript; Abu Sitta, *An Atlas of Palestine*; Yiftachel, "'Ethnocracy' and Its Discontents."

90 Abu Sitta, *An Atlas of Palestine*, 46.

91 Abu Sitta, *An Atlas of Palestine*, 49.

92 Ahmad Amara, Ismael Abu-Saad, and Oren Yiftachel, eds., *Indigenous (In)Justice: Human Rights Law and Bedouin Arabs in the Naqab/Negev* (Cambridge, MA: Harvard University Press, 2013), 28.

93 Amara, Abu-Saad, and Yiftachel, *Indigenous (In)Justice*, 42.

94 Amara, Abu-Saad, and Yiftachel, *Indigenous (In)Justice*, 42.

95 Amara, Abu-Saad, and Yiftachel, *Indigenous (In)Justice*.

96 Abu Sitta, *An Atlas of Palestine*, 46–48.

97 Bunton, *Land Legislation in Palestine*, 55; and see Kedar, "The Legal Transformation of Ethnic Geography," 936.

98 Yiftachel, Kedar, and Amara, "Questioning the 'Dead (*Mewat*) Negev Doctrine,'" 4.

99 See Abu Sitta, *An Atlas of Palestine*; Bisharat, "Land, Law and Legitimacy"; Kedar, "The Legal Transformation of Ethnic Geography."

100 Bisharat, "Land, Law and Legitimacy," 490.

101 Ronen Shamir, "Suspended in Space: Bedouins under the Law of Israel," *Law and Society Review* 30 (1996): 236.

102 Yiftachel, Kedar, and Amara, "Questioning the 'Dead (*Mewat*) Negev Doctrine,'" 2. For a detailed analysis of some of these judgments, see Kedar, "The Legal Transformation of Ethnic Geography." Kedar analyzes the ethnocratic definitions of landholding that transform the mewat doctrine into a tool of

expropriation of Bedouin lands, exposing the inherently political nature of the Israeli land regime.

103 See, for example, John Borrows, *Recovering Canada: The Resurgence of Indigenous Law* (Toronto: University of Toronto Press, 2007); Irene Watson, "Aboriginal Laws and the Sovereignty of Terra Nullius," *borderlands* 1, no. 2 (2002), http://www.borderlands.net.au/vol1no2_2002/watson_laws.html.

104 Alex Reilly, "From a Jurisprudence of Regret to a Regrettable Jurisprudence: Shaping Native Title from *Mabo* to *Ward*," *Murdoch University Electronic Journal of Law* 9, no. 4 (December 2002), http://www.austlii.edu.au/au/journals /MurUEJL/2002/50.html.

105 For further discussion, see Brenna Bhandar and Rafeef Ziadah, "Acts and Omissions: Framing Settler Colonialism in Palestine Studies," *Jadaliyya*, January 14, 2016, http://roundups.jadaliyya.com/pages/index/23569/acts-and-omissions _framing-settler-colonialism-in-.

106 The subheading is taken from the title of a publication by Suhad Bishara and Haneen Naamnih, *Nomads against Their Will: The Attempted Expulsion of the Arab Bedouin in the Naqab: The Example of Atir-Umm al-Hieran* (Haifa: Adalah, Arab Centre for Minority Rights, 2011). This report sets out in great detail the means by which the Bedouin have been cast out of their land and homes, focusing on the case of al-Hieran in particular, rendering them "nomads against their will."

107 *The State of Israel v. Tzalach Badaran*, P.D. 16(3) 1717 [1962], 2.

108 Kedar, "The Legal Transformation of Ethnic Geography," 955.

109 *The State of Israel v. Tzalach Badaran*, P.D. 16(3) 1717 [1962], 2.

110 David Lloyd, *Irish Culture and Colonial Modernity, 1800–2000* (Cambridge: Cambridge University Press, 2011), 61.

111 Lloyd, *Irish Culture and Colonial Modernity*, 62.

112 Weizman and Sheikh, *The Conflict Shoreline*, 55.

113 *Badaran*, 2.

114 Kedar, "The Legal Transformation of Ethnic Geography," 961.

115 Kedar, "The Legal Transformation of Ethnic Geography," 961.

116 Kedar, "The Legal Transformation of Ethnic Geography," 962.

117 See Kedar, "The Legal Transformation of Ethnic Geography," 964–65.

118 *Selim 'Ali Agdi'a al-Huashela et al. v. State of Israel* [1984], Civil Appeal No. 218/74.

119 Aharon Ben-Shemesh, *Land Law in the State of Israel* (Masadeh, 1953), cited in *al-Huashela v. State of Israel* (1984), para. 3.

120 Moshe Doukhan, *Land Law in Israel*, 2nd ed. (Ahva, 1952), 47, cited in *al-Huashela v. State of Israel* (1984), para. 3.

121 *Al-Huashela v. State of Israel* (1984), para. 4.

122 See Shamir, "Suspended in Space."

123 Weizman and Sheikh, *The Conflict Shoreline*, 54–55.

124 Bishara and Naamnih, *Nomads against Their Will*, 5.

125 Weizman and Sheikh, *The Conflict Shoreline*, 46.
126 *Al-Uqbi v. the State of Israel* (2015), para. 29.
127 *Al-Uqbi v. the State of Israel* (2015), para. 29.
128 *Al-Uqbi v. the State of Israel* (2015), para. 15.
129 *Al-Uqbi v. the State of Israel* (2015), para. 40.
130 *Al-Uqbi v. the State of Israel* (2015), para. 41.
131 *Al-Uqbi v. the State of Israel* (2015), para. 41.
132 *Al-Uqbi v. the State of Israel* (2015), para. 41.
133 *Al-Uqbi v. the State of Israel* (2015), para. 42.
134 Evidenced by the voluminous amount of Mandate-era correspondence, reports, and ordinances established in order to survey and register the land surrounding Be'er Sheva, which was driven by the needs, as noted above, to improve cultivation and settle land rights in a determinate way. See Bunton, *Land Legislation in Palestine*.
135 Aziz Alturi, interview with author, al-Araqib, April 2014.
136 Here I refer to the specific settlers encroaching on Palestinian land in the West Bank that is under the jurisdiction of the Palestinian Authority, as opposed to the general category of Israeli settlers.

4. STATUS

1 *McIvor v. The Registrar, Indian and Northern Affairs, Canada* [2007] BCSC 827, para. 7.
2 The British Columbia Court of Appeal radically narrowed the basis upon which Madame Justice Ross's judgment was made, by restricting the group of people against which those in McIvor's position were to be compared. Whereas Madame Justice Ross found that the registration provisions of the 1985 Indian Act "continue to prefer descendants who trace their Indian ancestry along the paternal line over those who trace their Indian ancestry along the maternal line" (para. 7), the Court of Appeal decided that the matrilineal and patrilineal dimensions of status determination were not "analogous grounds" under the charter (para. 99–100), and that the case was to be adjudicated simply on the basis of sex discrimination under section 15 of the charter. Finding that section 6 was discriminatory on the basis of sex, the Court of Appeal went on to find that the discrimination applied only to "the group caught in the transition between the old regime and the new one" (para. 122). They narrowed the question to whether section 6(1) of the 1985 Registration Provisions was underinclusive. They found, under the section 1 analysis (a four-part test devised to determine whether the charter violation is legally justifiable), that section 6(1) did not "minimally impair" the rights of Sharon McIvor's son, Mr. Grismer. The comparator group were those who had a modified status as a result of the Double Mother rule, a 1951 amendment which provided that children whose mother and paternal grandmothers had not been entitled to status except through marriage to an Indian man would have Indian status only to the age of twenty-one. This restriction was reversed in 1985 but created a distinction between the comparator

group and those in Mr. Grismer's position, that is, those whose mothers had been disenfranchised on the basis of marrying non-Indian men. It was on this much narrower basis that the Court of Appeal found a charter violation in favor of Mr. Grismer and his mother, Sharon McIvor.

3 Here, I draw on Foucault's concept of the *dispositif*, defined as a "certain manipulation of relations of forces, of a rational and concrete intervention in the relations of forces, either so as to develop them in a particular direction, or to block them, to stabilize them, and to utilise them." Indian status can be described as an apparatus insofar as it incorporates juridical processes, relations of power, and colonial forms of knowledge, in order to assert a hegemonic and strategic form of control over the lives of First Nations people. See Michel Foucault, *Power/ Knowledge: Selected Interviews and Other Writings, 1972–1977*, ed. Colin Gordon (New York: Pantheon, 1980), 194–96.

4 Joanne Barker, *Native Acts: Law, Recognition, and Cultural Authenticity* (Durham, NC: Duke University Press, 2011), 22, emphasis in original.

5 Barker, *Native Acts*, 5.

6 Barker, *Native Acts*, 82.

7 Aileen Moreton-Robinson, *The White Possessive: Property, Power, and Indigenous Sovereignty* (Minneapolis: University of Minnesota Press, 2015), 50.

8 Moreton-Robinson, *The White Possessive*, 50.

9 Davina Bhandar, "Decolonising the Politics of Status: When the Border Crosses Us," *Darkmatter* 14 (2016), http://www.darkmatter101.org/site/2016/05/16 /decolonising-the-politics-of-status-when-the-border-crosses-us/.

10 William Alexander Hunter, *Introduction to Roman Law* (London: W. Maxwell and Son, 1897), 129.

11 Stuart Elden, *The Birth of Territory* (Chicago: University of Chicago Press, 2013), 220–21.

12 Alain Pottage, "Law after Anthropology: Object and Technique in Roman Law," *Theory, Culture and Society* 31, no. 2–3 (March–May 2014): 147–66.

13 Elden, *The Birth of Territory*, 234–35.

14 Elden, *The Birth of Territory*, 221.

15 Hunter, *Introduction to Roman Law*, 670.

16 Orlando Patterson, *Slavery and Social Death: A Comparative Study* (Cambridge, MA: Harvard University Press, 1982), 30.

17 Patterson, *Slavery and Social Death*, 89.

18 Patterson, *Slavery and Social Death*, 31.

19 William Blackstone, *Commentaries on the Laws of England* (London: Routledge, 2001), 18.

20 Blackstone, *Commentaries on the Laws of England*, 31.

21 Blackstone, *Commentaries on the Laws of England*, 31.

22 Blackstone, *Commentaries on the Laws of England*, 17.

23 Carl Schmitt, *Constitutional Theory*, ed. and trans. J. Seitzer (Durham, NC: Duke University Press, 2008), 118, emphasis added.

24 Schmitt, *Constitutional Theory*, 118.
25 And see John Weaver, "Concepts of Economic Improvement and the Social Construction of Property Rights: Highlights from the English-Speaking World," in *Despotic Dominion: Property Rights in British Settler Societies*, ed. Andrew R. Buck, John MacLaren, and Nancy E. Wright (Vancouver: UBC Press, 2004).
26 The debates of the first Canadian Parliament in 1867 are rife with preoccupation about the viability of commercial exchange and markets, generally reflecting a view of political economy that accords with Adam Smith's emphasis on commercial exchange in a free market as the basis of economic development. See House of Commons Debates, 1st Parliament, 1st Session, Library of Parliament, 1867–68, http://parl.canadiana.ca/view/oop.debates_HOCo101_01/1?r=0&s=1.
27 John Milloy, "Indian Act Colonialism: A Century of Dishonour, 1869–1969" (Ottawa: National Centre for First Nations Governance, 2008), 2–4.
28 Milloy, "Indian Act Colonialism," 4, 6.
29 Milloy, "Indian Act Colonialism."
30 Shelagh Day, "The Charter and Family Law," in *Family in Canada: New Directions*, ed. E. Sloss (Ottawa: Canadian Advisory Council on the Status of Women, 1985), cited in *McIvor v. The Registrar*, para. 12; Glen Coulthard, *Red Skin, White Masks: Rejecting the Colonial Politics of Recognition* (Minneapolis: University of Minnesota Press, 2014).
31 *McIvor v. The Registrar*, para. 16.
32 Audrey Huntley and Fay Blaney, *Bill C-31: Its Impact, Implications and Recommendations for Change in British Columbia—Final Report* (Vancouver: Aboriginal Women's Action Network, 1999), 6.
33 See, for instance, Patricia Monture-Angus, *Journeying Forward: Dreaming First Nations' Independence* (Winnipeg: Fernwood, 1997); Emma La Roque, "The Colonisation of a Native Woman Scholar," in *Women of the First Nations: Power, Wisdom, and Strength*, ed. Christine Miller and Patricia Chuchryk (Winnipeg: University of Manitoba Press, 1996); Andrea Smith, *Conquest: Sexual Violence and the American Indian Genocide* (Boston: South End, 2005).
34 Sarah Carter, *Capturing Women: The Manipulation of Cultural Imagery in Canada's Prairie West* (Montreal: McGill-Queen's University Press, 1997), 51–52.
35 Bonita Lawrence, *"Real" Indians and Others: Mixed-Blood Urban Native Peoples and Indigenous Nationhood* (Lincoln: University of Nebraska Press, 2004), 73.
36 Lawrence, *"Real" Indians and Others*, 73.
37 Saidiya Hartman, *Scenes of Subjection: Terror, Slavery and Self-Making in Nineteenth-Century America* (Oxford: Oxford University Press, 1997), 195.
38 Smith, *Conquest*; Sherene Razack, "Gendered Racial Violence and Spatialized Justice: The Murder of Pamela George," in *Race, Space and the Law: Unmapping a White Settler Society*, ed. Sherene Razack (Toronto: Between the Lines, 2002).
39 Lawrence, *"Real" Indians and Others*, 47.
40 Lawrence, *"Real" Indians and Others*.

41 See discussion of homesteading in chapter 1.

42 Indian Act, 1886, section 85.

43 Indian Act, 1886, section 88; and see Lawrence, *"Real" Indians and Others*. The Act for the Gradual Civilization of the Indian Tribes in the Canadas, 1857, had as its aim the gradual assimilation of First Nations peoples into white society. The stated objectives of this act were to gradually bestow citizenship upon Indian subjects and thereby remove all legal distinctions between "Indians" and other "Canadian Subjects." Ironically, this act came into force at the same time that the category of Indian was legislated into being, a category of subjects that were defined as noncitizens. Although this act applied to Upper and Lower Canada, it did have consequences for native communities in the west (J. R. Miller, *Skyscrapers Hide the Heavens: A History of Indian-White Relations in Canada* [Toronto: University of Toronto Press, 2000], 139–40). The new dominion legislation in 1869, the Gradual Enfranchisement Act, set out similar requirements for the enfranchisement of the Indian population.

44 Robert Nichols, "Contract and Usurpation: Enfranchisement and Racial Governance in Settler-Colonial Contexts," in *Theorizing Native Studies*, ed. Audra Simpson and Andrea Smith (Durham, NC: Duke University Press, 2014), 105.

45 Nichols, "Contract and Usurpation," 105.

46 Nichols, "Contract and Usurpation," 106.

47 Nichols, "Contract and Usurpation," 105.

48 C. B. Macpherson, *The Political Theory of Possessive Individualism: Hobbes to Locke* (Oxford: Oxford University Press, 1962), 264.

49 James Tully, *An Approach to Political Philosophy: Locke in Contexts* (Cambridge: Cambridge University Press, 1993), 82.

50 Tully, *An Approach to Political Philosophy*, 138.

51 Neal Wood, *John Locke and Agrarian Capitalism* (Berkeley: University of California Press, 1984).

52 Tully, *An Approach to Political Philosophy*, 150; Barbara Arneil, *John Locke and America: The Defence of English Colonialism* (Oxford: Clarendon, 1996).

53 The idea that property is relational is a fairly standard way of understanding ownership. As Kevin Gray and Susan Frances Gray write in their widely consulted textbook, *Elements of Land Law*, "property law [is] a network of jural relationships between individuals in respect of valued resources." Kevin Gray and Susan Frances Gray, *Elements of Land Law* (Oxford: Oxford University Press, 2005), 5. The idea of absolute ownership, where the owner has exclusive power over the object of ownership, derives from the Roman law concept of *dominium* and has little relevance to the contemporary operation of the common law of property.

54 Gray and Gray, *Elements of Land Law*, 69–72, 426.

55 Étienne Balibar, " 'Possessive Individualism' Reversed: From Locke to Derrida," *Constellations* 9, no. 3 (2002): 303.

56 Étienne Balibar, *Identity and Difference: John Locke and the Invention of Consciousness*, trans. Warren Montag (London: Verso, 2013), 41; Jordana Rosenberg,

Critical Enthusiasm: Capital Accumulation and the Transformation of Religious Passion (Oxford: Oxford University Press, 2011), 38–39.

57 John Locke, *The Two Treatises of Government* (Cambridge: Cambridge University Press, 1960), 330, para. 28.

58 Locke, *The Two Treatises of Government*, 332, para. 31, emphasis in original.

59 Locke, *The Two Treatises of Government*, 334, para. 36.

60 Locke, *The Two Treatises of Government*, 341, para. 45.

61 Balibar, "'Possessive Individualism' Reversed," 303. A fairly standard interpretation of the Lockean subject is that it is abstract, bounded, and nonrelational. For instance, Margaret Davies discusses Macpherson's theory of the possessive individual and asserts that the "self has been defined through the idea of property: in this sense, we are said to be self-owning individuals, bounded, autonomous and distinct." Margaret Davies, *Property: Meanings, Histories, Theories* (Abingdon: Routledge-Cavendish, 2007), 26. Radin notes that self-consciousness for Locke is characterized by memory but argues that a "pure Lockean conception of personhood does not necessarily imply that object-relations . . . are essential to the constitution of persons, because that conception is disembodied enough not to stress our differentiation from one another." For Radin, Locke's concept of the person has "no inherent connection to the material world." Margaret Jane Radin, *Reinterpreting Property* (Chicago: University of Chicago Press, 1993), 42.

62 Locke, *The Two Treatises of Government*, para. 123.

63 Balibar, "'Possessive Individualism' Reversed," 303.

64 Balibar, "'Possessive Individualism' Reversed," 302.

65 Balibar, "'Possessive Individualism' Reversed," 302.

66 Balibar, *Identity and Difference*, 41.

67 Denise Ferreira da Silva, *Towards a Global History of Race* (Minneapolis: University of Minnesota Press, 2007).

68 Ferreira da Silva, *Towards a Global History of Race*, 60–61.

69 John Locke, *An Essay Concerning Human Understanding*, ed. Peter H. Nidditch (Oxford: Oxford University Press, 1998), x, emphasis added.

70 Locke, *An Essay Concerning Human Understanding*, 145.

71 Locke, *The Two Treatises of Government*, 328, 331.

72 Locke, *An Essay Concerning Human Understanding*, 44.

73 Locke, *An Essay Concerning Human Understanding*, 45.

74 We could contrast this with the temporality of recognition evident in First Nations' rights claims. Anne McClintock's term "anachronistic space" comes to mind here, where First Nations' cultural practices and relationships to land have been cast into the prehistory of modern law and sovereignty in the context of section 35 jurisprudence. See Brenna Bhandar, "Anxious Reconciliation(s): Unsettling Foundations and Spatializing History," *Society and Space* 22, no. 6 (2004): 831–45.

75 Balibar, *Identity and Difference*, 87.

76 Balibar, *Identity and Difference*, 87–88.

77　Mahmoud Darwish, *Journal of an Ordinary Grief*, trans. Ibrahim Muhawi (New York: Archipelago, 2010).

78　Indian Act, 1886, section 34.

79　Sections 30 through 32 provide penalties for the sale of "any grain or root crops or other produce" from reserves in the province of Manitoba, the North-West Territories, or the district of Keewatin. People who bought such crops or other produce contrary to the regulations were also liable to a monetary penalty or a short period of incarceration (Indian Act, 1886, section 30(2)). The harvesting and sale of timber, a very valuable natural resource, was strictly controlled by the colonial government. The superintendent general had the power to grant licenses (to anyone) to cut trees on reserves and ungranted Indian lands (section 54). The licensee was granted the right to "take and keep exclusive possession of the land so described subject to such regulations as are made" (section 56).

80　Indian Act, 1886, section 70.

81　Indian Act, 1886, section 73.

82　Status Indians living on reserve were given an annuity (an annual payment) by the federal government in an amount determined by the government.

83　Indian Act, 1886, section 81.

84　*Report of the Royal Commission on Aboriginal Peoples*, vol. 1: *Looking Forward, Looking Back* (Ottawa: Minister of Supply and Services, 1996), 279–86.

85　Indian Act, R.S.C. 1886, section 9–13.

86　The Indian Advancement Act, R.S.C. 1886, ch.44, sections 5 and 6.

87　John Lutz, "After the Fur Trade: The Aboriginal Labouring Class of British Co-lumbia 1849–1890," *Journal of the Canadian Historical Association* 3, no. 1 (1992): 69–93; James K. Burrows, "'A Much-Needed Class of Labour': The Economy and Income of the Southern Interior Plateau Indians, 1897–1910," *BC Studies* 71 (1986): 27–46.

88　Renisa Mawani, *Colonial Proximities: Crossracial Encounters and Juridical Trusts in British Columbia, 1871–1921* (Vancouver: University of British Columbia Press, 2009), 43; Lutz, "After the Fur Trade," 77.

89　Lutz, "After the Fur Trade," 81.

90　Mawani, *Colonial Proximities*, 46.

91　Lutz, "After the Fur Trade," 91.

92　Elizabeth Furniss, *The Burden of History: Colonialism and the Frontier Myth in a Rural Canadian Community* (Vancouver: University of British Columbia Press, 1999), 42.

93　Coulthard, *Red Skin, White Masks*, 85–88.

94　*The Attorney General of Canada v. Jeanette Lavalle, Richard Isaac et al. v. Ivonne Bedard* [1974] S.C.R. 1349; *Sandra Lovelace v. Canada, Communication No. R.6/24*, U.N. Doc. Supp. No. 40 (A/36/40) at 166 [1981].

95　*Lovelace v. Canada*, para. 13.2. For a much more thorough analysis of these cases as well as *Bédard v. Isaac* (1972), see Lawrence, *Real Indians and Others*, and Coulthard, *Red Skin, White Masks*, who in different ways place these cases in the longer history of First Nations women's resistance to the effects of the patriarchal settler colonial system.

96 Pamela Palmater, *Beyond Blood: Rethinking Indigenous Identity* (Saskatoon: Purich, 2011), 105.

97 McIvor was successful at trial, but on appeal, the scope of the trial judgment's vindication of her rights was narrowed dramatically. Her leave to appeal to the Supreme Court of Canada was denied.

98 *McIvor v. Canada* [2009] BCCA, 306 DLR (4th) 193, paras. 152–61.

99 See Library of Parliament, Legislative Summary, Bill C-3: Gender Equity in Indian Registration, November 15, 2010, http://www.parl.gc.ca/content/lop /legislativesummaries/40/3/40-3-c3-e.pdf.

100 Huntley and Blaney, *Bill C-31*, 9; James Anaya, "Report of the Special Rapporteur on the Rights of Indigenous Peoples, Addendum: The Situation of Indigenous Peoples in Canada" (New York: United Nations Human Rights Council, 2014), 16, http://www.ohchr.org/Documents/Issues/IPeoples/SR/A.HRC.27.52.Add.2 -MissionCanada_AUV.pdf.

101 Minister of Indian and Northern Affairs, *Impacts of the 1985 Amendments to the Indian Act (Bill C-31) Summary Report* (Ottawa: Ministry of Indian Affairs and Northern Development, 1990), iv. For an exemplary instance of the racially discriminatory nature of band membership rules, see *Jacobs v. Mohawk Council of Kahnawake* [1998] Canadian Human Rights Tribunal. Peter Jacobs's biological parents were black and Jewish, but he was adopted by two Mohawk Indians as a baby. He was raised in the Mohawk community and was schooled in Mohawk laws, traditions, and customs. When he was twenty-one, however, he was denied band membership on the basis that he was not racially or ethnically Mohawk.

102 Palmater, *Beyond Blood*.

103 Coulthard, *Red Skin, White Masks*, 95.

104 Lawrence, *"Real" Indians and Others*; Simpson, *Mohawk Interruptus*.

105 Palmater, *Beyond Blood*.

106 See *McIvor v. The Registrar* and *McIvor v. Canada*.

107 David Roediger and Elizabeth Esch, *The Production of Difference: Race and the Management of Labour in U.S. History* (Oxford: Oxford University Press, 2012).

108 Nadia Abu El-Haj, *The Genealogical Science: Genetics, the Origins of the Jews, and the Politics of Epistemology* (Chicago: University of Chicago Press, 2012).

109 Constantine George Caffentzis, *Clipped Coins, Abused Words and Civil Government* (New York: Autonomedia, 1989); Michel Foucault, *The Order of Things: An Archaeology of the Human Sciences* (London: Vintage, 1994).

110 In addition to the legal cases discussed above, Palmater notes that the Native Women's Association of Canada, for instance, has called outright for the repeal of section 6(2)'s second generation cutoff. Palmater, *Beyond Blood*, 128.

111 See Monture-Angus, *Journeying Forward*; Coulthard, *Red Skin, White Masks*; and Lawrence, *"Real" Indians and Others*, among others.

1 For example, see Joseph Singer, "Foreclosure and the Failures of Formality, or Sub-prime Mortgage Conundrums and How to Fix Them," *Connecticut Law Review* 46, no. 2 (2013): 497–559, for analysis of the Mortgage Electronic Registration System and its dire effects on people affected by the subprime mortgage crisis.

2 Avery F. Gordon, *Ghostly Matters: Haunting and the Sociological Imagination* (Minneapolis: University of Minnesota Press, 1997).

3 Heather Laird, for instance, in *Subversive Law in Ireland, 1879–1920: From "Unwritten Law" to the Dáil Courts* (Dublin: Four Courts, 2005), argues that Irish resistance to the imposition of agrarian capitalist property relations led to the creation of counterlegalities. Also see Peter Linebaugh, *Stop Thief! The Commons, Enclosures and Resistance* (Oakland, CA: PM Press, 2014).

4 Roderick Ferguson, *The Reorder of Things: The University and Its Pedagogies of Minority Difference* (Minneapolis: University of Minnesota Press, 2012); David Roediger and Elizabeth Esch, *The Production of Difference: Race and the Management of Labour in U.S. History* (Oxford: Oxford University Press, 2012); Miguel de Oliver, "Gentrification as the Appropriation of Therapeutic 'Diversity': A Model and Case Study of the Multicultural Amenity of Contemporary Urban Renewal," *Urban Studies* 53, no. 6 (2016): 1299–1316.

5 Nicholas Blomley, *Unsettling the City: Urban Land and the Politics of Property* (London: Routledge, 2003), 114.

6 Blomley, *Unsettling the City*, 114.

7 André van der Walt, *Property in the Margins* (Oxford: Hart, 2009), 15.

8 Van der Walt, *Property in the Margins*, 22.

9 Van der Walt, *Property in the Margins*, 43. This question could also be posed to other antieviction movements such as the Plataforma de Afectados por la Hipoteca in Spain, who have in some places halted evictions, taken over empty residential buildings to provide homes for the evicted, and started to negotiate with banks on how to formalize the rights of those in occupancy of residential buildings where they currently have no formal tenancy rights.

10 Examples, enumerated by Blomley among others, include "nuisance law (empowering the state to access private property in the interests of public aesthetics and hygiene, for example); the law of adverse possession (placing a time limit on the owners' right to exclude); the doctrine of public or private necessity (requiring an owner to allows others onto their property in moments of extreme need); the law of airplane over-flights . . . and the right to roam (allowing recreational access to certain wilderness areas)." Nicholas Blomley, "The Territory of Property," *Progress in Human Geography* 40, no. 5 (2016): 593–609.

11 Van der Walt, *Property in the Margins*, 161.

12 Van der Walt, *Property in the Margins*, 159.

13 Laurine Platzky and Cherryl Walker, *The Surplus People Project* (Johannesburg: Ravan, 1985), 80–83.

14 On labor requirements, see Platzky and Walker, *The Surplus People Project*, 83.
15 Gilbert Marcus, "Section 5 of the Black Administration Act: The Case of the Bakwena ba Mogopa," in *No Place to Rest: Forced Removals and the Law in South Africa*, ed. Christina Murray and Catherine O'Regan (Oxford: Oxford University Press, 1990), 13.
16 Platzky and Walker, *The Surplus People Project*, 74.
17 Platzky and Walker, *The Surplus People Project*, 80–81.
18 Platzky and Walker, *The Surplus People Project*, 81.
19 Platzky and Walker, *The Surplus People Project*, 83–84; Colin Bundy, "Land, Law and Power: Forced Removals in Historical Context," in *No Place to Rest: Forced Removals and the Law in South Africa*, ed. C. Murray and C. O'Regan (Oxford: Oxford University Press, 1990), 6.
20 Section 5(1)(b), Native Administration Act of 1927, as quoted in Marcus, "Section 5 of the Black Administration Act," 18.
21 Marcus, "Section 5 of the Black Administration Act," 19.
22 Platzky and Walker, *The Surplus People Project*, 92.
23 Platzky and Walker, *The Surplus People Project*, 89.
24 Platzky and Walker, *The Surplus People Project*, 90.
25 Michael Sutcliffe, Alison Todes, and Norah Walker, "State Urbanisation Strategies since 1986," in *No Place to Rest: Forced Removals and the Law in South Africa*, ed. C. Murray and C. O'Regan (Oxford: Oxford University Press, 1990), 98.
26 Van der Walt, *Property in the Margins*, 54.
27 Van der Walt, *Property in the Margins*, 56.
28 Van der Walt, *Property in the Margins*, 74.
29 Van der Walt puts the constitutional and legislative changes in South Africa into a comparative perspective with the political squatting movements of the 1970s and 1980s in the Netherlands, Germany, and England, and also makes brief reference to civil rights activism in the United States, in order to evaluate some of the political successes gained in housing and tenancy laws in the Netherlands and Germany, and the end of legalized racial segregation in the United States. Van der Walt, *Property in the Margins*, 146.
30 Constitution of the Republic of South Africa, Act no. 108 of 1996, section 26(3); see van der Walt, *Property in the Margins*, 147.
31 *Port Elizabeth Municipality v. Various Occupiers* [2005] 1 (SA) 217 (CC), para. 9.
32 *Port Elizabeth Municipality v. Various Occupiers*, para. 2.
33 *Port Elizabeth Municipality v. Various Occupiers*, para. 2.
34 *Port Elizabeth Municipality v. Various Occupiers*, para. 3.
35 *Port Elizabeth Municipality v. Various Occupiers*, para. 59.
36 *Port Elizabeth Municipality v. Various Occupiers*, para. 15.
37 *Port Elizabeth Municipality v. Various Occupiers*, para. 23.
38 Van der Walt, *Property in the Margins*, 158–59.
39 Van der Walt, *Property in the Margins*, 161.

40 Bradley Bryan, "Property as Ontology: Aboriginal and English Understandings of Ownership," *Canadian Journal of Law and Jurisprudence* 13, no. 1 (January 2000): 3–31.

41 Leanne Simpson, "Land as Pedagogy: Nishnaabeg Intelligence and Rebellious Transformation," *Decolonisation: Indigeneity, Education and Society* 3, no. 3 (2014), http://decolonization.org/index.php/des/article/view/22170.

42 Simpson, "Land as Pedagogy," 6.

43 Simpson, "Land as Pedagogy," 6.

44 Simpson, "Land as Pedagogy," 7.

45 Brenna Bhandar, "Anxious Reconciliation(s): Unsettling Foundations and Spatializing History," *Environment and Planning D: Society and Space* 22 (2004): 831–45.

46 See Patricia J. Williams, *The Alchemy of Race and Rights: The Diary of a Law Professor* (Cambridge, MA: Harvard University Press, 1991), 164–65.

47 Eva Mackey, *Unsettled Expectations: Uncertainty, Land and Settler Decolonization* (Halifax: Fernwood, 2016), 127.

48 Mackey, *Unsettled Expectations*, 125–27.

49 Avery Gordon, *The Hawthorn Archives: Letters from the Utopian Margins* (New York: Fordham University Press, 2017), 112, manuscript on file with author.

50 Cedric J. Robinson, *Black Movements in America* (London: Routledge, 1997), 13.

51 Robin D. G. Kelley, *Freedom Dreams: The Black Radical Imagination* (Boston: Beacon, 2003), 101.

52 Kelley, *Freedom Dreams*, 101.

53 Gordon, *The Hawthorn Archives*, 52.

54 Gordon, *The Hawthorn Archives*, 52.

55 Gordon, *The Hawthorn Archives*, 184.

56 Gordon, *The Hawthorn Archives*, 184.

57 Frederick Douglass, *Narrative of the Life of Frederick Douglass* (Oxford: Oxford University Press, 2009), 81.

58 Douglass, *Narrative of the Life of Frederick Douglass*, 82.

59 Richard Wright, *Twelve Million Black Voices* (New York: Basic Books, 2008), 33.

Bibliography

Abu El-Haj, Nadia. *The Genealogical Science: Genetics, the Origins of the Jews, and the Politics of Epistemology*. Chicago: University of Chicago Press, 2012.

Abu Hussein, Hussein, and Fiona McKay. *Access Denied: Palestinian Land Rights in Israel*. London: Zed, 1993.

Abu Sitta, Salman. *An Atlas of Palestine, 1917–1966*. London: Palestine Land Society, 2010.

Agamben, Giorgio. *The Highest Poverty: Monastic Rules and Forms of Life*. Stanford, CA: Stanford University Press, 2013.

Aguilar, Delia. "From Triple Jeopardy to Intersectionality: The Feminist Perplex." *Comparative Studies of South Asia, Africa and the Middle East* 32, no. 2 (2012): 415–48.

Alemany, Adrià, and Ada Colau. *Mortgaged Lives*. Los Angeles: Journal of Aesthetics and Protest Press, 2014.

Alexander, Gregory. *Commodity and Propriety: Competing Visions of Property in American Legal Thought, 1776–1970*. Chicago: University of Chicago Press, 1997.

Althusser, Louis. *For Marx*. London: Verso, 2005.

Altman, J. C., C. Linkhorn, and J. Clarke. "Land Rights and Development Reform in Remote Australia." Discussion paper no. 276/2005. Canberra: Centre for Aboriginal Economic Policy Research, 2005.

Amara, Ahmad, Ismael Abu-Saad, and Oren Yiftachel, eds. *Indigenous (In)Justice: Human Rights Law and Bedouin Arabs in the Naqab/Negev*. Cambridge, MA: Harvard University Press, 2013.

Anaya, James. "Report of the Special Rapporteur on the Rights of Indigenous People." New York: United Nations Human Rights Council, 27th session, May 7, 2014.

Anderson, J. Stuart. *Lawyers and the Making of English Land Law, 1832–1940*. Oxford: Clarendon, 1992.

Anderson, Warwick. *The Cultivation of Whiteness: Science, Health and Racial Destiny in Australia*. Melbourne: Melbourne University Press, 2002.

Arneil, Barbara. *John Locke and America: The Defence of English Colonialism*. Oxford: Clarendon, 1996.

Athanasiou, Athena, and Judith Butler. *Dispossession: The Performative in the Political*. London: Polity, 2013.

Avineri, Shlomo. *Arlosoroff*. London: Peter Halban, 1989.

Bacon, Francis. *Novum Organum: Or, A True Guide to the Interpretation of Nature*. London: Bell and Daldy, 1859.

Bakan, Joel, et al., eds. *Canadian Constitutional Law*, 3rd ed. Toronto: Emond Montgomery, 2003.

Balibar, Étienne. *Cinq études de matérialisme historique*. Paris: Francois Maspéro, 1974.

Balibar, Étienne. *Identity and Difference: John Locke and the Invention of Consciousness*. Translated by Warren Montag. London: Verso, 2013.

Balibar, Étienne. " 'Possessive Individualism' Reversed: From Locke to Derrida." *Constellations* 9, no. 3 (2002): 299–317.

Banner, Stuart. "Conquest by Contract: Wealth Transfer and Land Market Structure in Colonial New Zealand." *Law and Society Review* 34, no. 1 (2000): 47–96.

Barker, Joanne. *Native Acts: Law, Recognition and Cultural Authenticity*. Durham, NC: Duke University Press, 2011.

Barnard, T. C. "Sir William Petty as Kerry Ironmaster." *Proceedings of the Royal Irish Academy Section C: Archeology, Celtic Studies, History, Linguistics, Literature* 82C (1982): 1–32.

Bein, Alex, ed. *Arthur Ruppin: Memoirs, Diaries, Letters*. Translated by Karen Gershon. London: Weidenfeld and Nicolson, 1971.

Bentham, Jeremy. *Theory of Legislation*. London: Kegan Paul, Trench, Trübner, 1896.

Bernier, François. "The Division of the Earth According to the Different Types of Races of Men Who Inhabit It." *History Workshop*, no. 51 (spring 2001): 247–50 (originally published 1684).

Bhandar, Brenna. "Anxious Reconciliation(s): Unsettling Foundations and Spatializing History." *Environment and Planning D: Society and Space* 22, no. 6 (2004): 831–45.

Bhandar, Brenna. "Resisting the Reproduction of the Proper Subject of Rights: Recognition, Property Relations and the Movement towards Post-colonialism in Canada." PhD diss., University of London, 2007.

Bhandar, Brenna, and Davina Bhandar. "Cultures of Dispossession: Rights, Status and Identities." *Darkmatter* 14 (2016). http://www.darkmatter101.org/site/2016/05/16/cultures-of-dispossession/.

Bhandar, Brenna, and Alberto Toscano. "Race, Real Estate and Real Abstraction." *Radical Philosophy* 194 (November/December 2015): 8–17.

Bhandar, Brenna, and Rafeef Ziadah. "Acts and Omissions: Framing Settler Colonialism in Palestine Studies." *Jadaliyya*, January 14, 2016. http://www.jadaliyya.com /pages/index/23569/acts-and-omissions_framing-settler-colonialism-in-.

Bhandar, Davina. "Decolonising the Politics of Status: When the Border Crosses Us." *Darkmatter* 14 (2016). http://www.darkmatter101.org/site/2016/05/16 /decolonising-the-politics-of-status-when-the-border-crosses-us/.

The Bill on London: Or, the Finance of Trade by Bills of Exchange. London: Gillett Brothers Discount Company Ltd., 1952.

Birge, Silma, and Patricia Hill Collins. *Intersectionality*. London: Polity, 2016.

Birla, Ritu. *Stages of Capital: Law, Culture, and Market Governance in Late Colonial India*. Durham, NC: Duke University Press, 2009.

Bishara, Suahd, and Haneen Naamnih. *Nomads against Their Will: The Attempted Expulsion of the Arab Bedouin in the Naqab: The Example of Atir-Umm al-Hieran*. Haifa: Adalah, Arab Centre for Minority Rights, 2011.

Bisharat, George. "Land, Law and Legitimacy and the Occupied Territories." *American University Law Review* 43 (1994): 467–561.

Blackstone, William. *Commentaries on the Laws of England*. London: Routledge, 2001.

Blomley, Nicholas. "The Boundaries of Property: Complexity, Relationality, and Spatiality." *Law and Society Review* 50, no. 1 (2016): 224–55.

Blomley, Nicholas. "The Territory of Property." *Progress in Human Geography* 40, no. 5 (2016): 593–609.

Blomley, Nicholas. *Unsettling the City: Urban Land and the Politics of Property*. London: Routledge, 2003.

Bolaria, B. Singh, and Peter S. Li. *Racial Oppression in Canada*. Toronto: Garamond, 1988.

Borrows, John. *Nookomis' Constitution: Revitalizing Law in Canada*. Toronto: University of Toronto Press, forthcoming.

Borrows, John. *Recovering Canada: The Resurgence of Indigenous Law*. Toronto: University of Toronto Press, 2007.

Boylan, Thomas A., and Timothy P. Foley. *Political Economy and Colonial Ireland: The Propagation and Ideological Function of Economic Discourse in the Nineteenth Century*. London: Routledge, 1992.

Brace, Laura. "Colonisation, Civilisation and Cultivation: Early Victorians' Theories of Property Rights and Sovereignty." In *Land and Freedom: Law, Property Rights and the British Diaspora*, edited by A. R. Buck, John McLaren, and Nancy E. Wright, 23–38. Aldershot: Ashgate, 2001.

Brace, Laura. *The Politics of Property: Labour, Freedom and Belonging*. Edinburgh: Edinburgh University Press, 2004.

Brah, Avtar. *Cartographies of Diaspora: Contesting Identities*. London: Routledge, 1996.

Bryan, Bradley. "Property as Ontology: Aboriginal and English Understandings of Ownership." *Canadian Journal of Law and Jurisprudence* 13, no. 1 (2000): 3–31.

Bundy, Colin. "Land, Law and Power: Forced Removals in Historical Context." In *No Place to Rest: Forced Removals and the Law in South Africa*, edited by C. Murray and C. O'Regan, 3–13. Oxford: Oxford University Press, 1990.

Bunton, Martin. "'Home,' 'Colony,' 'Vilayet': Frames of Reference for the Study of Land in Mandate Palestine." Paper presented at workshop, Brown University, March 2014.

Bunton, Martin. *Land Legislation in Palestine*. Cambridge: Cambridge University Press, 2009.

Burrows, James K. "'A Much-Needed Class of Labour': The Economy and Income of the Southern Interior Plateau Indians, 1897–1910." *BC Studies*, no. 71 (1986): 27–46.

Byrd, Jodi. *The Transit of Empire: Indigenous Critiques of Colonialism*. Minneapolis: University of Minnesota Press, 2011.

Caffentzis, George G. *Clipped Coins, Abused Words and Civil Government: John Locke's Philosophy of Money*. New York: Autonomedia, 1989.

Carter, Sarah. *Capturing Women: The Manipulation of Cultural Imagery in Canada's Prairie West*. Montreal: McGill-Queen's University Press, 1997.

Chakrabarty, Dipesh. *Provincialising Europe: Postcolonial Thought and Historical Difference*. Princeton, NJ: Princeton University Press, 2007.

Cotterrell, Roger. "Power, Property and the Law of Trusts: A Partial Agenda for Critical Legal Scholarship." *Journal of Law and Society* 14, no. 1 (1987): 77–85.

Coulthard, Glen. *Red Skin, White Masks: Rejecting the Colonial Politics of Recognition*. Minneapolis: University of Minnesota Press, 2014.

Crosby, A. W. *The Measure of Reality: Quantification and Western Society, 1250–1600*. Cambridge: Cambridge University Press, 2007.

Cunningham, Frank. "Could Canada Turn into Bosnia?" In *Cultural Identity and the Nation-State*, edited by Carol C. Gould and Pasquale Pasquino. Lanham, MD: Rowman and Littlefield, 2001.

Curran, Andrew S. *The Anatomy of Blackness: Science and Slavery in an Age of Enlightenment*. Baltimore, MD: Johns Hopkins University Press, 2011.

Darwish, Mahmoud. *Journal of an Ordinary Grief*. Translated by Ibrahim Muhawi. New York: Archipelago, 2010.

Davies, Margaret. *Property: Meanings, Histories, Theories*. Abingdon: Routledge-Cavendish, 2007.

Day, Shelagh. "The Charter and Family Law." In *Family in Canada: New Directions*, edited by E. Sloss, 27–61. Ottawa: Canadian Advisory Council on the Status of Women, 1985.

Dayan, Colin. *The Law Is a White Dog: How Legal Rituals Make and Unmake Persons*. Princeton, NJ: Princeton University Press, 2011.

de Oliver, Miguel. "Gentrification as the Appropriation of Therapeutic 'Diversity': A Model and Case Study of the Multicultural Amenity of Contemporary Urban Renewal." *Urban Studies* 53, no. 6 (2016): 1299–316.

de Soto, Hernando. *The Mystery of Capital*. Reading: Bantam Press, 2000.

Douglass, Frederick. *Narrative of the Life of Frederick Douglass*. Oxford: Oxford University Press, 2009.

Dyal-Chand, Rashmi. "Leaving the Body of Property Law? Meltdowns, Land Rushes, and Failed Economic Development." In *Hernando de Soto and Property in a Market Economy*, edited by D. Benjamin Barros, 83–96. Surrey: Ashgate, 2010.

Elden, Stuart. *The Birth of Territory*. Chicago: University of Chicago Press, 2013.

Fanon, Frantz. *The Wretched of the Earth*. London: Penguin, 2001.

Federici, Silvia. *Revolution at Point Zero: Housework, Reproduction, and Feminist Struggle*. Oakland, CA: PM Press / Common Notions, 2012.

Ferguson, Roderick. *The Reorder of Things: The University and Its Pedagogies of Minority Difference*. Minneapolis: University of Minnesota Press, 2012.

Ferreira da Silva, Denise. *Towards a Global History of Race*. Minneapolis: University of Minnesota Press, 2007.

Fisher, Robin. *Contact and Conflict: Indian-European Relations in British Columbia, 1774–1890*. 2nd ed. Vancouver: University of British Columbia Press, 1992.

Fisher, Robin. "Joseph Trutch and Indian land Policy." *BC Studies*, no. 12 (winter 1971–72): 12–16.

Fitzmaurice, Edmond. *The Life of Sir William Petty, 1623–1687*. London: Murray, 1895.

Fitzpatrick, Peter. *Modernism and the Grounds of Law*. Cambridge: Cambridge University Press, 2001.

Fitzpatrick, Peter. *The Mythology of Modern Law*. London: Routledge, 1992.

Fitzpatrick, Peter. " 'No Higher Duty': *Mabo* and the Failure of Legal Foundation." *Law and Critique* 13, no. 3 (2002): 233–52.

Fletcher, Ruth. "Legal Form, Commodities and Reproduction: Reading Pashukanis." In *Feminist Encounters with Legal Philosophy*, edited by Maria Drakopoulou, 138–57. London: Routledge, 2013.

Forman, Geremy. "Settlement of the Title in the Galilee: Dowson's Colonial Guiding Principles." *Israel Studies* 7, no. 3 (2002): 63.

Foucault, Michel. *The Order of Things: An Archaeology of the Human Sciences*. New York: Vintage, 1994.

Foucault, Michel. *Power/Knowledge: Selected Interviews and Other Writings, 1972–1977*. Edited by Colin Gordon. New York: Pantheon, 1980.

Foucault, Michel. *The Punitive Society*. Basingstoke: Palgrave Macmillan, 2015.

Fox, Adam. "Sir William Petty, Ireland, and the Making of a Political Economist, 1653–87." *Economic History Review*, New Series, 62, no. 2 (May 2009): 388–404.

Fraenkl, Josef. *Herzl: A Biography*. Jerusalem: Ararat, 1946.

Frank, Thomas. "Exploring the Boundaries of Law in the Middle Ages: Franciscan Debates on Poverty, and Inheritance." *Law and Literature* 20, no. 2 (summer 2008): 243–60.

Franklin, Sarah. *Dolly Mixtures: The Remaking of Genealogy*. Durham, NC: Duke University Press, 2007.

Furniss, Elizabeth. *The Burden of History: Colonialism and the Frontier Myth in a Rural Canadian Community*. Vancouver: University of British Columbia Press, 1999.

Ghandour, Zeina. *A Discourse on Domination in Mandate Palestine: Imperialism, Property and Insurgency*. London: Routledge, 2009.

Gilmore, Ruth Wilson. "Fatal Couplings of Power and Difference: Notes on Racism and Geography." *Professional Geographer* 54, no. 1 (2002): 15–24.

Gilmore, Ruth Wilson. *The Golden Gulag: Prisons, Surplus, Crisis, and Opposition in Globalizing California*. Berkeley: University of California Press, 2007.

Gilroy, Paul. *After Empire: Melancholia or Convivial Culture?* London: Routledge, 2004.

Girard, Philip. "Land Law, Liberalism, and the Agrarian Ideal: British North America, 1750–1920." In *Despotic Dominion: Property Rights in British Settler Societies*, edited by John MacLaren, Andrew R. Buck, and Nancy E. Wright, 120–43. Vancouver: University of British Columbia Press, 2005.

Godden, Lee. "Grounding Law as Cultural Memory: A 'Proper' Account of Property and Native Title in Australian Law and Land." *Australian Feminist Law Journal* 19, no. 1 (2003): 61–80.

Godden, Lee. "The Invention of Tradition: Property Law as a Knowledge Space for the Appropriation of the South." *Griffith Law Review* 16, no. 2 (2007): 375–410.

Gordon, Avery F. *Ghostly Matters: Haunting and the Sociological Imagination*. Minneapolis: University of Minnesota Press, 1997.

Gordon, Avery F. *The Hawthorn Archives: Letters from the Utopian Margins*. New York: Fordham University Press, 2017.

Gordon, Avery F. " 'I'm Already in a Sort of Tomb': A Reply to Philip Scheffner's *The Halfmoon Files*." *South Atlantic Quarterly* 110, no. 1 (winter 2011): 121–54.

Gordon, Avery F. "The Prisoner's Curse." In *Towards a Sociology of the Trace*, 17–57. Minneapolis: University of Minnesota Press, 2010.

Gould, Stephen J. "The Geometer of Race." *Discover*, November 1, 1994.

Gould, Stephen J. *The Mismeasure of Man*. New York: Norton, 1996.

Gray, Kevin, and Susan Gray. *Elements of Land Law*. Oxford: Oxford University Press, 2005.

Gross, Ariela J. *What Blood Won't Tell: A History of Race on Trial in America*. Cambridge, MA: Harvard University Press, 2008.

Guha, Ranajit. *A Rule of Property for Bengal: An Essay on the Idea of Permanent Settlement*. Durham, NC: Duke University Press, 1996.

Hadawi, Sami. *Land Ownership in Palestine*. New York: Palestine Arab Refugee Office, 1957.

Haldar, Piyel. *Law, Orientalism and Postcolonialism: The Jurisdiction of the Lotus Eaters*. London: Routledge, 2007.

Hall, Stuart. "Gramsci's Relevance for the Study of Race and Ethnicity." *Journal of Communication Inquiry* 10, no. 5 (1986): 5–27.

Hall, Stuart. "Race, Articulation and Societies Structured in Dominance." In *Sociological Theories: Race and Colonialism*, edited by UNESCO, 305–45. Paris: UNESCO, 1980.

Hall, Stuart. "Signification, Representation, Ideology: Althusser and Post-structuralist Debates." *Critical Studies in Mass Communication* 2, no. 2 (June 1985): 91–114.

Hanieh, Adam. *Lineages of Revolt: Issues of Contemporary Capitalism in the Middle East*. London: Haymarket, 2013.

Hannaford, Ivan. *Race: The History of an Idea in the West*. Baltimore, MD: Johns Hopkins University Press, 1996.

Harris, Cheryl. "Whiteness as Property." *Harvard Law Review* 106, no. 8 (June 1993): 1707–91.

Harris, Cole. *Making Native Space: Resistance, Colonialism and Reserves in British Columbia*. Vancouver: UBC Press, 2002.

Hartman, Saidiya. *Scenes of Subjection: Terror, Slavery and Self-Making in Nineteenth-Century America*. Oxford: Oxford University Press, 1997.

Hayton, David J. *Registered Land*. London: Sweet and Maxwell, 1981.

Herzl, Theodor. *The Jewish State* (1896). Translated by Sylvie D'Avigdo. MidEastWeb. http://www.mideastweb.org/jewishstate.pdf.

Hirst, Paul. *On Law and Ideology*. London: Macmillan, 1979.

Hogg, Peter. *Constitutional Law of Canada*. Toronto: Thompson Reuters, 2000.

Holdsworth, William Searle. *The History of English Law*, vol. 2. London: Sweet and Maxwell, 1936.

Hooykaas, R. "The Rise of Modern Science: When and Why?" In *The Scientific Revolution*, edited by Marcus Hellyer, 19–43. Oxford: Blackwell, 2003.

Hunter, William Alexander. *Introduction to Roman Law*. London: W. Maxwell and Son, 1897.

Huntley, Audrey, and Fay Blaney. *Bill C-31: Its Impact, Implications and Recommendations for Change in British Columbia—Final Report*. Vancouver: Aboriginal Women's Action Network, 1999.

Hussain, Nasser. *The Jurisprudence of Emergency: Colonialism and the Rule of Law*. Ann Arbor: University of Michigan Press, 2003.

Imai, Shin. *Aboriginal Law Handbook*. Toronto: Carswell, 1999.

Isac, Jac, and Fida' Abdul-Latif. *Jerusalem and the Geopolitics of De-Palestinianisation*. Jerusalem: Arab League Educational, Cultural and Scientific Organisation, 2007.

Jickling, Nicholas (Customs Officer). *A Digest of the Laws of the Customs Comprising a Summary of the Statutes in Force in Great Britain and Its Foreign Dependencies Relating to Shipping, Navigation, Revenue and other matters within the cognizance of the officers of the Customs, from the earliest Period to the 53 Geo. III inclusive, Part II*. London: No. 41, Pall Mall, 1815.

Johnson, Walter. *River of Dark Dreams: Slavery and Empire in the Cotton Kingdom*. Cambridge, MA: Harvard University Press, 2013.

Kedar, Alexandre (Sandy). "The Legal Transformation of Ethnic Geography: Israeli Law and the Palestinian Landholder 1948–1967." *NYU Journal of International Law and Politics* 33, no. 4 (2001): 923–1000.

Kēhaulani Kauanui, J. *Hawaiian Blood: Colonialism and the Politics of Sovereignty and Indigeneity*. Durham, NC: Duke University Press, 2008.

Kelley, Robin D. G. *Freedom Dreams: The Black Radical Imagination*. Boston: Beacon, 2003.

Kelley, Robin D. G. "What Did Cedric Robinson Mean by Racial Capitalism?" *Boston Review*, January 12, 2017.

Khalidi, R., and S. Samour. "Neoliberalism as Liberation: The Statehood Programme and the Remaking of the Palestinian National Movement." *Journal of Palestine Studies* 40, no. 2 (2011): 6–25.

Khalidi, Walid. "The Jewish-Ottoman Land Company: Herzl's Blueprint for the Colonisation of Palestine." *Journal of Palestine Studies* 22, no. 2 (winter 1993): 30–47.

Laird, Heather. *Subversive Law in Ireland, 1879–1920: From "Unwritten Law" to the Dáil Courts*. Dublin: Four Courts, 2005.

La Roque, Emma. "The Colonisation of a Native Woman Scholar." In *Women of the First Nations: Power, Wisdom, and Strength*, edited by Christine Miller and Patricia Chuchryk. Winnipeg: University of Manitoba Press, 1996.

Lawrence, Bonita. *"Real" Indians and Others: Mixed-Blood Urban Native Peoples and Indigenous Nationhood*. Lincoln: University of Nebraska Press, 2004.

Lefebvre, Henri. *State, Space, World: Selected Essays*. Edited by N. Brenner and S. Elden. Translated by G. Moore, N. Brenner, and S. Elden. Minneapolis: University of Minnesota Press, 2009.

Levy, Jonathan. *Freaks of Fortune: The Emerging World of Capitalism and Risk in America*. Cambridge, MA: Harvard University Press, 2012.

Linebaugh, Peter. *Stop Thief! The Commons, Enclosures and Resistance*. Oakland, CA: PM Press, 2014.

Lloyd, David. *Irish Culture and Colonial Modernity, 1800–2000*. Cambridge: Cambridge University Press, 2011.

Lloyd, David. *Irish Times: Temporalities of Modernity*. Dublin: Field Day, 2008.

Lloyd, David, and Patrick Wolfe. "Settler Colonial Logics and the Neoliberal Regime." *Settler Colonial Studies* 6, no. 2 (2016): 109–18.

Locke, John. *An Essay Concerning Human Understanding*. Edited by Peter H. Nidditch. Oxford: Oxford University Press, 1998.

Locke, John. *The Two Treatises of Government*. Cambridge: Cambridge University Press, 1960.

Lowe, Lisa. *The Intimacy of Four Continents*. Durham, NC: Duke University Press, 2015.

Lutz, John. "After the Fur Trade: The Aboriginal Labouring Class of British Columbia 1849–1890." *Journal of the Canadian Historical Association* 3, no. 1 (1992): 69–93.

Lynch, Hollis R. "Sir Joseph William Trutch, a British-American Pioneer on the Pacific Coast." *Pacific Historical Review* 30, no. 3 (August 1961): 243–55.

Mackey, Eva. *Unsettled Expectations: Uncertainty, Land and Settler Decolonization*. Halifax: Fernwood, 2016.

Mackey, Eva. "(Un)Settling Expectations: (Un)Certainty, Settler States of Feeling, Law and Decolonization." *Canadian Journal of Law and Society* 29, no. 2 (2014): 235–52.

Macklem, Patrick. *Indigenous Difference and the Constitution of Canada*. Toronto: University of Toronto Press, 2001.

Macpherson, C. B. *The Political Theory of Possessive Individualism: Hobbes to Locke.* Oxford: Oxford University Press, 1962.

Mamdani, Mahmood. *Citizen and Subject: Contemporary Africa and the Legacy of Late Colonialism.* Princeton, NJ: Princeton University Press, 1996.

Mamdani, Mahmood. *Define and Rule: Native as Political Identity.* W. E. B. Du Bois Lectures. Cambridge, MA: Harvard University Press, 2012.

Mamdani, Mahmood. *Saviours and Survivors: Darfur, Politics, and the War on Terror.* New York: Pantheon, 2009.

Mamdani, Mahmood. *When Victims Become Killers: Colonialism, Nativism and the Genocide in Rwanda.* Princeton, NJ: Princeton University Press, 2002.

Marcus, Gilbert. "Section 5 of the Black Administration Act: The Case of the Bakwena ba Mogopa." In *No Place to Rest: Forced Removals and the Law in South Africa,* edited by Christina Murray and Catherine O'Regan. Oxford: Oxford University Press, 1990.

Marx, Karl. *Capital,* vol. 1. London: Penguin, 1990.

Marx, Karl. *Grundrisse: Foundations of the Critique of Political Economy.* Translated by Martin Nicolaus. London: Penguin, 1993.

Marx, Karl. "On the Jewish Question." In *Early Writings,* translated by D. McLellan. London: Penguin, 1972.

Maurer, Bill, and Gabriele Schwab. *Accelerating Possession: Global Futures of Property and Personhood.* New York: Columbia University Press, 2006.

Maurer, Sara L. *The Dispossessed State: Narratives of Ownership in 19th-Century Britain and Ireland.* Baltimore, MD: Johns Hopkins University Press, 2012.

Mawani, Renisa. *Colonial Proximities: Crossracial Encounters and Juridical Trusts in British Columbia, 1871–1921.* Vancouver: University of British Columbia Press, 2009.

Mbembe, Achille. *On the Postcolony.* Los Angeles: University of California Press, 2001.

McAuslan, Patrick. *Bringing the Law Back In: Essays in Land, Law and Development.* Abingdon: Ashgate, 2003.

McLaren, John, Andrew R. Buck, and Nancy E. Wright, eds. *Despotic Dominion: Property Rights in British Settler Societies.* Vancouver: University of British Columbia Press, 2005.

McNeil, Kent. *Common Law Aboriginal Title.* Oxford: Clarendon, 1989.

Meiksins Wood, Ellen. *Liberty and Property: A Social History of Western Political Thought from the Renaissance to Enlightenment.* London: Verso, 2011.

Mendyk, Stanley G. *Speculum Britanniae: Regional Study, Antiquarianism, and Science in Britain to 1700.* Toronto: University of Toronto Press, 1989.

Miéville, China. *Between Equal Rights: A Marxist Theory of International Law.* London: Pluto, 2005.

Miller, J. R. *Skyscrapers Hide the Heavens: A History of Indian-White Relations in Canada.* Toronto: University of Toronto Press, 2000.

Milloy, John. "Indian Act Colonialism: A Century of Dishonour, 1869–1969." Ottawa: National Centre for First Nations Governance, 2008.

Mitchell, Timothy. *Rule of Experts: Egypt, Techno-politics, Modernity.* Berkeley: University of California Press, 2002.

Mitchell, Timothy. "The Work of Economics: How a Discipline Makes Its World." *European Journal of Sociology* 46, no. 2 (2005): 297–320.

Mogel, Lize, and Alexis Bhagat. *An Atlas of Radical Cartography.* Los Angeles: Journal of Aesthetics and Protest Press, 2009.

Moloney, Pat. " 'Strangers in Their Own Land': Capitalism, Dispossession and the Law." In *Land and Freedom: Law, Property Rights and the British Diaspora*, edited by A. R. Buck, John McLaren, and Nancy E. Wright. Aldershot: Ashgate, 2001.

Monture-Angus, Patricia. *Journeying Forward: Dreaming First Nations' Independence.* Winnipeg: Fernwood, 1997.

Moreton-Robinson, Aileen. *The White Possessive: Property, Power, and Indigenous Sovereignty.* Minneapolis: University of Minnesota Press, 2015.

Morris-Reich, Amos. "Arthur Ruppin's Concept of Race." *Israel Studies* 11, no. 3 (fall 2006): 1–30.

Mundy, Martha, and Richard Saumarez Smith. *Governing Property, Making the Modern State: Law, Administration and Production in Ottoman Syria.* London: I. B. Tauris, 2007.

Nedelsky, Jennifer. "Law, Boundaries, and the Bounded Self." *Representations*, no. 30 (spring 1990): 162–89.

Nedelsky, Jennifer. *Private Property and the Limits of American Constitutionalism.* Chicago: University of Chicago Press, 1990.

Nedelsky, Jennifer. "Should Property Be Constitutionalized? A Relational and Comparative Approach." In *Property on the Threshold of the 21st Century*, edited by G. E. van Maanen and A. J. van der Walt. Antwerp: Maklu, Blackstone, Nomos, Jurdik and Samhaelle, Schulthess, 1996.

Nichols, Robert. "Contract and Usurpation: Enfranchisement and Racial Governance in Settler-Colonial Contexts." In *Theorizing Native Studies*, edited by Audra Simpson and Andrea Smith, 99–121. Durham, NC: Duke University Press, 2014.

Nichols, Robert. "Disaggregating Primitive Accumulation." *Radical Philosophy*, no. 194 (November/December 2015): 18–28.

Noked, Orit. *Israel's Agriculture.* Tel Aviv: The Israel Export and International Cooperation Institute. http://www.a-id.org/pdf/israel-s-agriculture.pdf.

Offer, Avner. *Property and Politics, 1870–1914: Land Ownership, Law, Ideology and Urban Development in England.* Cambridge: Cambridge University Press, 1981.

O'Malley, Michael. *Face Value: The Entwined Histories of Money and Race in America.* Chicago: University of Chicago Press, 2012.

Palgi, Michael. "Organization in Kibbutz Industry." In *Crisis in the Israeli Kibbutz: Meeting the Challenge of Changing Times*, edited by U. Leviatan, H. Oliver, and J. Quarter. New York: Praeger, 1998.

Palmater, Pamela. *Beyond Blood: Rethinking Indigenous Identity.* Saskatoon: Purich, 2011.

Pashukanis, Evgeny. *Law and Marxism: A General Theory.* London: Pluto, 1989.

Pasternak, Shiri. "How Capitalism Will Save Colonialism: The Privatization of Reserve Lands in Canada." *Antipode* 47, no. 1 (January 2015): 179–96.

Patterson, Orlando. *Slavery and Social Death: A Comparative Study*. Cambridge, MA: Harvard University Press, 1982.

Perrin, Colin, and Kay Anderson. "Reframing Craniometry: Human Exceptionalism and the Production of Racial Knowledge." *Social Identities: Journal of Race, Nation and Culture* 19, no. 1 (2013): 90–103.

Petty, William. *The Economic Writings of Sir William Petty*. Edited by Charles Henry Hull. Cambridge: Cambridge University Press, 1899.

Petty, William. *Political Anatomy of Ireland with the establishment for that kingdom when the late Duke of Ormond was Lord Lieutenant: to which is added Verbum sapienti, or, An account of the wealth and expences of England, and the method of raising taxes in the most equal manner*. London: D. Brown and W. Rogers, 1691.

Pietz, William. "Material Considerations: On the Historical Forensics of Contract." *Theory, Culture and Society* 19, no. 5/6 (2002): 35.

Piterberg, Gabriel. *Returns of Zionism: Myths, Politics and Scholarship in Israel*. New York: Verso, 2008.

Platzky, Laurine, and Cherryl Walker. *The Surplus People Project*. Johannesburg: Ravan, 1985.

Poovey, Mary. *A History of the Modern Fact: Problems of Knowledge in the Sciences of Wealth and Society*. Chicago: University of Chicago Press, 1998.

Pottage, Alain. "Conflict of Laws: Comparing Autochthonous Legal Cultures." In *Territorial Conflicts in World Society: Modern Systems Theory, International Relations and Conflict Studies*, edited by Stephan Stetter. New York: Routledge, 2007.

Pottage, Alain. "Introduction: The Fabrication of Persons and Things." In *Law, Anthropology and the Constitution of the Social: Making Persons and Things*, edited by Alain Pottage and Martha Mundy. Cambridge: Cambridge University Press, 2004.

Pottage, Alain. "Law after Anthropology: Object and Technique in Roman Law." *Theory, Culture and Society* 31, no. 2–3 (March–May 2014): 147–66.

Pottage, Alain. "The Measure of Land." *Modern Law Review* 57, no. 3 (May 1994): 361–84.

Pottage, Alain. "The Originality of Registration." *Oxford Journal of Legal Studies* 15, no. 3 (1995): 371–401.

Pottage, Alain, and Brad Sherman. *Figures of Invention: A History of Modern Patent Law*. New York: Oxford University Press, 2010.

Povinelli, Elizabeth. "The Governance of the Prior." *interventions* 13, no. 1 (2011): 13–30.

Pratt, Mary Louise. *Imperial Eyes: Travel Writing and Transculturation*. London: Routledge, 1992.

Quio, Shitong. "Planting Houses in Shenzhen: A Real Estate Market without Legal Titles." *Canadian Journal of Law and Society*, no. 29 (2013): 253–72.

Radin, Margaret Jane. *Reinterpreting Property*. Chicago: University of Chicago Press, 1993.

Razack, Sherene. *Dying from Improvement: Inquests and Inquiries into Indigenous Deaths in Custody*. Toronto: University of Toronto Press, 2015.

Razack, Sherene. "Gendered Racial Violence and Spatialized Justice: The Murder of Pamela George." In *Race, Space and the Law: Unmapping a White Settler Society*, edited by Sherene Razack. Toronto: Between the Lines, 2002.

Raz-Krakotzkin, Amnon. "Exile, History and the Nationalisation of Jewish Memory: Some Reflections on the Zionist Notion of History and Return." *Journal of Levantine Studies* 3, no. 2 (winter 2013): 37–70.

Raz-Krakotzkin, Amnon. *Exil et Souveraineté: Judaïsme, sionisme, et pensée binationale*. Paris: La Fabrique, 2007.

Reilly, Alex. "From a Jurisprudence of Regret to a Regrettable Jurisprudence: Shaping Native Title from *Mabo* to *Ward*." *Murdoch University Electronic Journal of Law* 9, no. 4 (December 2002). http://www.austlii.edu.au/au/journals/MurUEJL/2002/50.html.

Robinson, Cedric J. *Black Marxism: The Making of the Black Radical Tradition*. Chapel Hill: University of North Carolina Press, 1983.

Robinson, Cedric J. *Black Movements in America*. London: Routledge, 1997.

Robinson, Cedric J. *Forgeries of Memory and Meaning: Blacks and the Regimes of Race in American Theater and Film before World War II*. Chapel Hill: University of North Carolina Press, 2007.

Roediger, David, and Elizabeth Esch. *The Production of Difference: Race and the Management of Labour in U.S. History*. Oxford: Oxford University Press, 2012.

Rose, Carol. *Property and Persuasion: Essays on the History, Theory, and Rhetoric of Ownership*. Boulder, CO: Westview, 1994.

Rosenberg, Jordana. *Critical Enthusiasm: Capital Accumulation and the Transformation of Religious Passion*. Oxford: Oxford University Press, 2011.

Rosser, Ezra. "Anticipating de Soto: Allotment of Indian Reservations and the Dangers of Land-Titling." In *Hernando de Soto and Property in a Market Economy*, edited by D. Benjamin Barros, 61–81. Surrey: Ashgate, 2010.

Ruppin, Arthur. *The Agricultural Colonisation of the Zionist Organisation in Palestine*. London: M. Hopkinson, 1926.

Ruppin, Arthur. *Three Decades of Palestine: Speeches and Papers on the Upbuilding of the Jewish National Home*. Jerusalem: Schocken, 1936.

Said, Edward. *After the Last Sky*. Somerset: Butler and Tanner, 1986.

Said, Edward. *Culture and Imperialism*. New York: Vintage, 1993.

Sanyal, Kalyan. *Rethinking Capitalist Development: Primitive Accumulation, Governmentality and Post-Colonial Capitalism*. New Delhi: Routledge, 2013.

Sayer, Derek. *The Violence of Abstraction: The Analytical Foundations of Historical Materialism*. London: Basil Blackwell, 1987.

Sayigh, Rosemary. *The Palestinians: From Peasants to Revolutionaries*. Chicago: University of Chicago Press, 2007.

Schiebinger, Londa, and Claudia Swan, eds. *Colonial Botany: Science, Commerce, and Politics in the Early Modern World*. Philadelphia: University of Pennsylvania Press, 2007.

Schmitt, Carl. *Constitutional Theory*. Edited and translated by J. Seitzer. Durham, NC: Duke University Press, 2008.

Scott, James. *Seeing Like a State: How Certain Schemes to Improve the Human Condition Have Failed*. New Haven, CT: Yale University Press, 1998.

Shafir, Gershon. *Land, Labor and the Origins of the Israeli-Palestinian Conflict, 1882–1914*. Cambridge: Cambridge University Press, 1989.

Shalhoub Kevorkian, Nadera. "Stolen Childhood: Palestinian Children and the Structure of Genocidal Dispossession." *Settler Colonial Studies* 6, no. 2 (2016): 142–52.

Shamir, Ronen. "Suspended in Space: Bedouins under the Law of Israel." *Law and Society Review* 30, no. 2 (1996): 231–57.

Shehadeh, Raja. *Occupier's Law: Israel and the West Bank*. Beirut: Institute for Palestine Studies, 1988.

Shohat, Ella. "The Narrative of the Nation and the Discourse of the Modernization: The Case of the Mizrahim." *Critique: Critical Middle Eastern Studies* 6, no. 10 (1997): 3–18.

Silva, Noenoe K. *Aloha Betrayed: Native Hawaiian Resistance to American Colonialism*. Durham, NC: Duke University Press, 2004.

Simpson, Alfred William Brian. *An Introduction to the History of Land Law*. Oxford: Oxford University Press, 1961.

Simpson, Audra. *Mohawk Interruptus: Political Life across the Borders of Settler States*. Durham, NC: Duke University Press, 2014.

Simpson, Leanne. "Land as Pedagogy: Nishnaabeg Intelligence and Rebellious Transformation." *Decolonisation: Indigeneity, Education and Society* 3, no. 3 (2014). http://decolonization.org/index.php/des/article/view/22170.

Simpson, Stanhope Rowton. *Land Law and Registration*. London: HMSO, 1986.

Singer, Joseph W. *Entitlement: The Paradoxes of Property*. New Haven, CT: Yale University Press, 2000.

Singer, Joseph W. "Foreclosure and the Failures of Formality, or Subprime Mortgage Conundrums and How to Fix Them." *Connecticut Law Review* 46, no. 2 (2013): 497–559.

Slack, Paul. "Material Progress and the Challenge of Affluence in Seventeenth-Century England." *Economic History Review*, New Series, 62, no. 3 (August 2009): 576–603.

Smith, Andrea. *Conquest: Sexual Violence and the American Indian Genocide*. Boston: South End, 2005.

Spivak, Gayatri. *A Critique of Postcolonial Reason: Toward a History of the Vanishing Present*. Cambridge, MA: Harvard University Press, 1999.

Stark, David. "Recombinant Property in East European Capitalism." In *Laws of the Market*, edited by Michel Callon, 117–46. Oxford: Blackwell, 1998.

Stein, Robert T. J., and Margaret A. Stone. *Torrens Title*. London: Butterworths, 1991.

Stepan, Nancy. *The Idea of Race in Science: Great Britain, 1800–1960*. London: Macmillan, 1982.

Stuckey, Sterling. *Slave Culture: Nationalist Theory and the Foundations of Black America*. Oxford: Oxford University Press, 1987.

Stuurman, Siep. "François Bernier and the Invention of Racial Classification." *History Workshop*, no. 50 (autumn 2000): 1–21.

Sugarman, David, and Ronnie Warrington. "Land Law, Citizenship, and the Invention of Englishness: The Strange World of the Equity of Redemption." In *Early Modern Conceptions of Property*, edited by John Brewer and Susan Staves, 111–43. London: Routledge, 1996.

Sutcliffe, Michael, Alison Todes, and Norah Walker. "State Urbanisation Strategies since 1986." In *No Place to Rest: Forced Removals and the Law in South Africa*, edited by C. Murray and C. O'Regan, 86–106. Oxford: Oxford University Press, 1990.

Taylor, Greg. *The Law of the Land: The Advent of the Torrens System in Canada*. Toronto: University of Toronto Press, 2008.

Tennant, Paul. *Aboriginal Peoples and Politics: The Indian Land Question in British Columbia, 1849–1989*. Vancouver: University of British Columbia Press, 1990.

Thompson, E. P. *Customs in Common*. London: New Press, 1992.

Thring, Henry. *A Memorandum of the Merchant Shipping Law Consolidation Bill; Pointing Out and Explaining the Points in Which the Existing Acts Are Altered*. London: George E. Eyre and William Spottoswoode (HM Stationery Office), 1854.

Tomlins, Christopher. "The Legalities of English Colonising: Discourses of European Intrusion upon the Americas, c. 1490–1830." In *Law and Politics in British Colonial Thought: Transpositions of Empire*, edited by Shaunnagh Dorsett and Ian Hunter, 51–70. New York: Palgrave Macmillan, 2010.

Torrens, Richard Robert. *Notes on a System of Conveyancing by Registration of Title (with instructions for the guidance of parties dealing, illustrated by copies of the books and forms in use in the land titles office)*. Adelaide: Register and Observer General Printing Office, 1859.

Toscano, Alberto. "The Culture of Abstraction." *Theory, Culture and Society* 25, no. 4 (2008): 57–75.

Toscano, Alberto. "The Open Secret of Real Abstraction." *Rethinking Marxism: A Journal of Economics, Culture and Society* 20, no. 2 (2008): 273–87.

Tucker, William H. *The Science and Politics of Racial Research*. Chicago: University of Illinois Press, 1994.

Tully, James. *An Approach to Political Philosophy: Locke in Contexts*. Cambridge: Cambridge University Press, 1993.

Underkuffler, Laura. *The Idea of Property*. Oxford: Oxford University Press, 2003.

Vallier, Ivan. "Social Change in the Kibbutz Economy." *Economic Development and Cultural Change* 10, no. 4 (July 1962): 337–52.

van der Walt, André J. *Property in the Margins*. Oxford: Hart, 2009.

van der Walt, André J. "Un-doing Things with Words: The Colonization of the Public Sphere by Private Property Discourse." *Acta Juridica* (1998): 235–81.

Watson, Irene. "Aboriginal Laws and the Sovereignty of Terra Nullius." *borderlands* 1, no. 2 (2002). http://www.borderlands.net.au/vol1no2_2002/watson_laws.html.

Watson, Irene. "Aboriginal Women's Laws and Lives: How Might We Keep Growing the Law?" *Australian Feminist Law Journal* 26, no. 1 (2007): 95–109.

Weaver, John. "Concepts of Economic Improvement and the Social Construction of Property Rights: Highlights from the English-Speaking World." In *Despotic Dominion: Property Rights in British Settler Societies*, edited by Andrew R. Buck, John MacLaren, and Nancy E. Wright, 79–102. Vancouver: UBC Press, 2004.

Weizman, Eyal, and Fazal Sheikh. *The Conflict Shoreline: Colonization as Climate Change in the Negev Desert*. New York: Steidl, 2015.

West, Cornel. "Race and Social Theory: Towards a Genealogical Materialist Analysis." In *The Year Left: Toward a Rainbow Socialism*, vol. 2, edited by Mike Davis, Manning Marable, Fred Pfeil, and Michael Sprinkler. London: Verso, 1987.

Williams, Eric. *Capitalism and Slavery*. Chapel Hill: University of North Carolina Press, 1944.

Williams, Patricia J. *The Alchemy of Race and Rights*. Cambridge, MA: Harvard University Press, 1991.

Wolfe, Patrick. "Purchase by Other Means: The Palestine *Nakba* and Zionism's Conquest of Economics." *Settler Colonial Studies* 2, no. 1 (2012): 133–71.

Wolfe, Patrick. "Settler Colonialism and the Elimination of the Native." *Journal of Genocide Research* 8, no. 4 (December 2006): 387–409.

Wolfe, Patrick. *Traces of History: Elementary Structures of Race*. London: Verso, 2016.

Wood, Neal. *John Locke and Agrarian Capitalism*. Berkeley: University of California Press, 1984.

Wright, Richard. *Twelve Million Black Voices*. New York: Basic Books, 2008.

Yiftachel, Oren. "'Ethnocracy' and Its Discontents: Minorities, Protests and the Israeli Polity." *Critical Inquiry* 26, no. 4 (summer 2000): 725–56.

Yiftachel, Oren. *Ethnocracy: Land and Identity Politics in Israel/Palestine*. Philadelphia: University of Pennsylvania Press, 2006.

Yiftachel, Oren, Alexandre (Sandy) Kedar, and Ahmad Amara. "Questioning the 'Dead (*Mewat*) Negev Doctrine': Property Rights in Arab Bedouin Space." Paper prepared for "Socio-Legal Perspectives on the Passage to Modernity in the Middle East," Ben Gurion University, Be'er Sheba, June 2012.

TABLE OF CASES

The Attorney General of Canada v. Jeanette Lavalle, Richard Isaac et al. v. Ivonne Bedard [1974] S.C.R. 1349.

C.A. 518/61. *The State of Israel v. Tzalach Badaran*, 16(3) P.D. 1717.

Calder v. Attorney General of British Columbia [1973] S.C.R. 313.

Civil Appeal No. 218/74. *Selim 'Ali Agdi'a al-Huashela et al. v. State of Israel* [1984].

Civil Appeal 4220/12. *Suliman Mohammed El-Uqbi v. the State of Israel* [2015].

Civil Case File nos. 7161/06 . . . *El-Uqbi v. the State of Israel*.

Delgamuukw v. British Columbia [1997] 3 S.C.R. 1010.

el-Okbi v. the State of Israel (June 2, 2014, Case 4220/12).

Haida Nation v. British Columbia (Minister of Forests) [2004] 3 S.C.R. 511.

Jackson et al. v. MERS Inc 770 N.W.2d 487 [Minn. 2009].

Jacobs v. Mohawk Council of Kahnawake [1998] Canadian Human Rights Tribunal.

Mabo v. Queensland (No.2) [1992] 175 CLR 1.

McIvor v. Canada [2009] BCCA, 306 DLR (4th) 193.

McIvor v. The Registrar, Indian and Northern Affairs, Canada [2007] BCSC 827.

Mitchell v. M.N.R. [2001] 1 S.C.R. 911.

Musqueam Indian Band v. Glass [2000] 2 S.C.R. 633.

Port Elizabeth Municipality v. Various Occupiers [2005] 1 (SA) 217 (CC).

R. v. Bernard [2000] 3 C.N.L.R. 184 [2003] 262, N.B.R. (2d) 1.

R. v. Gladstone [1996] 2 S.C.R. 723.

R. v. Marshall [1993] 3 S.C.R. 456.

R. v. Marshall [1999] 3 S.C.R. 566.

R. v. Marshall [2001], 191 N.S.R. (2d) 323, [2003], 218 N.S.R. (2d) 78.

R. v. Marshall; R. v. Bernard [2005] 2 S.C.R. 220.

R. v. Oakes [1986] 1 S.C.R. 103.

R. v. Secretary of State for Foreign and Commonwealth Affairs [1981], 4 C.N.L.R. 86
   [1982] 2 All E.R. 118.

R. v. Sparrow [1990] 1 S.C.R. 1075.

R. v. Van der Peet [1996] 2 S.C.R. 507.

Sandra Lovelace v. Canada, Communication No. R.6/24, U.N. Doc. Supp. No. 40
   (A/36/40) at 166 [1981].

The State of Israel v. Tzalach Badaran, P.D. 16(3) 1717 [1962].

St. Catherine's Milling and Lumber Co. v. The Queen [1888] 14 App. Cas.46.

Tsilhqot'in Nation v. British Columbia [2014] 2 S.C.R. 256.

REPORTS, COMMISSIONS, AND GOVERNMENT PAPERS

*Copy of the Second Report made to His Majesty by the Commissioners appointed to
   inquire into the Law of England respecting Real Property*. 1830.

Fourth Annual Report of the Colonization Commissioners for South Australia. 1839.
   London: House of Commons, 1836–40.

Minister of Indian and Northern Affairs. *Guide to Understanding Bill C-7, the First
   Nations Governance Act*. Ottawa: Ministry of Indian Affairs and Northern Development, 2003.

Minister of Indian and Northern Affairs. *Impacts of the 1985 Amendments to the
   Indian Act (Bill C-31) Summary Report*. Ottawa: Ministry of Indian Affairs and
   Northern Development, 1990.

Papers Connected with the Indian Land Question 1850–1875. Victoria: Government
   Printing Office, 1875.

Report of the Royal Commission on Aboriginal Peoples. Vol. 1: *Looking Forward, Looking Back*. Ottawa: Minister of Supply and Services, 1996.

Report of the Royal Commission on Aboriginal Peoples. Vol. 3: *Gathering Strength.* Ottawa: Supply and Services Canada, 1996.

South Australia Parliamentary Debates, January 27, 1858.

South Australia Parliamentary Debates, June 4, 1857.

Sproat, Gilbert Malcolm. "Sir Joseph William Trutch, K.C.M.G." Provincial Archives of British Columbia (PABC).

Tithe Commission and Ordnance Survey. *First Report of the Registration and Conveyancing Commission* PP. London: House of Commons, 1850.

Trutch Archives. University of British Columbia Library, Vancouver, BC.

STATUTES AND BILLS

Act for the Gradual Civilization of the Indian Tribes in the Canadas, 1857.

An Act for Gradual Enfranchisement of Indians, the Better Management of Indian Affairs, and to Extend the Provisions of the Act 31st of Victoria, Chapter 42, S.C. 1869, c.6.

An Act Further to Amend the "Dominion Lands Act, 1883," 1886 R.S.C. ch.27.

An Act Providing for the Organisation of the Department of the Secretary of State of Canada, and for the Management of Indian and Ordinance Lands, S.C. 1868, c.42 (31 Vict.).

An Act Respecting the Land of the Crown, RSBC, 1911, vol. 2, ch.128.

An Act to Amend and Consolidate the Laws Affecting Crown Lands in British Columbia, Statutes of the Province of British Columbia, 4th Session of First Parliament of BC, 1875.

An Act to Amend and Consolidate the Laws Respecting Indians, S.C. 1876, c.18.

An Act to Amend the Indian Act (Bill C-31).

An Act to Amend the "Land Act, 1875" Statues of the Province of British Columbia, 1879.

An Act to Consolidate and Amend the Acts Respecting the Public Lands of the Dominion ("The Dominion Lands Act"), 1908, ch.20, 7–8.

An Act Respecting Indians ("The Indian Act") R.S.C. 1886, ch.43.

Canada Act 1982 (including "The Constitution Act 1982") c.11 (U.K.).

Constitution Act 1867 ("The British North America Act"), 31 & 31 Victoria, c.6.

Constitution of the Republic of South Africa, Act No. 108 of 1996.

First Nations Governance Act (Bill C-7).

First Nations Land Management Act, S.C. 1999, c.24.

Indian Act, R.S.C. 1985, c.32.

Indian Advancement Act, R.S.C. 1886, ch.44.

Law of Property Act, 15 Geo. V ch.20.

Mewat Land Ordinance of 1921.

Native Title Act, No. 110, 1993.

Index

Fanon, Frantz, 5, 58
Federation of Saskatchewan Indian Nations, 62
fee simple title, 31, 42, 59, 67, 70, 79–80, 162
Fertile Memory (Khleifi film), 112
film industry, American, 14–15, 16. *See also specific films*
First Nations: aboriginal title to land, 64–75, 139; abstract thought and, 58; appropriation of land, 27, 30–31, 38, 54, 56, 58; British Crown obligations to, 61–62; expulsion of, 161; improvement ideology and, 28, 36, 38, 53, 57; Indian, legally defined, 158–59, 171; property ownership of, 13, 52–54, 60–75, 79, 138, 139, 144; racial regimes of ownership, 30, 38, 48, 50, 56, 67, 70, 74, 170; recognition of, 24; resistance to appropriation, 25, 27, 51, 170; status of, 24, 30, 37, 138, 148, 153–63, 170–74, 175, 182. *See also* aboriginal/indigenous populations
Fisher, Robin, 51, 54
Fitzmaurice, Edmond, 40
Fitzpatrick, Peter, 4
Forgeries of Memory and Meaning (Robinson), 14
Forman, Geremy, 108
Foucault, Michel, 15, 36–37, 44, 230n3
Franciscan property ownership, 33–34
Frank, Thomas, 34
freedom: Canadian Charter, 62; concept of, 20, 194; knowledge formation and, 194–95; as practice, 197–200; from reliance, 163; from sex discrimination, 175

gender: Canadian indigenous, 176; feminist challenges to Indian Act, 175–79; forms of labor, 203n25; property ownership and, 5, 30–31, 59, 171, 187; racial regimes of ownership and, 30–31; status and, 149–53, 157, 159, 161, 175–79; women as property, 161, 167
Gender Equity in Indian Registration Act (2010), 175–76
George III, King of Great Britain, 62

Ghandour, Zeina, 108–9
Gilmore, Ruth Wilson, 8
Gitksan Nation, 64–66
Glen Grey Act (1894), 187–88
God TV (television channel), 116
Gordon, Avery F., 9–10, 181, 183, 197–98
Gould, Stephen J., 105
Gramsci, Antonio, 11
Grant, Peter R., 66
Green Patrol, 117, 133–34, 136
Grey, George, 62, 187
Grundrisse (Marx), 100
Guha, Ranajit, 18
Günther, Hans F. K., 125

Hadawi, Sami, 134
Hall, Stuart, 5; on articulation theory, 9, 12–13, 183; on race and class, 10–11, 14; on social formation, 11
Harris, Cheryl, 7–8, 10, 152, 177
Harris, Cole, 52
Hartman, Saidiya, 20, 161
Hawai'i: displacement in, 79; land ownership, 18, 78–79
Hawthorn Archives, The (Gordon), 197–99
Herzl, Theodor, 118, 119, 120, 122, 126–28, 130
Hill, Elias, 162
Hirst, Paul, 99–100
Hogg, Peter, 61
Hohfeldian rights, 19–20
homesteading: defined, 59; land appropriation and, 28, 38, 51, 212n104; racial/gender bias and, 59–60, 61, 212n104
Hooykaas, R., 45
Hope-Simpson, John, 147
housing, social, 33
Hübbe, Ulrich, 88
Hudson's Bay Company, 51
Hussain, Nasser, 4

ILA. *See* Israel Land Authority (ILA)
improvement, ideology of: Blackstone on, 47–50; Locke on, 38–39, 47–50; ownership and, 8, 10, 26, 28, 34, 35, 36, 38, 50, 71; Petty on, 37, 43, 48, 97, 181; in

Schwab, Gabriele, 80–81

science, racial. *See under* race and racialism

Scott, James, 51, 92

Scott, Walter, 2, 3, 44

segregation, racial, 16, 104, 187–89, 191

"Selection of the Fittest, The" (Ruppin), 125

self-possession, 163–64, 182–83

seminomad, use of term, 28, 71, 73–74

Sepoys, 107

Shafir, Gershon, 129

Shamir, Ronen, 138

Sharon, Ariel, 117

shipping system registration, 88–91

Shohat, Ella, 126

Simpson, Audra, 25

Simpson, Leanne, 194

Singer, Joseph W., 19, 20

Sitta, Abu, 133, 135

slave trade, 6–7, 15, 20, 86, 102–3, 154–55, 157, 196, 198

Smith, Adam, 35–36, 46

social formations, 3, 11, 12–14, 164

Sociology of the Jews (Ruppin), 126

South Africa: displacement from, 185; eviction law in, 185–93; land surveying in, 188; racial regimes of ownership in, 185–86, 188–89, 193

South Australia: displacement from, 106; indigenous sovereignty in, 3–4; land surveying in, 81, 93–94; as *terra nullius*, 94–96; Torrens system in, 3, 82, 95

South Australian Company, 94

Spain, foreclosures and evictions in, 33

status: of First Nations, 24, 30, 37, 138, 148, 153–63; gender and, 149–53, 157, 159, 161; legal concept of, 153–55; property as, 155–57

Stepan, Nancy, 104

Stuurman, Siep, 46

subjectivity: human, 58, 163, 164, 165, 168; racial, 2, 5, 9, 10, 21–22, 56, 182

Sugarman, David, 86

Supreme Court of Canada, 28, 38, 50, 63, 64, 70, 72, 73–74, 139, 141. *See also* specific cases

Supreme Court of Israel, 132–33, 139–40, 142, 144

surplus population, 27–28, 36

surveying: in British Columbia, 17, 28, 37, 38, 50–59, 68, 72, 161; imposition of, 193; in Ireland, 39, 40–41; land appropriation and, 17, 28, 37, 38, 53–59; land occupation and, 68, 72; land value and, 28, 35–41, 48, 55, 181; in South Africa, 188; in South Australia, 81, 93–94; Torrens system and, 92–93. *See also* mapping

Tanzimat, 129

taxation, 41, 44, 80, 128

terra nullius doctrine, 49; in Australia, 83, 95–96; Bedouin land rights and, 143; centrality of, 93; purpose of, 92; racist underpinnings, 102; Tsilhqot'in tribe, effect on, 74; in Vancouver Island, 82

Theory of Legislation (Bentham), 86

Thomas, Yan, 154

Thring, Henry, 90

title registration, 3, 77–83, 182; logics of abstraction and, 96–101; Ottoman system, 79, 83, 109–10, 111, 116, 128–29, 133–34, 136–37, 145–46; Torrens system, 82, 84–85, 92, 95, 96, 108–10. *See also* conveyance, deeds of

Torrens, Robert Richard, 84–86, 88–90, 92–93, 95–96; system of registration, 82, 84–86, 92, 95, 96, 108–10

Treatise of Taxes (Petty), 44

Trutch, Joseph: on improvement, 54, 57, 69; individual greed of, 17, 38, 40–41, 51, 53, 54–56; racism of, 54, 56; on savagery, 58; surveying and appropriation by, 17, 28, 37, 38, 53–58

Tsilhqot'in hangings, 50–51, 61

Tsilhqot'in Nation v. British Columbia, 28, 38, 50, 63, 70–74, 139, 145–46

Two Treaties of Government (Locke), 165–66, 169–70

Underkuffler, Laura, 19–20

United Kingdom, title registration, 85–88